THE INDY CAR WARS

THE INDY CAR WARS

*The 30-Year Fight for
Control of American
Open-Wheel Racing*

Sigur E. Whitaker

McFarland & Company, Inc., Publishers
Jefferson, North Carolina

All photographs courtesy Indianapolis Motor Speedway.

LIBRARY OF CONGRESS CATALOGUING-IN-PUBLICATION DATA [new form]

Names: Whitaker, Sigur E., 1948–
Title: The Indy Car wars : the 30-year fight for control of American open-wheel racing / Sigur E. Whitaker.
Description: Jefferson, North Carolina : McFarland & Company, Inc., Publishers, 2015. | Includes bibliographical references and index.
Identifiers: LCCN 2015034195| ISBN 9780786498321 (softcover : acid free paper) | ISBN 9781476619804 (ebook)
Subjects: LCSH: Indianapolis Speedway Race—History. | Championship Auto Racing Teams (Organization)—History.
Classification: LCC GV1033.5.I55 W44 2015 | DDC 796.720977252—dc23
LC record available at http://lccn.loc.gov/2015034195

BRITISH LIBRARY CATALOGUING DATA ARE AVAILABLE

ISBN (print) 978-0-7864-9832-1
ISBN (ebook) 978-1-4766-1980-4

Front cover: Hélio Castroneves (bottom) and Scott Dixon on the track in the Indy Japan 300 at the Twin Ring Motegi in Motegi, Japan, on April 20, 2008 (Morio)

Printed in the United States of America

 McFarland & Company, Inc., Publishers
Box 611, Jefferson, North Carolina 28640
www.mcfarlandpub.com

Table of Contents

Preface

The world of open-wheel racing was rocked by a series of seismic events, over a 30-year period that brought the sport to its knees. Rather than the races and the drivers being the focus, the sport's internal turmoil gained the attention of the press and fans. Meanwhile, rival NASCAR was ascending in prestige and fan loyalty.

The seeds of division were planted long before 1978, the year Championship Auto Racing Teams (CART) was formed in frustration with the United States Auto Club (USAC). Up through the 1950s, Champ Car racing was primarily a sportsman's hobby. Just as the Indianapolis Motor Speedway was built by four businessmen whose financial wealth enabled them to build the first super-speedway, Champ Car racing was, by and large, the purview of wealthy individuals who enjoyed the sport and were willing to dip into their own pockets to support it.

In the early days of the sport, local businesses began supporting the races by providing trophies. Car manufacturers also realized the commercial value of winning races for the sale of their product to consumers. It didn't take long for the tire and oil companies to recognize the value to their franchises, leading to financial support of the individual teams.

As the cost of racing escalated in the 1960s, others saw an opportunity to expand their brand images by supporting racing teams. It became a vicious cycle. The more sponsorships a team garnered, the more sponsorships it needed to maintain the status quo. Underlying the Indy car wars was the cost of supporting a racing team, which had by the 1970s outpaced the ability of individual sportsmen. Teams had become the norm. Long gone were the days when a car would race for multiple years. The technology—exotic engines and ground effects—drove annual equipment changes for those teams that could afford it. The teams without the financial wherewithal fell further and further behind.

The individuals involved in the Indy car wars are all passionate about racing. All wanted the championship circuit to be successful. The underlying schism was for the control of the sport. Unfortunately, there were multiple missed opportunities to reunify the sport. There were no winners in this fight for control. The sport, which had dominated auto racing, fell from grace. The task is now to regain the luster the sport once enjoyed.

This book would not have been possible without the sports journalists who documented this period of automobile racing, including Curt Cavin, Robin Miller, Ron Lemasters, Jr., Chris Economaki, Bruce Martin, Steve Mayer, and John Oreovicz. Many thanks to Laura Dodson, Inter-Library Loan Librarian at Norfolk (VA) Public Library, who was able to provide multiple reels of microfilm. Pictures were provided by Mary Ellen Loscar of the Indianapolis Motor Speedway.

Prologue

In the 1930s and 1940s, the top spectator sports in the United States included horse racing and auto racing. Horse racing had three primary events—the Kentucky Derby, the Preakness, and the Belmont—while auto racing had the Indianapolis 500. These were the races that garnered national attention. But all of the other races, horse racing or auto racing, were local.

This was before the days of television. The broadcasting of live sporting events changed the landscape of spectator sports. No longer did fans have to go to the event; they could sit in the comfort of their loungers and enjoy the event on their televisions even if the event was being held halfway across the country. It was before the days of Kentucky Derby and Super Bowl parties.

By 2007, the top-rated spectator sport was the National Football League, followed by college football, college basketball, Major League Baseball, and the National Basketball Association. In sixth place, leading all types of auto racing, was NASCAR. The National Hot Rod Association (NHRA) was twelfth while Formula One racing, dominant in Europe, was nineteenth. Open-wheel racing, which had been the pinnacle of auto racing for decades, couldn't be found in the top twenty spectator sporting events.[1]

What happened? The seeds of change were sown in the 1960s. As with so many other things in life, it comes down to money. For decades prior to the 1960s, most forms of auto racing in the United States were strictly American events—American team owners, American drivers, and primarily American-built cars. Although Europe had Formula One racing, which is very similar to American open-wheel racing, European teams did not usually cross the Atlantic. But that changed in 1961 when a British-built race car was brought to the Indianapolis Motor Speedway.

Brian Lisles, the Newman/Haas racing team's general manager, attributed the "British invasion" in auto racing of the early 1960s to the possibility of earning significantly more money racing in the United States. He explained,

"A lot of European drivers came to the United States to race because there was much bigger prize money in CanAm series and at Indianapolis. Colin Chapman didn't come and do Indy out of the goodness of his heart. He came because he could win in one race probably ten times what he could win during an entire Formula 1 series."[2]

Historically, Formula One racing, just like American open-wheel racing, had a front engine design until John Cooper designed the Cooper-Climax, a rear-engine racer. This car turned Grand Prix racing upside down when it won the 1959 International Grand Prix Championship. Just two short years later, the entire field in Grand Prix racing had abandoned the front-engine concept.[3]

Lured by the possibility of winning big money in the United States, defending world champion Jack Brabham and the car's designer, John Cooper, came to the United States in the fall of 1960 for a road race. They stopped by the Indianapolis Motor Speedway, where Brabham tested the car. The American open-wheel community should have thought about the speed that Brabham obtained at the Speedway—144.8 miles per hour—in a car whose engine was about two-thirds the size of an American Offenhauser powered racer.[4] But the American racing community yawned. The world was about to change.

Although Cooper was interested in participating in the Indianapolis 500, he needed financial backing. In stepped James H. Kimberly, the president of the Sports Car Club of America and heir to the Kimberly-Clark fortune, which was built upon Kleenex tissues. He provided Cooper with $30,000 to finance the building of a Cooper-Climax car to be raced in the Indianapolis 500.[5]

Cooper brought a rear-engine Cooper-Climax to the 1961 Indianapolis 500. In an effort to entice participation from abroad, which hadn't happened since before World War I, a United States Auto Club (USAC) exception to its standard rules for Champ Car racing allowed foreign entrants' cars to have a wheelbase of 92 inches rather than the longer 96-inch wheelbase required for Indianapolis 500 cars. The shorter car, combined with a 2.75-liter engine rather than the standard 4.2-liter Offenhauser engine, resulted in the car's weighing a mere 1,050 pounds. The standard open-wheel racer in 1961 weighed 500 pounds more. The lighter weight offset the car's lower horsepower, making the car competitive.[6]

Jack Brabham easily qualified for the Indianapolis 500, placing 13th with a qualifying speed of 145.144 miles per hour.[7] Although the car was fast in the corners, it couldn't hold a candle to the power of the Offenhauser engine on the straightaways. Despite finishing 9th in the race, this underpowered car was quickly dismissed by the American racing establishment.[8]

Another rear-engine design would turn the American racing establishment upside down and would soon threaten the Offenhauser engine for the dominance of Champ Car racing stateside. With a passion for racing, Briton Colin Chapman was designing the Lotus race cars for Formula One. American Dan Gurney, who drove in the Formula One circuit, was introduced to Chapman's Lotus 25 at the Dutch Grand Prix at Zandvoort in 1962. This car was revolutionary, with its rear engine, full-monocoque chassis construction. Upon seeing the car in action, Gurney said to Chapman, "My God, you know if someone took a car to Indianapolis like this, they could win with it."[9]

Gurney believed rear-engine racers were the wave of the future for American open-wheel racing. He hatched a plan to introduce Chapman, the British engineer and founder of Lotus Engineering Company, and racing officials at Ford Motor Company. Step number one was to get Chapman to the 1962 Indianapolis 500, which he accomplished by paying Chapman's way.[10]

Step number two was arranging a meeting between Chapman and Ford Motor Company officials. Mission accomplished. After a meeting at Ford headquarters on July 23, 1962,[11] Ford and Chapman agreed to bring the Lotus-Ford rear-engine racer to participate in the Indianapolis 500.[12] Gurney became Ford's driver for the testing of its new engine that would power the Lotus-Ford. In March 1963, this car was tested at the Indianapolis Motor Speedway, confirming its quickness—the car recorded a speed of 150.5 miles per hour, which was, at the time, the second fastest time in Speedway history.[13]

The 1963 Indianapolis 500 saw the unveiling of the Lotus-Ford, with Lotus teammates Dan Gurney and Scotsman Jim Clark at the wheel. This time, with power provided by a 256-cubic-inch, V-8 pushrod engine built by Ford Motor Company, the rear-engine car was much more competitive. The race would be controversial, as the eventual winner, Parnelli Jones, was not black flagged despite having spewed oil over the track. The second place finisher was Clark, driving one of the two Lotus-Fords entered in the race.[14] Dan Gurney finished ninth.

Later in the season, both Clark and Gurney participated in the Milwaukee Mile and left their competitors in the dust during the practice and competition. Clark easily won the 200-mile race, having led from the first lap.[15] This broke the domination of the Offenhauser engine and started the revolution that would lead to the Indy car wars. Although the Offenhauser engine powered the winning car at the 1964 Indianapolis 500, by the next year the rear-engine car had taken hold and was the power-plant of choice for 27 of the 33 entrants. This time, the 1965 Indianapolis 500 was won by Jimmy Clark in a Lotus-Ford.

The revolution continued when Andy Granatelli, one of the owners of STP auto treatment and a fan of Indy car racing, brought the Novis to the Indianapolis 500 from 1961 through 1965. Walking away without winning the Borg-Warner Trophy, given to the winners of the Indianapolis 500, Granatelli, determined to win, created a new style of racing auto that would revolutionize the sport. In secrecy inside the California STP facilities, the new racing machine took shape in 1967. Its design was revolutionary. On the left-hand side, there was a bulge where the engine was located. On the right-hand side was another, smaller bulge, which held the driver tub. The center of the racing car was the frame.

Granatelli had wanted Parnelli Jones to drive for him since the mid–1960s. In the years when Granatelli had brought the Novis to the Indianapolis Motor Speedway, drivers could handle the machines at about 141 miles per hour—not enough to power the Novi to Victory Circle. One day Granatelli asked Jones to take one of the Novis for a spin around the fabled track. After Jones obtained a lap speed of 148 miles per hour, Granatelli was determined for Jones to pilot the Novi. But it was not to be. When originally approached to drive for the STP team, Jones was driving for the Agajanian team. Granatelli didn't push Jones to change his loyalties. Then Jones retired from racing.

When the STP turbine was ready to be tested, the first person on Granatelli's short list, not surprisingly, was Jones.[16] With Jones at the wheel, a secret trial of the car was held at the Phoenix International Raceway on March 16, 1967. The car, powered by a 280-pound Pratt and Whitney aircraft engine, set a new track record for a mile run at more than 120 miles per hour.[17] Jones described his reaction to the car: "I was pretty impressed with it. But, I heard it might be dangerous. If it ever exploded, I could see shrapnel going through my body. But, as I ran it, I became very impressed with it."[18]

Impressed with the car, Jones listened to Granatelli's proposal to drive it in the Indianapolis 500. Would Jones come out of retirement to drive the turbine? What got Jones' attention was a retainer of between $100,000 and $150,000. At the time, there were a few drivers who received minor retainers, but nothing of this magnitude. Jones accepted Granatelli's offer in room 239 of the Indianapolis Motor Speedway Motel. It was not known at the time, but the retainer paid by Andy Granatelli to Parnelli Jones was another inroad of big business into the racing scene. Down the track would come well-heeled racing teams to dominate the auto racing landscape.

While the car attracted a lot of attention at the Speedway, Mario Andretti snagged the pole for the 1967 Indianapolis 500 with an average speed of 168.982 miles per hour, while Jones' sixth-place effort was at 166.075 miles per hour. When the car failed to win the pole, Jones vehemently denied speculation that he was sandbagging.[19] Race day was a different story. With superior cornering ability, the STP Special was able to drive anywhere on the track. Jones passed the first five cars coming out of the second turn on the first lap to take the lead. Jones' car clearly had an advantage over the competition and was cruising to an easy victory. Those thinking Jones would win the Indianapolis 500 left the Speedway to get a head start on the impending traffic jam. They missed the end of the race when, on lap 197, a bearing broke in Jones' car and the race was won by A. J. Foyt.[20]

In 1970, another seismic change occurred in auto racing, but it was far away from the track. Responding to the apparent linkage between smoking, lung cancer and chronic bronchitis, Congress passed the Public Health Smoking Act, which was signed into law on April 1, 1970, by President Richard Nixon. Not only did this act require a warning on all cigarette packages, it also banned the advertising of cigarettes on the radio and television.

Recognizing that the Act would adversely impact its marketing campaigns, the cigarette manufacturers sought other mediums. Philip Morris reached an agreement with USAC for its flagship brand, Marlboro, to become the title sponsor of its National Championship Series. The announcement was made on May 28, 1970, in conjunction with the Indianapolis 500. As part of the agreement, Philip Morris agreed to provide $50,000 for the top three drivers in championship points in 1970. The fund would increase to $300,000 to be divided among the top drivers in 1971. The other two dominant cigarette manufacturers followed Philip Morris' lead very quickly. Liggett & Meyers announced their L&M brand would sponsor the Sports Car Club of America's (SCCA) Continental Championship. Joining the ranks in December 1971, R. J. Reynolds announced that Winston cigarettes would become the title sponsor for NASCAR's Grand National Championship.

The benefit to the cigarette manufacturers was that although they could no longer run advertising on television, the law did not prohibit incidental showing of cigarette logos. So, instead of paying for television advertising, the cigarette manufacturers simply paid the major auto racing leagues, and then they could display their logos on the team cars, which would be caught by the television cameras. It also provided for indirect advertising as the various leagues incorporated the sponsors' names into the league name. The United States Auto Club (USAC) now was the Marlboro-USAC National Driving Championship, and NASCAR became known as the Winston Cup

Grand National Series. Meanwhile, the SCCA National Championship had the L&M National Championship Trophy.[21]

Over the next several years, sponsorships became essential to racing. Sponsors became important to the car owners and to the tracks themselves. With big money chasing the races, the costs of fielding a racing team increased, and increased, and increased. Gone were the days of when a person would enter a car in races for the sport of it. Racing was now becoming big business.

CART Is Born

For several years, the cost of fielding a racing team had escalated, while the monetary benefits of racing had not kept pace. By 1978, few teams at the Indianapolis Motor Speedway could financially support their operations. The well-heeled teams, included those led by Pat Patrick and Roger Penske, dominated championship racing.

Patrick, who made his money through oil exploration,[1] recognized the problem and was concerned that the independent, small racing teams were being priced out of the competition. His solution was to slow the race speeds down. Patrick told the *Indianapolis Star*, "It's imperative that the 200-mph speed be reduced or the less affluent can't stay in racing. The stupid rule restricting fuel is the most expensive in racing history. If they don't do something to reduce the size of the rear wings, you will see a 205 lap next year and a 210 the year after. That's too fast … way too fast. I think the rear wing size should be reduced 20 percent to start, then another 20 percent, and more from there until they cut the speeds 20 mph."[2]

Also recognizing the problem was Dan Gurney, a successful driver at the top levels of racing who, upon retirement, transitioned into the role of team owner. In later years Gurney talked about the relationship between the USAC and the Indianapolis Motor Speedway: "USAC was a child of the Speedway. USAC was there to run the month of May and it was also allowed to run its own additional races that made up the national championship series."

USAC successfully ran the Indianapolis 500, which had the largest purse in auto racing. Gurney's focus was on the problems with the remainder of USAC's National Championship: "The rest of the championship series was bogged down. It didn't have any leadership and was more or less derelict. Each particular promoter at each track was free to either promote or not promote. It was a very loose organization and there wasn't much linkage between all the other races and the Indy 500. The rest of the races were sort of orphans that nobody paid attention to." The remainder of Gurney's comments provides a glimpse of the future: "Nor had anybody heard the word marketing. The waters were stagnant. You can't run the business of a racing team with just one big race a year and the rest of them are a bunch of losers, unless you're doing it as a hobby and not a real business."[3]

As a team owner, Gurney talked with the stakeholders of championship racing: drivers, team owners, promoters and track owners, corporate sponsors and fans over several years. He came to the conclusion that championship racing needed a major overhaul. This resulted in Gurney's writing the "white paper" sent to several team owners including Roger Penske and Pat Patrick. The letter outlined the need for change, saying, "At the moment, we the car owners are the ones who have put forth by far the most effort, by far the most financial stake with little or no chance of return. And yet, because we have been so busy fighting each other, we have let the track owners or promoters and the sanctioning body lead us around by the nose while they reap the benefits."[4]

Having spent much of his racing career participating in the Formula One Grand Prix circuit, Gurney pointed to the Formula One Constructors' Association, led by Bernie Ecclestone, as a prototype. In the white paper, Gurney provided the historical parallel to the plight of the championship racing teams: "Back in the early '70s the status of Formula One Grand Prix racing was similar to our own USAC championship racing right now. The crowds were quite small, sponsors were hard to find, the news media was not overly interested, expenses were high and going higher and the entire scene was one of disorganization."

He then went on to paint the picture of how the banding together of the Formula One teams had improved the sport for all: "Sponsors are numerous

Dan Gurney's white paper led to the formation of CART. After a successful racing career, Gurney became a team owner.

and happy to be involved. The media is vigorous in covering all the events on TV and so are weekly magazines and daily newspapers on a worldwide basis. And money is coming back to the constructors and track owners in the form of larger ticket sales, more sponsorship, more prize money and expense money and the spectator is getting a much bigger, better spectacular for his ticket money."[5] Gurney's white paper concluded with a call for action.

In April 1978, USAC officials and staff attended a race in New Jersey. On the return flight to Indianapolis, the chartered plane met with unsettled weather. Winds were estimated at up to 100 miles per hour and the plane was being pelted with sleet. In order to get below the turbulence, the pilot requested permission to lower the plane's altitude to 5,000 feet. After attaining that level, he asked the Indianapolis control tower to allow him to fly at 3,000 feet. The Indianapolis flight control tower responded affirmatively. Whether or not the plane descended to this level is not known. What is known is that the plane crashed into a plowed field, creating a five-foot-deep crater and killing all nine aboard. This crash decimated the leadership at USAC, taking the lives of technical director Frank DelRoy, publicist Ray Marquette, registrar Stanley Worley, Midget supervisor and Championship flagman Shim Malone, Sprint supervisor Donald Peabody, typographist Judith F. Phillips, deputy technical director Ross Teeguarden, and USAC physician Dr. Bruce White, as well as Don Mullendore, the plane's pilot.[6] With the loss of the USAC officials, there was a leadership void at USAC.

Just six months before in October 1977, Tony Hulman, who had rescued the Indianapolis 500 after it was closed during World War II, died of an aneurism. He was also the driving force behind the establishment of USAC when the AAA Contest Board exited auto racing in 1955. Well beloved by the racing community, Hulman's death was another loss of leadership in Championship racing.

Seizing the opportunity created by the leadership void, several team owners, including Penske, Gurney, Patrick and Jim Hall, formed Championship Auto Racing Teams (CART). Initially, the goal for CART was to be similar to the Formula One Constructors Association. Penske and Patrick were pushing the team owners in Indy car racing to have more of a say in the sport.

Concerned about the escalating costs of fielding a race team,[7] some team owners felt they weren't being properly compensated and the television rights should accrue to them. The team owners also felt that USAC did a poor job in promoting open-wheel racing.[8] Wally Dallenbach, a former driver for the Patrick Racing team, remembered the frustrations of the team owners: "They were truly frustrated with the lack of response from USAC. The owners were not making any money. They believed the sanctioning body had to do more to help the sport grow. USAC had the opportunity to take the owners seriously then, but it fell on deaf ears."[9] Patrick was at a breaking point. He recalled, "My motivation was the U.S. Auto Club was so inept at enforcing the rules and managing the operation, I was going to change it or quit."[10]

At issue was the control of open-wheel racing. Should it be controlled by the promoters and USAC, or should it be controlled by the racing teams? Gurney's white paper clearly lays out the position that the car owners should control the sport: "In all of our discussions as car owners and team leaders, we have agreed that it is essential that we continue to support USAC as the sanctioning body for Championship racing. The only improvement will be that USAC will work for us and support our causes and our policies." Gurney's white paper continued, "It should be clearly understood that the purpose of this organization is to make racing better in an overall way. Not just for the car owners and drivers, but also for the track owners and promoters and the sanctioning body and the sponsors and supporters and last but certainly not least, the racing fans and paying spectators."[11]

Roger Penske is a very successful team owner who was one of the founders of CART.

Despite these lofty goals, the battle for the control of open-wheel racing soon developed into various factions. On one side there were the team owners and on the other side there were the promoters and track owners. There were also divisions within the ranks of the team owners. One camp included the movers and shakers of CART, whose racing teams had adapted the V-8 Cosworth engine—Penske, Patrick and Hall. The other constituency consisted of those teams using the Offenhauser engine. The Offy engine, which had powered the Indy cars since the 1950s, wasn't competitive with the exotic Cosworth, but it was more affordable for those teams without deep pockets. By August 1978, open-wheel racing was in turmoil.

The V-4 Offenhauser contingent was so upset by their racing disadvantage that they staged a slowdown at the Texas World Speedway. The solution to the disparity in racing could be easily fixed by changing the boost allowed for the V-4 engines. The V-4 group also wanted the fuel mileage restrictions eased. Without action by USAC, the V-4 contingent was threatening "unspecified action" to bring about parity.[12] Soon the "unspecified action" became focused. When the 4-cylinder group threatened to boycott the Bettenhausen 200-mile race at the Wisconsin Fairgrounds Speedway, USAC called an emergency meeting of the competition committee. The committee decided to lower the boost level from 80 inches of mercury to 74 inches of mercury. They also gave more fuel to the racers by lowering the mileage requirement from 1.8 miles per gallon to 1.5 miles per gallon.[13]

When the final 500-mile race for 1978 was held at Ontario over Labor Day weekend, only 31 racers took to the field, compared to 47 entrants for the Indianapolis 500. Although this was the third richest race of the season, many of the 4-cylinder cars which were Indy 500 entrants did not participate in the race because they were not competitive. By the end of the race, only 5 cars were still running.[14]

In response to the 4-cylinder revolt, the USAC board made several changes for the 1979 racing season, including changing the fuel mileage from 1.8 miles per gallon to 1.5 miles per gallon, keeping the boost regulation to 80 inches of mercury for the 4-cylinder cars, and reducing the rear wing size from 43 inches to 36 inches.[15]

Goodyear Tire and Rubber Company, supplier of the racing tires not only for the Indianapolis 500 but for the entire championship racing circuit, was not pleased with the rule changes made by USAC. Underlying the company's discontent was an expansion of championship races from 14 in 1977 to 18 in 1978, including 2 in England. With the cost of supplying tires for the championship circuit at more than $1 million per year, Goodyear officials were upset that USAC didn't consult with them as other sanctioning bodies did before making the changes to the schedule and the rules. A Goodyear spokesman said, "The others call us and ask our opinion on even minor changes but USAC adds two championship races in England and one at Atlanta without ever finding out what effect it would have on us."[16] With displeasure over the rules changes and not being consulted, Leo Mehl, Goodyear's point man, said, "We're in the process of re-evaluating our entire racing program. We are studying the new USAC regulations to determine what effect they will have on Goodyear's future participation, with respect to additional expense, increased types of tires involved, and the expense and manpower required for future development of fuel cells, tires and other components.

Until these decisions are finalized, Goodyear is not in a position to participate in any discussions involving its future role in racing."[17]

Underlying the team owners' dissatisfaction with USAC was the fact that the cost of racing had increased significantly over what the teams earned in winnings. As the Indianapolis 500 was the largest, most significant race on the USAC schedule, most racers depended upon it to support the remainder of the season. Unfortunately, the Indianapolis 500 purse had not kept up with the cost of racing. As proof, CART members pointed to the winnings Al Unser enjoyed with his victories in 1970 and 1978. Although the cost of racing had nearly doubled during that time, the fruits of his labor had increased only 14.5 percent. Also underlying the dissatisfaction with the Indianapolis 500 purse was the construction of the $7 million Hall of Fame Museum; increased seating, which resulted in more spectators during the month of May; and an increase in ticket prices. Indianapolis Motor Speedway sources indicated that the majority of the Hall of Fame Museum financing was through the Hulman Trust, not the operations of the Speedway itself. Unconfirmed rumors circulated that CART's goal was to increase their payout from racing to $5 million for the series, of which $2 million would be from the Indianapolis 500. CART's Pat Patrick said this rumor was "totally false."[18]

The various speedways negotiated separately for the television broadcasts of the races, which accrued solely to the speedways; this also contributed to the unrest. CART member Dan Gurney laid out the case for the drivers' dissatisfaction with the television revenues: "It's not that we want all the TV money but those who negotiate the TV rights aren't selling us for what we are worth. People in TV tell us that Mario Andretti and Al Unser are driving around for one-quarter to one-third of what some minor league basketball players' teams command."[19]

In an attempt to work within USAC's framework, Penske and Patrick met with Reynold MacDonald, USAC's chairman, and Dick King, USAC's CEO, in October 1978. Although they wanted greater input in championship racing, including limiting the number of races to 12–14 and determining the race car specifications, the primary focus was the race purses, including the television rights. At the time of the split, USAC's policy on purses had races of 150 miles with a guaranteed payout of $50,000, while 200 miles had a guaranteed payment of $85,000. CART wanted a payout of $75,000 for 150-mile races and $100,000 for races of 200 miles.[20]

The CART entourage came to the meeting prepared with a plan to give them more say in championship racing. They proposed an 11-man board with 6 members from CART and 5 members from USAC. Although the board would be under the USAC umbrella, it would function independently for all decisions relating to championship racing.[21] The role model for this plan was the Formula One Constructors' Association, which made most of the decisions regarding the Grand Prix series. The proposed board would be responsible for the car specifications, the racing schedule and the monies paid.

Joseph Cloutier, president of the Indianapolis Motor Speedway and a member of the USAC board, also attended the meeting. Among the items discussed, he heard the CART members asking for a doubling of the Indianapolis 500 purse and participation in the television revenues that the Speedway enjoyed from ABC Sports. Being the largest one-day sporting event in the nation, the Indianapolis 500 purse of $1 million was by far the largest in auto racing, overshadowing the rest of the season.[22]

CART's desire to double the Indianapolis 500 purse was laid out in Gurney's white paper, which had singled out the Indianapolis 500 as the first target of CART. Just like a robber targeting banks because that is where the money is, Gurney wrote, "It appears that a 'showdown' with the Indianapolis Motor Speedway is or should be the first target. They are the ones who can afford it. We should negotiate the TV rights (our rights—not theirs) and we should double the purse." Gurney also addressed the other racing facilities: "Other tracks should be negotiated with on the basis of what is a reasonable amount of revenue to come from all sources such as TV, gate receipts, advertising, sponsors, etc. The entire picture should be shaped from the standpoint of cooperation rather than killing each other."[23]

Joe Cloutier was a close associate of Tony Hulman and assumed the presidency of the Indianapolis Motor Speedway after Hulman's death.

USAC's board held an emergency meeting to discuss the CART initiatives. The result of this meeting was a rejection of the separate board for championship racing.[24] The Indy car wars were on.

CART Goes Racing

As a result of the proposals being turned down by USAC, CART's Patrick said, "We were very disappointed in the action taken by USAC because we've been fair and tried to act like gentlemen. But the people spending the money have no vote in the rules. We have no input into what USAC says or does." He then laid down the gauntlet and made the future of CART very clear: "As a result of USAC's rejection of this proposal, CART is going to function separately from United States Auto Club in 1979 and will run the entire Championship Trail under a separate sanctioning organization."[1]

CART looked to somebody they knew to head the organization. James A. Melvin, president of the Michigan International Speedway, was named CART's president by the end of November.[2] They didn't have to look far to find Melvin as his boss, Roger Penske, was the owner of the Michigan International Speedway. Melvin also had previous experience in the auto racing industry as the Sports Car Club of America (SCCA) administrator.[3]

CART was also able to announce a tentative schedule of fourteen races for 1979. In early December, in addition to establishing its bylaws and electing officers, CART's membership listened to a proposal by the SCCA to be the sanctioning body.[4] Within a week of the membership meeting, CART garnered from SCCA what it had wanted from USAC—control over championship racing. The five-year agreement allowed CART to set the racing schedule, establishing their own racing rules including car specifications, the setting of purses and television rights.[5]

The big question was how did the Indianapolis 500 fit into this mix? The history of the race's being sanctioned by USAC had deep roots. When the AAA Contest Board, which had sanctioned the race from its beginning in 1911, announced it was getting out of the auto racing business in 1955, Tony Hulman, the owner of the Indianapolis Motor Speedway, was the driving force behind the establishment of USAC. There had been a close relationship throughout the intervening years.

In early December 1978, there was a meeting of Dick King, USAC's president, Henry Ryder, USAC's attorney, and Joseph Cloutier, president of the Indianapolis Motor Speedway. The topic at hand was the car regulations for the 1979 Indianapolis 500. USAC hoped to encourage new participants to the race by adopting a stock-block engine. Used by USAC's dirt race division, stock-block engines were more affordable than the turbocharged Offys or the exotic Cosworths. USAC leadership also hoped that by adopting the stock-block engine for the Indianapolis 500, some Detroit manufacturers might be enabled to reenter the racing circuit. This was a very similar tactic to that taken by Eddie Rickenbacker when he banned superchargers in the early 1930s[6] to encourage Detroit manufacturers to enter semi-stock cars in the race.[7] To make the stock-block engine competitive if adopted, the Offys and the Cosworth engines would need to have their power reduced either through a restrictor plate similar to the one used in NASCAR or through lowering the manifold pressure.

When the entry forms were distributed for the Indianapolis 500, the stock-block engines were given parity to the turbocharged engines. This brought immediate protests from the CART crowd that USAC was being vindictive, as to run at the Indianapolis 500 would cost the CART teams more money. Dick King, USAC president, explained USAC's actions: "We don't have any responsibility to those who left, ours is to those people who have stayed with us, and they are saying stock blocks. We have known for a long time that we've had serious problems with the Championship Car racing, and when those people took their circus down the road we acted. We're not trying to hurt anyone's investment, but we're trying to give everyone an equal shot at winning, and thus bring a new look into the sport."[8]

As would be expected, there was unrest among some of the CART members over the severed relationships of the tightly knit championship-racing fraternity. Sherman Armstrong, an Indiana businessman, owner of the Armstrong Mould racing team, was the first to leave CART and return to USAC. Amid rumors of dissatisfaction by some drivers, including Danny Ongais and four-time Indianapolis 500 winner A. J. Foyt, and other teams, the folks at USAC hoped this would turn into a mass migration. But a flood of teams returning to USAC did not happen.[9]

As the 1979 racing season approached, CART had lined up two race tracks—Michigan International Speedway, owned by Roger Penske, and Phoenix International Raceway. The other tracks, including Indianapolis, Ontario, Pocono, Trenton and the Wisconsin Fairgrounds, remained committed to running USAC races. Pat Patrick did not hide the intentions of CART to have other oval tracks as part of their series. Speaking of USAC,

Patrick said, "Their actions are a little frustrating, but we're getting our schedule ready and our plans haven't altered. Roger [Penske] is in Hawaii at the moment looking at their track and motorsport, Mid-Ohio and Watkins Glen [all road courses] are all very interested. But of course, we don't want this thing to become a road course circuit and we intend to pursue other oval tracks around the country."[10]

In mid–January 1979, CART announced the beginning of their racing schedule for the year. If there had been any question about the animosity between the two groups, the scheduling made it quite clear that CART was out to destroy USAC. By negotiating a change of date of the race at Phoenix

A. J. Foyt, a very successful driver who became a team owner. He was among the first team owners to return to USAC after the split in 1979.

International Raceway from March 25 to March 11, CART insured that they would have the first Indy car race of the season. An even bigger shock followed with the announcement that CART had scheduled a race on April 22, 1979, at the Atlanta International Speedway in direct competition with USAC's Trenton race. CART also tentatively announced races at the North Carolina Motor Speedway and at Mosport, Ontario's road course.[11]

With these announced dates, the total open-wheel races scheduled increased to seventeen, four more than what Goodyear Tire and Rubber Company had announced they would support. Goodyear and the television networks would become important players in the increasing rift between the two sides. Although Goodyear publicly maintained neutrality, it was believed they were supporting the breakaway group.

Because named-drivers'

participation in the races was essential for viewership, which translates to advertising revenues, the television contracts with USAC required a "representative field" for the races. For one network, this meant that fifteen of the top twenty drivers would need to participate in the race to be televised. This put USAC in a difficult position, as the top drivers, by and large, were associated with CART. Without these drivers participating, the USAC races wouldn't be broadcast on television—and one very important source of revenue to the sanctioning body would be lost. Trying to maintain a "representative field," USAC modified its rules regarding driver eligibility at an emergency board meeting. Instead of limiting the top twenty USAC drivers determined by championship points for the prior season to participating only in USAC races or international races, USAC opened the gate, allowing the drivers to participate in CART races once permission had been given. The one exception where approval would be denied was if both USAC and CART scheduled races on the same date. In this instance, the USAC driver would not have the option to participate in the CART race.[12]

The elephant in the room was what would the Indianapolis 500 do? Historically, the race was open to all drivers holding a Federation Internationale de l'Automobile (FIA) license. Rumors floated around Indianapolis that the Speedway would drop its FIA licensing. This would benefit USAC as it would basically require drivers to be a part of USAC in order to drive in the Indianapolis 500, the race with the largest purse and upon which most teams depended in order to be solvent. Joseph Cloutier solved the question when he announced the Indianapolis 500 would be open to all drivers with international licenses, meaning that those drivers aligned with CART could participate.[13] With this announcement, Cloutier guaranteed that the Speedway should be able to field a competitive event on Memorial Day.

In late January 1979, USAC established the racing engine configuration for the year. Since the Indianapolis 500 would continue to run under USAC sanctioning but the majority of the race cars would be regular participants in the CART racing circuit, they needed to achieve parity between those cars running with Cosworth engines, Offy engines and USAC's proposed stock-block engines. To do this, they put limitations on the amount of manifold boost the engine could produce. The new limits were 50 inches of boost for 8-cylinder (Cosworth) engines, 55 inches of boost for 4-cylinder (Offenhauser and Drake) racing engines and 58 inches for American stock production engines.[14]

USAC's only advantage was that they had the racing promoters, and therefore the tracks, in their camp. Since CART had the named drivers and the strongest racing teams, what it needed was a shift of allegiance of the promoters from USAC. CART set its next focus on breaking this lock. They approached Trenton Speedway's George Hamid about running an event on April 8 for CART and canceling the April 22 race sponsored by USAC. The real kicker was that the proposed race on April 8 would be in direct conflict with USAC's 200-mile race at the Texas World Speedway. This not only would damage USAC's race schedule but would also take away one of the valuable television broadcasts for the league.[15] A week later, Roger Penske announced that he had leased the Trenton track from George Hamid and would control open-wheel racing events at that facility. This caused USAC to cancel its two races at Trenton. Putting on the best spin possible, Dick King said of Penske's announcement, "They couldn't play ball in our park so they went out and bought the ballpark. They must be desperate if they have to go around leasing facilities because they can't get promoters to run their races because of the costs involved."[16]

While absorbing this blow, USAC learned it also lost its primary series sponsor, Citicorp.[17] USAC was on the ropes—CART not only had the teams and the drivers but they were also being successful in getting the remaining part of the puzzle to fall into place, with tracks abandoning their allegiance to USAC. The bad news continued for USAC when Montgomery Ward Auto Club canceled both its mini-Indy and Robert Bosch Super Vee sponsorships. Instead, they would shift their sponsorship monies to the support of rally races. The announcement provided yet more proof that the split between CART and USAC was doing damage to the sport. The announcement blamed "the controversy among the major sanctioning bodies involved, and, the time limitations to develop a sound marketing approach around a yet unannounced series schedule."[18]

As rumors circulated through the racing community that USAC was in dire straits, speculation grew about whether or not it would be able to hold its pre–Indianapolis 500 races at Trenton, Ontario and the Texas World Speedway. If it was unable to hold this racing season together, most felt that would be the end of USAC championship racing. Joseph Cloutier, Indianapolis Motor Speedway president, expressed his concern about the future of USAC: "I just don't think that two rival series will make it. I don't know which group will come out, but I wonder what will happen to the other types of racing USAC conducts if they're the losers."[19]

By the end of January, CART was able to add another piece to the puzzle. President James Melvin[20] had negotiated an agreement with NBC to telecast three of their races—the Phoenix race on March 11, the Michigan International race on July 3 and one yet to be specified. Not only was the announcement important in the scope of race promotions, but the agreement also gained one of the desires of the car owners. The race revenues would flow to CART, owned by the race teams, rather than to the sanctioning body (in this case SCCA).

A CART meeting in mid–January in Indianapolis provided a glimmer of hope for USAC. As is normal in the Midwest during the winter, there was always the possibility of inclement weather. As it turned out, two of CART's team owners couldn't make it to Indianapolis for the meeting. A. J. Foyt was snowed in in Memphis and Jim Hall was snowed in in Little Rock. Foyt called Patrick requesting the meeting be postponed for several days in order to allow Foyt and Hall to attend. Patrick quickly dismissed this request.

Foyt later recounted his conversation with Patrick to the *Indianapolis Star*: "Patrick started saying 'we gotta go forward' and all this and that we couldn't have another one that soon. I said we'd agreed to have 100 percent representation and that if I wasn't going to get mine, then maybe I'd see you cats later. Patrick said 'If you want to stay fine, and if you want to leave, fine.'" Foyt, unhappy with his treatment by Patrick, decided to return to the USAC fold. In the announcement of his decision made in early February, Foyt said, "We formed CART to improve the benefits of car owners and form a more workable relationship with the USAC Board of Directors on areas such as rules. The USAC board definitely needed to make some changes and it took some time, but they agreed to work with us. I don't think CART should be sanctioning and promoting its own races and I think it's in the best interest of racing to stay with USAC." Foyt also accused CART's leadership of lying. He said, "I asked two or three questions that I already knew the answers to, and received flat-assed lies. They used me to get CART formed and now there are only one or two guys doing all the talking. They're on an ego trip and they want to conquer the racing world, but I have no desire to do that."[21]

With USAC apparently on the ropes, behind the scenes Leo Mehl of Goodyear Tire and Rubber was making efforts to reunite the two sides. Mehl was successful in getting CART's Patrick and USAC's King together for a meeting in Florida in early March. Mehl proposed an eleven member Championship Racing board composed of five CART representatives and six USAC representatives. Unfortunately, this meeting fell apart. One of the reasons given by CART for not being able to reunite open-wheel racing was their sanctioning contract with SCCA. Another obstacle was the CART rulebook banning CART licensed drivers from participating in any non-CART race other than the Indianapolis 500.[22]

Not only was the CART/USAC split damaging championship racing, but there was also the threat by President Jimmy Carter to close all retail gasoline stations between noon Friday and midnight Sunday due to the energy crisis. One racing insider commented on the proposed ban: "These planned closures mean virtual house arrest for every American on weekends, unless something is done about it."[23]

CART opened its racing season in early March with a 150-mile event at the Phoenix International Raceway. As USAC got ready to open its racing season, ABC pulled the plug on broadcasting the Ontario and Texas World Speedway races. Then ABC chose to broadcast CART's Atlanta International Speedway race on April 22 rather than the USAC race at Dover Downs on the same day. ABC was willing to broadcast the Dover Downs event if USAC would change the date of the race. The underlying problem for USAC was that without the big-name drivers, the race wouldn't have a draw for the television audience. This was a big blow to USAC, as there would not be a televised USAC race prior to the 1979 Indianapolis 500.[24] The skirmishes between CART and USAC/Indianapolis 500 continued with the Ontario 500 race in March, which the CART teams boycotted.[25] Despite the lack of CART racers, USAC had a field of 21 cars for the race. Surprisingly, the lack of big-name drivers did not appear to hurt attendance. Race officials reported about the same attendance as the prior year, perhaps slightly higher.[26]

Although the Indianapolis Motor Speedway officials were pleased with the 100 entries for the upcoming May classic, they were concerned about rumors of a potential boycott. The issue at hand was the boost pressure that USAC had set, trying to equalize the stock-block engines with the turbocharged engines. The CART teams felt they would be at a disadvantage if their cars were not given more boost. In fact, they were concerned about whether they would even qualify for the field of 33.

Trying to resolve this issue, Pat Patrick negotiated with the Indianapolis Motor Speedway over the acceptable boost pressure for the Cosworth and Offenhauser engines. Patrick said, "The CART teams feel very strongly that such maneuvering by USAC is the result of unlawful, arbitrary and malicious motivation."[27] Unable to convince USAC and Indianapolis Motor Speedway to change the boost pressure for V-8 and V-4 turbocharged engines, talk of a potential boycott of the Indianapolis 500 circulated throughout the Championship racing community. The boycott rumors speculated that to do the most damage to USAC and the Indianapolis Motor Speedway, after qualifications, the CART teams would "park" their entries that qualified for the race in order to get their demands for increased boost met. There was also some discussion of holding a race at Penske's Michigan International Speedway in direct competition with the Indianapolis 500. With CART representing some of the strongest race teams, the potential boycott could have disastrous results for the Indianapolis classic.[28]

Despite the submission by the CART teams of their entry forms for the 1979 Indianapolis 500, the concern about a boycott of the race remained. Underlying this concern was the action by the CART owners regarding the Ontario Motor Speedway 200-mile race. CART owners had advised their drivers that they would not be allowed to participate in this race, which had full international FIA listing. USAC president King wondered, "What evidence do we have that the situation at Indianapolis would be any different than it was at Ontario?"[29] Concern in the Indianapolis 500 camp about the potential for a boycott of the race was evident when Indianapolis Motor Speedway attorney Harry Ice later commented, "Even when they turned their entries in, Mr. Patrick presented a veiled threat when he said they turned in their entries only to avoid technical disqualification. The actions of the plaintiffs in this case are detrimental to the integrity of the operation of the Indianapolis 500."[30]

On April 13, 1979, representatives from the Ontario, Texas, Pocono and Milwaukee tracks along with Dick King, president of USAC, and Joe Cloutier, president of the Indianapolis Motor Speedway, met to discuss ways to "combat CART." Options debated at this meeting included (1) rejecting all CART teams for the Indianapolis 500; (2) rejecting the entries for the six CART leaders; (3) diverting the Indianapolis 500 purse money for appearance money at other USAC races; (4) diverting Indianapolis 500 funds into a USAC point fund; and 5) withholding two-thirds of the Indianapolis 500 purse.[31]

Four days later, Penske and Patrick met with King and Tom Binford, Indianapolis 500 chief steward, to discuss ways to bring the two sides together. Patrick proposed a board consisting of four representatives from CART and four from USAC to control championship racing. Patrick left the meeting with a positive outlook for the remainder of the season: "We agreed to get together and run the rest of the season together—using USAC rules and officials at USAC races and CART rules and officials at CART races. We even agreed to change our schedule and move the Trenton date so we wouldn't be in conflict with their Milwaukee race."[32] The next day Patrick and Penske conveyed to the CART board in New York the results of the conversations with King and Binford indicating that the eight-member governing board was acceptable in principle.[33] But King left the meeting with a very different perspective:

> It was an 8-man board with four from each group alright, but they wanted to specifically disallow certain people from being on the USAC board. And this was all based on the premise that a new entity would be established separately from USAC. We'd run under USAC sanction, but basically— other than our four men—we'd have nothing to do with any of the actual

business at hand. Basically, it was no different from the proposal they gave us back in January and, in fact, I think we lost ground. Before we'd have a separate board to run champ racing and the new concept was to be completely autonomous of USAC.[34]

When the USAC board met on April 19, the members voted unanimously on the fifth ballot to reject the entries for the six CART teams. King said his vote was influenced by his uncertainty over whether the six CART teams would run at Indianapolis.[35] Interestingly, four-time Indianapolis 500 winner A. J. Foyt, who was not on the board of USAC, attended the board meeting of April 19. He was given a voice and later in a deposition was quoted as saying, "Now is the time to act, USAC must take a stand. I'm in favor of rejecting the entries."[36]

Tom Binford, former chief steward of the Indianapolis 500. He was the CEO of the Indy Racing League.

USAC notified the six affected teams (Team McLaren, Patrick Racing, Penske Racing, Inc., Chaparral Racing, Fletcher Racing and All-American Racers, Inc.) by telegram when they arrived at Atlanta for an upcoming CART race that their entries had been rejected by USAC because they were "not in good standing" with the sanctioning body.[37] These teams had submitted entries for nineteen cars. The drivers impacted included four who had won the Indianapolis 500 a total of eight times—Al Unser (three), Bobby Unser (two), Johnny Rutherford (two) and Gordon Johncock (one).[38] Patrick responded publicly, saying, "It shows a complete disregard for the fans who have purchased tickets. It shows complete disregard for the sponsors who have helped make the Indianapolis '500' the great sporting spectacle it is." Fellow CART board member Dan Gurney voiced his opinion: "USAC appears to be using the Indianapolis '500' as a pawn in its efforts to destroy CART as a viable racing organization. We will not let this happen."[39]

Needless to say, the telegrams only increased the animosity between the two groups. And since the six teams impacted were all headed by CART board members and were among the strongest racing teams, they were going to fight for their chance to be in the field. Patrick immediately sent a telegram to Cloutier, president of the Indianapolis Motor Speedway; Mary Hulman, widow of Tony Hulman and chair of the board of the Indianapolis Motor Speedway; and Mari Hulman George, daughter of Tony Hulman and vice president of the Indianapolis Motor Speedway. The telegram read,

> First, we must know whether USAC is acting in behalf of the Indianapolis Motor Speedway with regard to the above referenced entries for the 500-Mile International Sweepstakes. If USAC is acting on your behalf with regard to these entries, we must assume until notified otherwise that the entry blanks as submitted are still pending with the Speedway, since it is our understanding that the right to refuse any entry is reserved to the Speedway. If USAC is speaking on your behalf with regard to these entries, we must request immediate clarification of the grounds of the rejection for the entries. Since some 25 CART entries have apparently been accepted and a select few refused, none of which are USAC members, we must immediately know the basis of this distinction. Failing a satisfactory response to these inquiries, we will be compelled to resort to our available remedies.[40]

CART also asked its sanctioning body, SCCA, to intervene on their behalf with Automobile Competition Committee for the United States (ACCUS), the ruling body for all auto racing organizations in the United States.[41]

Cloutier answered the telegram by simply stating the decision was made by the sanctioning body. For more clarification, he referred to the entry blank, which stated, "An automobile race for cars and drivers in good standing with the United States Auto Club, the Organizing Committee, subject to all USAC rules and Approved Supplementary Regulations will be held as described hereafter...."[42]

King explained to the public that the six CART team entries were not in good standing with USAC because of "the tremendous amount of detrimental information put out in conflict with the ideals of USAC. Indianapolis is an event of ours sanctioned by us and we do not have to consent to the entries of those who have been doing harm to us." King continued expressing concern about their intent to run in the Indianapolis 500: "They said publicly that they filed their entries to satisfy the technical requirements, but that did not necessarily indicate that they were going to race."[43] Understanding the financial importance of the Indianapolis 500 for the CART teams, Patrick offered to post a bond guaranteeing that those teams qualifying for the race would run.[44]

In an effort to avoid the legal wrangling, the two sides met in early May 1979. The meeting concluded with the two sides being at an impasse. The statements issued by both sides indicated how far apart they were and left little hope of a resolution before the Indianapolis 500. King said the "CART reps refused to mend the split on a long range basis. They insisted they be allowed to compete in the Indianapolis 500 before ever considering any permanent settlement to the problems. We would have preferred a settlement to litigation, but it just didn't happen this way."[45] A CART representative said, "They [the USAC] presented us with a proposal that said if we would agree to come back within the USAC structure, they would withdraw their ban of our six teams. We told them that we felt their actions were illegal and we suggested they rescind those actions. If they agreed, we would then sit down and conduct some good faith negotiations."[46]

With the attempt at mediation of the split failing, the suit headed to court. CART sought reinstatement of the six banned teams through a preliminary injunction. They maintained USAC's action was "arbitrary, capricious and totally without foundation or rational basis" and was a violation of the Sherman Antitrust Act. They further asserted that the real reason for USAC's action was "to penalize the principals of the plaintiff racing teams for establishing a competitive championship racing organization and sought to divide the loyalties of the CART organization."[47] Johnny Rutherford, a driver for a CART team, also filed legal action requesting the documentation surrounding the entries and the rejection of the CART teams be produced in court.[48] USAC's argument was that CART's boycott of the Ontario race, and the threatened boycott of the Indianapolis 500 unless changes were made to the rules around manifold pressure, were evidence of CART trying to destroy the existing sanctioning body.[49]

As part of the legal maneuvering, CART's suit added Gary Bettenhausen, Roger McCluskey, car owner Rolla Vollstedt, Cloutier, members of the USAC board of directors, and A. J. Foyt, who attended the board meeting as defendants.[50] Their complaint was also expanded to include those eight drivers who were contractually obligated to the banned CART teams, including Al and Bobby Unser, Gordon Johncock, Rick Mears, Wally Dallenbach, Mike Mosley and Steve Krisiloff.[51]

On May 3, 1979, Federal District Court Judge James E. Noland ruled in favor of CART and allowed the six teams to participate in the Indianapolis 500. In his ruling, Judge Noland wrote, "The plaintiffs have no accurate remedy by law, and the threatened injury to the plaintiffs outweighs the threatened damage of the defendants. Therefore, a preliminary injunction was granted in the best public interest." Even though Judge Noland ruled in favor of the CART teams, he told the packed courtroom, "The plaintiffs have not provided sufficient proof that there was a per se violation of the Sherman

Antitrust Act. There is considerable evidence that the owners tried to coerce the IMS management into rule changes and the court will keep this under advisement."[52]

When the Indianapolis Motor Speedway opened for practice, a controversy bloomed over the manifold pressure on the cars. In order to boost their speeds, some competitors had crimped the tailpipes on their cars while others blocked off the wastegate exhaust valves. This allowed teams to effectively override the pop-off valve, resulting in increased speeds. When these modifications were brought to the attention of USAC officials prior to the start of the time trials and they took no action, some competitors believed the changes were acceptable. On the first weekend of qualifying, twenty-five cars qualified for the race, many of which reportedly had modified their tailpipes. USAC did not find any of the teams qualifying guilty of manipulating the manifold pressure.[53]

Suddenly, on the second weekend of qualifying, the modification of tailpipes became a big issue. Three drivers (Dick Ferguson, Steve Krisiloff and Tom Bigelow) were disqualified from the race.[54] The outcry was immediate. Seven teams filed protests, which were denied by the race officials. Al Loquesto, one of the drivers involved in the protest, said, "They [USAC officials] are wrong, know they are wrong and won't admit it. They just are trying to cover up for their own mistakes. I have a feeling that many of us are going to go to another organization."[55] The drivers felt that action taken by USAC was unfair. John Martin circulated a petition in the garage area requesting the size of the field be increased from 33 cars to allow those disqualified cars to run. In a statement to the *Indianapolis Star*, Martin said, "We got rooked. We've just plain been eliminated due to the incompetence of the USAC technical staff. They were told before the first weekend of qualifications how the boost was being overridden and they didn't do anything about it."[56]

With the protest having been dismissed by USAC officials, team owner Wayne Woodward planned to pursue legal action to get his car reinstated in the race. He said, "I've retained an attorney and I'm going to seek an injunction to reinstate my car in the race. I want an injunction to halt the race until the issue is resolved."[57]

After the disqualification of the seven cars, USAC issued a bulletin stating that the inside diameter of the tailpipe must be 1.47 inches. Since the standard tailpipe was 2.5 inches, teams interpreted the bulletin as allowing the use of washers to reduce the size of the tailpipe, effectively overriding the pop-off valve.[58]

CART teams supported the disqualified teams in their efforts to get reinstated. Representing the group, CART president Patrick said, "Due to the unfortunate circumstances surrounding qualifying, we have polled our CART membership and we sincerely believe that every car unfairly removed from the field should have an equal opportunity to qualify for the Indianapolis 500. We feel that USAC officials should have made this decision themselves instead of transferring the responsibility for it to the entire starting field. It was their mistake and they should have remedied it."[59] Bowing to the pressure, USAC relented and agreed to allow the eleven cars that had been disqualified from the race to attempt to re-qualify, subject to the consent of all of the cars qualified for the race. Excluded from the opportunity to re-qualify was Wayne Woodward, who had filed legal action.[60]

The battle lines were drawn. In less than a year, the split between CART and USAC/Indianapolis Motor Speedway had resulted in two controversies resulting in legal action. The new leadership at USAC had stumbled badly on the qualification trials. As the hours ticked down to the start of the race, the Indianapolis Motor Speedway was getting many requests for refunds on the tickets. This might have been attributed to the gas crisis or it might have been the result of the infighting between the two factions.[61]

The attempt to get all of the qualified racers to sign a consent form allowing the disqualified teams to reattempt their qualifying runs failed. This resulted in the protest going through USAC's appeals process.[62] In a surprise to many, the appeals process allowed qualifications to be reopened to the disqualified teams with the proviso that to get into the field, the teams would need to go at least 183.908 miles per hour, the speed of the slowest qualifier, Roger McCluskey. The USAC appeals board issued a statement that said, "The appeals have merit and call for a solution which will cause the least disruption to entrants, the United States Auto Club and the Indianapolis Motor Speedway, because of a rule on manifold restrictions that became difficult to enforce due to developments that continued to change throughout the period of qualifications for the 1979 Indianapolis 500-Mile Race."[63]

On race day, thirty-five cars lined up for the beginning of the field. Although eight teams made qualifying runs only two, Billy Vukovich and George Snider, qualified.[64] On the legal front, Marion County Superior Court Judge Michael T. Dugan ruled against Wayne Woodward's efforts to have his driver, Dick Ferguson, reinstated in the race. In his ruling, Dugan said, "The plaintiff [Woodward] is a voluntary private member of a private racing association. It is not the role of the courts to operate or [supervise] a private organization whose activities are bound by internal rules."[65]

An Attempt at Reconciliation

Some within the open-wheel fraternity recognized the damage being done to the sport. Among those was driver Roger McCluskey, who organized a meeting before the running of the 1979 Indianapolis 500 in an effort to bring the two warring sides together. At the meeting he proposed a nine-member committee to try to reunify open-wheel racing. His proposal included USAC's being represented by Tom Binford (chief steward of the Indianapolis 500), King (president of USAC) and himself. CART's proposed representatives were Dan Gurney (team owner), Jerry O'Donnell (team owner) and Tim McLauren (crew chief for Tyler Alexander). The final third of the committee included Larry Conrad (Indiana secretary of state), Clarence Cagle (former grounds superintendent for the Indianapolis Motor Speedway) and Gordon Betz (former USAC official). What was distressing to those in the racing community about the committee being formed was the lack of a time frame for action. Johnny Rutherford said, "There's no timetable on this. In fact, there hasn't been a future date set for the committee to meet."[1] The lack of a timetable ultimately resulted in this proposed committee never meeting.

Despite all of the turmoil leading up to the Indianapolis 500, there was a sense of camaraderie at the dinner celebrating the victory of Rick Mears, who had started the race in the pole position. Penske, owner of the winning car, thanked the folks at the Indianapolis Motor Speedway for "a great race." He went on to express hope for the future: "I am hoping by next year things can be smoothed out. Time can do a lot to solve problems." On behalf of the Indianapolis Motor Speedway, chief steward Tom Binford also struck a conciliatory tone: "By the 1980 race we've got to pull ourselves together. There's no way we can do the job right unless we're all chasing the same rabbit."[2]

The good feelings at the victory banquet didn't last long. Less than a week after the Indianapolis 500, the Speedway announced that the automatic invitations to the 1980 Indianapolis 500 would be extended to those teams participating in the USAC-sanctioned races at Pocono and the Labor Day race at Ontario. The Speedway added another proviso that those teams hoping to get the automatic invitations were also expected to participate in "other races designated by the Indianapolis Motor Speedway 10 days prior to the closing of entries for such races." Racing insiders saw this move as USAC's trying to protect its existing relationship with race tracks and possibly increasing the number of tracks loyal to USAC. It was also perceived as the Speedway's trying to avoid the potential of litigation by making this event by invitation only; they could exclude anyone from participating. Patrick reacted to the announcement, saying, "It's unfortunate that the Indianapolis Motor Speedway has chosen to use its power and influence as the organizer of the world's greatest auto race in what obviously is a last-ditch effort to salvage the 1979 USAC race schedule and its viability as a racing sanctioning body."[3]

Racing resumed with head-to-head competition on June 10. USAC ran a race at Milwaukee, while CART ran a competing race at Trenton. The next race on USAC's schedule was the Music 500 at Pocono on June 24. Rumors circulated CART would run a 500-kilometer (310-mile) race on the same day at the New Jersey State Fairgrounds. Adding fuel to the embers, Penske stated he would consider honoring the tickets to the Music 500 race at the CART race.[4]

Meanwhile on the legal front, the CART antitrust lawsuit against USAC was amended to include triple damages. They stated they were "damaged in [their] trade or business and in [their] competitive position."[5] Not to be outdone, USAC filed its own antitrust case against CART, and like CART was seeking treble damages. The issue went back to the CART boycott of the Ontario race in March. USAC alleged that the "concerted action of CART has damaged the business and trade and competitive position of USAC and, is aimed at eliminating USAC as a sanctioning organization in competition with CART. The concerted action of [CART] has the purpose and effect of subjecting USAC to a group boycott, and therefor constitutes a per se violation of Section 1 of the Sherman Act."[6]

Behind the scenes, Ray Smartis, the general manager at the Ontario Motor Speedway, tried his hand at brokering a truce between the two sides. He proposed a Champ Car governing board to CART's leadership team. The Champ Car board would have eleven members—three from USAC, three from CART, three track operators, one CART driver and one other representative from USAC. But this structure was dead on arrival. Smartis proposed Dr. Joseph Mattioli from Pocono International Raceway, Bob Fletcher from Phoenix International Raceway, and himself as the track operators. Fletcher was also on the CART board of directors. Under the Smartis plan, the grand-daddy of them all, the Indianapolis Motor Speedway, wasn't going to have representation. Another complication to this plan was CART's contract with the SCCA. Would they become the sanctioning body for the Champ Car governing board or would it remain with USAC? Certainly the people from SCCA wanted their share of the deal. A SCCA spokesman said, "What we want to see is peace, but under the SCCA. If it doesn't work out that way, I don't know what will happen."[7]

The two sides got together in Indianapolis in mid–June, where two plans were presented highlighting the chasm between USAC and CART. The plan presented by Ray Smartis had an interim board to govern the remainder of the 1979 races. It would consist of Dan Gurney, Jim Hall, Tyler Alexander (McLaren team manager), Smartis, Mattioli, Fletcher and Wally Dallenbach. Additionally, there would be two "independents," one of whom would be CART's legal counsel, John Frasco; the other would be either Dick King or Gordon Betz (a former USAC official). With six of the nine representatives clearly in the CART camp, this was clearly a non-starter for the USAC folks. USAC's proposal had a fourteen-member "Indy Car Commission" that would operate within the USAC framework. Composition of the commission was more balanced, with five members coming from USAC, five members from CART, and four from the promoter ranks. Of the promoters, three permanent members would be representatives from the three tracks on which 500-mile contests were run—Indianapolis, Ontario and Pocono—and one selected annually. The USAC representatives would include team owners, mechanics and a driver. CART would choose their five representatives. The weakness in the USAC proposal was that any rule passed would need to have been approved by 70 percent of the commission—ten members. This requirement alone could hang the commission up indefinitely. If CART or USAC voted as a block, there would be five votes against a proposal.[8] This attempt at reconciliation was not successful.

Remaining on the USAC calendar was the California 500 at the Ontario Motor Speedway on Labor Day. Soon, another shoe dropped for USAC when Smartis announced that Ontario would work with CART for the remainder of 1979 and for 1980. Smartis gave the rationale for the decision: "We feel the decision to go with CART is in the best interest of the race as well as the fans. I think we owe it to the fans to provide the best field of cars and drivers available and under the present circumstances, I don't think that's possible with USAC."[9] Understandably, the folks at USAC were disappointed by this decision. Not only did it give CART another track in their camp, it also provided them with a 500-mile race. King said, "I am disappointed that Ray chose to go this way. USAC has stood behind all the tracks it has dealt with in the past. We stuck by them when things were rough for them. It's unfortunate they didn't remember that."[10]

In September, Dr. Mattioli filed legal action against CART for antitrust action for its running of a race in direct competition with the Music 500 at the Pocono International Raceway on June 24. As a result of the CART race, attendance at the Music 500 was down 50 percent, resulting in Pocono's experiencing a $2 million loss for the race. In addition to CART, defendants named in the action included Penske, Patrick, Penske Corporation, Penske Racing, and Gould, Inc., Gould, Inc. was one of Penske's major sponsors and a 21 percent owner of Penske Corporation. Seeking treble damages, the suit asked for $6.3 million.[11] In early August, CART reaffirmed its contract with SCCA for 1980. Reunification under sanctioning by USAC would remain very difficult.

With USAC spinning out of control, the Indianapolis Motor Speedway sought to find a leader to replace Cloutier, the trusted assistant to Tony Hulman who had stepped into the president's role after Hulman's death. It was hoped that a path towards reunification might be found with new leadership at the Speedway. The man ultimately selected was John Cooper. With a love of auto racing, Cooper brought a wealth of knowledge and experience to the job. He had been USAC's first public relations man and rose to the level of vice president. He later gained valuable experience as the president of the Ontario Motor Speedway. After serving as a director of the Automobile Competition Committee of the United States (ACCUS), he joined NASCAR as a vice president. With his hiring, it was hoped he could reunite open-wheel racing.[12]

Cooper clearly understood there would be challenges. He said, "This USAC-CART dispute has been going on one year now and it's not going to go away. I don't think a Henry Kissinger type is going to come down, out of the clouds and solve this thing. I'm not that guy, but I'll do my share."[13] Cooper also recognized the potential damage to the Indianapolis 500 if the warring factions couldn't start working together: "I think the Indianapolis 500 must be a part of something. It must be a part of a series and the fans have shown during this past season they want a single championship."[14]

In October 1980, CART passed another major hurdle when they landed PPG Industries as a series sponsor. This sponsorship was valued at $250,000. Additionally, CART had negotiated four broadcasts of their races on the NBC television network.[15]

Taking a page from the CART playbook, the Indianapolis Motor Speedway inked a one-year deal with the Pocono International Raceway, which was having cash flow difficulties. The deal included financial assistance for the Pocono 500-mile race and a NASCAR race. This action assured, at least temporarily, USAC's having two 500-mile races for 1980.[16]

The impact of the USAC/CART split upon Championship racing was highlighted in the Goodyear Tire and Rubber 1979 annual report of attendance at the various racing series. Overall, racing attendance was down 6 percent (roughly 300,000), which was attributed to the gasoline shortage and the CART/USAC war. But the impact upon Championship racing was significant. Indy car races were down by 305,400 spectators. As a comparison, NASCAR spectator count was down only 2,000 per event. Goodyear's Leo Mehl said, "It appears that racing fans have registered their votes at the box office and what they seem to be calling for is a single, unified champ-car series."[17]

Goodyear wasn't at all happy with the chain of events in Championship racing. They were upset with all of the bad publicity and concerned about the significant drop in attendance at the races. Goodyear's participation in the races, which included giving free tires to the participants, wasn't intended to be charitable. Rather, it was part of their corporate advertising strategy. Having cars run on Goodyear tires would hopefully result in an increase in retail sales. Mehl told United Press International, "Regardless of the intent or motives behind CART's formation and breakaway from USAC, the results have been a disaster for all concerned."[18] Mehl delivered a wake-up message to both CART and USAC. Goodyear was considering cutting back its support for Championship racing by limiting the free tires provided to the teams. He indicated Goodyear might also cut back on research and development on some of the racing tires.

Given the pressure from Goodyear, Mehl was able to get the two sides together for a meeting. In attendance were King, Rolla Vollstedt, McCluskey, Tom Binford and Henry Ryder from USAC and Patrick, Penske, John Frasco, James Melvin (CART president), and Bob Fletcher from CART. They discussed the possibility of a seven-member championship racing board consisting of three CART members, three USAC representatives and one independent member.[19] The meeting concluded abruptly when the CART delegation walked out. Objecting to the races being run under the USAC banner, the CART delegation wanted one schedule and one set of officials, but the races would be run under the individual sanctioning bodies depending upon who scheduled the race. Showing a significant amount of distrust, the CART delegation also wanted a separate accounting firm to keep the financial records for the championship races.[20]

After the negotiations fizzled, Goodyear advised the two sides they would support only seventeen races in 1980 including the three 500-mile races and seven additional races for each side. Between USAC and CART, twenty-three races had been scheduled.[21] To apply pressure to both sides to seek a compromise, Goodyear's stance hardened within a week. With the exception of the three 500-mile races, Goodyear decided to start charging for the tires. They would provide one free set of tires to the top 15 teams if there were at least 20 teams entered in a race or the top 20 teams if at least 30 teams were entered a race. All other sets of tires would have to be purchased by the teams. This would cause the teams financial challenges, as during most races, three to four sets of tires were utilized. A Goodyear spokesman explained, "The two groups have reached a firm stalemate and Goodyear will not subsidize the fight any longer. The two groups are going to have to stand on their merit and not ride along on Indy's coattails anymore. Goodyear has to justify its means and supplying free tires to groups that draw 3,000 people (i.e. CART's shoddy Atlanta turnout and USAC's Texas debacle) while IMSA draws 35,000 and all but a couple of teams have to buy their tires."[22]

In January, the Indianapolis Motor Speedway modified the rules for entering the 1980 Indianapolis 500. They had tried to prop up USAC by providing automatic invitations to the Indianapolis 500 for those teams that entered and were qualified for the races. When only one team received an automatic invitation for the Indianapolis 500 Speedway officials, concerned about a potential lack of participants, modified their stance and decided to issue invitations to members of CART. Cooper explained the change in heart: "There was a possibility they wouldn't be invited but I've been doing a lot of soul searching lately. This is a major sports entertainment and the paying customers want to see the entertainers. In this case, it's the drivers and they didn't bring this feud about, so why should they be penalized along with the fans?"[23]

Behind the scenes, A. J. Foyt had been instrumental in getting the two sides together for talks, and some progress was being made. Both sides agreed to a championship board, and CART finally relented and agreed that it could be under the USAC banner. With apparent victory at hand, USAC suddenly decided this structure wasn't acceptable. Dick King, USAC's president, said, "After a great deal of soul-searching, we have concluded that USAC cannot allow a single-faction entity to be structured within the basic organization framework. In this instance, it would create a car owners entity, using the USAC name. It would have control over everything and we don't see how participants can hire and fire the officials. In other words, if four of the six car owners decided to fire an official, then that's all it would take. And we don't see any way that would work because you've got to have more representation than just owners."[24]

This latest attempt at reunification resulted in Foyt's resigning from USAC. He said, "It hurt me that USAC didn't consult me in the peace meetings and it hurt me that USAC didn't buy the proposal." He was also miffed that USAC didn't include him on the six-man championship board. "I'm certainly not the smartest man in the world but I've spent my whole life in racing and I think I'm qualified to make good decisions. USAC made a lot of bad decisions last year and I kept my mouth shut but maybe it's time for the old wives' tale about the new broom that sweeps clean."[25]

The Short-Lived Championship Racing League

With reunification apparently dead, John Cooper was about to try his hand at brokering a peace between the two sides. His approach was different in that he did not go to King, Penske and Patrick with a plan but rather approached Roger McCluskey and Wally Dallenbach, the competition directors for USAC and CART, respectively.

The plan had many similarities to previous plans. Championship racing would have a separate board with the authority to set the racing schedule and the car specifications, negotiate the purses, and approve the race officials proposed by USAC. They would also have a quarterly review of the financial statements for Championship racing. For 1980, the board would have seven members—three from USAC, three from CART and one selected by the six members. In subsequent years, the seven-man governing board would include three car owners, one driver, one track operator, the USAC president and one to be elected by the other six representatives. The plan also addressed one of the main complaints of the CART faction: money. Cooper proposed the creation of the Hulman Cup, honoring Tony Hulman, who had rescued the Indianapolis 500 after it was shuttered during World War II. The Hulman Cup would include a trophy for the national champion as well as a prize from the Hulman Cup Award Fund, combining the award funds for CART and USAC. Cooper hoped the Hulman Cup, supplemented by $100,000 from the Indianapolis Motor Speedway, would grow from $1,000,000 to $2,000,000 within three years.[1]

This plan appeared to be viable to Dallenbach and McCluskey, although they recommended increasing the board to ten members to include five car owners, a driver, a mechanic, an Indianapolis Motor Speedway representative, a promoter of a non-500-mile race and USAC's president.[2] Would this plan be acceptable to the two warring factions? USAC signaled they were in agreement in principle with the plan. CART also sent a positive response in a letter where they agreed in principle to the two main components of the Cooper peace plan—the independent board and USAC sanctioning the races.[3]

But not all in the CART camp agreed with the plan. Patrick had multiple objections. Once again, the idea of the governing board being under the USAC banner was an issue. Believing that the proposed board could not operate independently within the USAC framework, Patrick declared that this proposal, if adopted, would be illegal under the current USAC policies. Additionally, he objected to USAC's sanctioning the races. Patrick pointedly said CART would never agree to use USAC race officials because "they're not competent, that's why we left."[4] He also believed they could bring in more revenues by negotiating the television rights for the series rather than for individual races.

Underlying Patrick's objections was Cooper's strategy to approach Dallenbach and McCluskey with the plan, not those who were in charge. Patrick said, "I am mystified as to why this plan was addressed to two employees instead of the principals involved."[5]

Within both the CART and USAC camps, pressure was building for reunification. All sides understood that the split wasn't good for the sport and that ultimately, it wasn't good for the warring factions. Both sides started offering suggestions and agreed to another pow-wow. CART suggested Dan Gurney, whose white paper had led to the formation of CART, be included in the negotiations. And despite Patrick's objections of Cooper's initial proposal being made to Dallenbach and McCluskey, CART recommended they also be part of the discussion. USAC recommended that the board be expanded to ten members and made suggestions as to the 1980 composition. Proposed representation included Penske, Patrick, Hall, Sherman Armstrong (team owner who was part of the formation of CART but whose cars raced with USAC in 1979), Rolla Vollstedt (USAC team owner), Jud Phillips as the mechanic representative, A. J. Foyt as the driver representative, John Cooper, Dick King and Bob Fletcher (owner of the Phoenix International Speedway). Behind the scenes, Cooper was working with the companies who controlled the competition budgets—Goodyear, Valvoline, Champion Spark Plug, STP, Sears, Monroe Equipment and Bear Wheel Alignment.[6]

Although it seems that consensus was building about the composition of the board, there were other issues where the two sides were far apart. One sticking point continued to be the boost pressure, which had caused friction between those teams running the Cosworth engine and those running the other more traditional engines. Another issue was the use of skirts on the cars. There was also the additional complication of the lawsuit filed by Joseph

Mattioli of the Pocono International Speedway against CART, Penske, Penske Corporation and Gould, Inc.[7]

It looked like the reunification was going to happen. CART accepted the modified Cooper plan and suggested a meeting in Detroit with Penske, Patrick, Fletcher, Cooper, King and McCluskey to get the ball rolling. Significantly, there were to be no attorneys at the meeting. The progress was sidetracked when King sent a letter to Patrick saying the organizational meeting was premature. Rather, King's letter suggested a meeting between Patrick and King and their respective legal counsels. It also brought into discussion the rules surrounding fuel consumption and manifold pressure. King's desire for the USAC rules to be used for the 1980 racing season would be a disadvantage to the CART-aligned racers.

Needless to say, the reception of this news by the CART contingency was not positive. One CART member said,

> This latest mail-o-gram is just a flak job from USAC. At one time or another, this proposal has been accepted by USAC, CART and Cooper. Now this thing is getting twisted and kicked around. We had a lengthy discussion on boost today in our CART meeting and of course there are some owners who feel strongly about sticking with 60 inches. But we all agreed that we were willing to accept the fate of what these 10 men decide. Either we take these 10 and let them decide our future or we don't. The CART nominees to the Board of Governors are ready to meet and get organized right now. So what are we waiting for? Let's get on with it.[8]

By the end of March, all signs were pointing to reunification of the two racing series. Both sides had agreed on the composition of the governing board containing five car owners—Penske, Patrick, and Hall for the CART side, Vollstedt and Foyt for the USAC side. The two sides agreed that four of the six votes would carry any particular motion. Significantly, USAC's executive committee agreed to a bylaw change making this group the sole body to run Championship racing during the season.[9]

The Championship Racing League became a reality on April 3. This group would reunite the racing community for the 1980 season, with USAC sanctioning the races. The two sides also agreed that for the 1980 racing season, the engine configurations at the tracks in 1979 would be applicable.[10] With agreement reached, the two sides went racing.

The peace was short lived. The source of the problem was the composition of the board with five of the six members being car owners. Cooper said, "I thought the six-man board might have a chance but there have been six or seven meetings since qualifying at Indy and I've heard the talk in every one of them has been, 'We can't have him as an official or we don't run this track.' Some of the promoters are up in arms because of some of the demanding letters they've received from one of the board members."

Cooper's solution? According to Roger Penske, on June 20 Cooper wrote a letter to USAC's president King saying, "It becomes increasingly clear that USAC hasn't met the criteria of independent sanctioning authority, at least with regard to championship racing. It appears as though selected car owners alone control the policymaking and administration. If this is the case, we will no longer be able to consider USAC as the sanctioning body for our 500 mile championship car race. If it is not the case, I would appreciate evidence of that fact by July 1 as we must proceed with our 1981 activities."[11]

With the vast majority of USAC's income coming from the Indianapolis 500, this action was a real blow. Fighting for survival, USAC attempted to get the members of the Championship Racing League to agree on a different composition of the board with only three car owners. But they were unable to gain the required 100 percent agreement. So, USAC took action to rescind the bylaw changes made in late March enabling the formation of the Championship Racing League. In its place, USAC would expand its competition committee to twelve members to include four car owners, two drivers, a mechanic representative, a promoter, two at-large members, Tom Binford and Roger McCluskey.[12] Requiring only a simple majority of the board, this proposal passed. King attributed the change in the bylaws to the "unauthorized assumption of administrative authority of the Championship Racing League by its Board of Governors and its chairman, Pat Patrick, and for failure of some other essential conditions, including the dismissal of lawsuits with regards to USAC." Patrick had sent a letter to all Championship car participants that he would be the only person to negotiate the television rights for 1981 and to deal with the sponsors.[13]

This attempt to appease the Indianapolis Motor Speedway reopened the rift between USAC and CART. Penske made it clear that CART intended to resume independent operations when he said, "I'm sorry the marriage was so short-lived. Now USAC doesn't have a championship division. CART now has control of the 3 television dates remaining on the schedule."[14] Shortly thereafter, CART announced they would resume racing under the CART banner.

On July 10, 1980, King sent a letter to the CART membership. The Championship Racing League was folded and sanctioning of the Indianapolis 500 was returned to USAC.[15] USAC took the long-urged step of restructuring its board, reducing it from nineteen members to six. They thought the smaller board would give USAC greater responsiveness to its constituency. Significantly, the reformulated USAC board did not have any car owner representation.

This was in great contrast to CART, which was controlled by the car owners.[16] Additionally, USAC took the step of establishing a separate competition commission for each level of racing. King explained, "These people will be charged with making the rules for their own type of racing. The direction in which a particular division goes will not be affected in any way by someone from another division, voting on something which does not interest or involve him. The input will be where it rightfully belongs—with the people who compete in a particular division."[17]

Back at the Speedway, Cooper asked for proposals for sanctioning the Indianapolis 500 from SCCA, the National Hot Rod Association (NHRA), NASCAR and the International Motor Sport Association (IMSA).[18] Cooper, wanting the Indianapolis 500 to be part of a series of six to twelve races, indicated that the Speedway wouldn't establish another sanctioning body.[19]

While trying to get back in the Indianapolis Motor Speedway's good graces, USAC received another blow. During the 1979 racing season the promoter of the Bettenhausen 200, Wisconsin Auto Racing, remained with USAC and experienced a significant decline in attendance. With the prospect of A. J. Foyt being the only big name in the race if sanctioned by USAC, Wisconsin Auto Racing decided to switch their race from being sanctioned by USAC to CART. Jim Engel, vice president of Wisconsin Auto Racing, Inc., said, "We have to consider the interests of our fans who buy the tickets. CART can assure us of having the big name drivers here for the Bettenhausen. USAC cannot present a similar package."[20]

The efforts made by USAC to reshape its structure were evidently good enough in terms of independence for Cooper to reaffirm USAC as the sanctioning body for the Indianapolis 500 for 1981. As the 1980 racing season ended, USAC had only two tracks for championship races—Pocono International Raceway and the Indianapolis Motor Speedway—and one of them, Pocono, was in financial difficulty.[21] The Indianapolis Motor Speedway had financially supported this track in 1980 but made the decision not to continue the support in 1981.

CART saw this as an opportunity to take away USAC's only track other than Indianapolis. In mid–February John Frasco, CART's president, and Penske reached an agreement with Dr. Mattioli to lease the track for three years. But there was a fly in the ointment. First Pennsylvania Bank, which financed the racetrack's loan, was also having financial difficulties. The previous year its parent, First Pennsylvania Corporation, had received a $1.5 billion cash infusion from 26 other banks with the proviso that the equity of the bank be increased. Frasco continues with the story: "The documents had been prepared and Roger [Penske] and I flew to Philadelphia a week ago

Tuesday to sign a three-year agreement with an option for two more. It was very satisfactory with Dr. Mattioli and his attorney and we all thought it was just a matter of signing the papers. But when we got to Philly, suddenly the bank told us it wouldn't lease Pocono for longer than a year at a time. That was undesirable to us." Failing to secure the lease on the Pocono race track, CART announced they would run a pair of 125-mile races in Atlanta on the last weekend in June instead of running the Pocono 500. They also scheduled a 500- mile race for Michigan in the middle of July.[22]

With the lease deal having fallen through, Dr. Mattioli found a silent investor to guarantee the funding for the Pocono 500 race. In order to save money for both the track and the race teams, it would have a different format than in previous years. Historically, the track had been open for a week to include practice, qualifying and the race. This year, practice would only be held on Friday, with qualifications on Saturday and the race with a $290,000 purse on Sunday.[23]

In order to try to generate some momentum, USAC announced that the 1981 championship year would begin January 1, 1981, and conclude May 31, 1982. Since the Indianapolis 500 is the biggest event in Championship racing, this would put the race at the end of the season, hopefully making a more exciting conclusion. King explained, "We think a split-year racing season will have many advantages. The biggest, perhaps, is that the Indianapolis 500, which until now has been an early season event, will become racing's Super Bowl, our World Series, our Stanley Cup. Because of the number of points available at Indianapolis, the national championship almost always will be decided there—and that is as it should be."[24]

Meanwhile, for CART, things continued to look up. They announced thirteen championship races for 1981, including two at new venues and five road courses.[25] They also announced a $1 million point fund established by their sponsor, PPG Industries.[26] The good news continued when CART announced NBC's live telecast of the Michigan 500 race. This would be the first live telecast of a championship circuit race.[27]

In early January 1981, USAC announced its engine formulations for the 1982–1984 racing seasons.

For the first time in 30 years, USAC's championship circuit would only run with production stock-block engines. This meant those teams with Cosworth engines would need a separate car to compete in the biggest race of the season, the Indianapolis 500. The motivation behind the move was to fulfill one of the goals they had when CART broke away in 1979—to reduce the cost of racing. The move to a production stock-block engine would hopefully bring lower-budget teams back to championship racing.[28] Speedway president Cooper lauded the move: "The production-based engine formula for 1982 could produce one of the most exciting years yet in championship racing. And we anticipate many entries built to those specifications for our 1981 500 which will be run under the same basic specifications as last year. The announcement by USAC seems to be the kind of bold move that most participants and fans have been asking for."[29]

As qualification trials were underway in Indianapolis, only 18 entries had been received for the Pocono 500, USAC's only other championship race. Rumors circulated that the CART teams were planning to boycott. CART's president, John Frasco, explained that CART teams hadn't entered the Pocono race because he had not received any requests for a waiver. But Patrick driver Gordon Smiley said, "It's not a boycott—don't use that word—but we're not going."[30]

Despite all of the turmoil at USAC, the 1981 Indianapolis 500 had a banner year with a record 104 entries.[31] Unfortunately, qualifying was marred by controversy. On the final day of qualifying, Jerry Karl was bumped from qualifying by Tom Sneva. That is where the intrigue began. Based upon a tip from driver Steve Krisiloff, Karl filed a protest indicating that Sneva's car had exceeded the allowable manifold pressure, as a bolt had been inserted in the pop-off valve. USAC held a hearing, and based upon the testimony of Krisiloff and Rich Vogler as well as the examination of the car, Sneva's car was disqualified.[32] This resulted in Sneva's filing an appeal.[33] The appeal board did not reinstate Sneva to the race, stating, "There was insufficient evidence to reverse the previous ruling of the steward's committee."[34]

If the qualifying controversy wasn't enough, the Indianapolis 500 was also filled with drama. People at the race saw Bobby Unser take the checkered flag. Later when USAC officials reviewed the race tapes, they noticed that Unser had passed eight cars under the yellow flag. USAC imposed a one-lap penalty on Unser for this rule violation. This resulted in the victory being taken away from Unser and granted to Mario Andretti.[35] Needless to say, an appeal of this decision was made to USAC. On the appeal, USAC determined that Unser had benefited from the passing during the yellow flag but ruled the penalty was too severe. They restored the victory to Unser and assessed him a $40,000 penalty.

Upon hearing his 1981 victory had been taken away by the USAC appeals court, Andretti filed an appeal with the Automobile Competition Committee of the United States (ACCUS). Andretti maintained that USAC did not have the authority to hear the appeal since this was an FIA-sanctioned race. According to Andretti, ACCUS was the proper ruling body.[36] Andretti maintained that he had not been given proper notice of the USAC hearing, but in fact he had. USAC was required to give the entry the notice of the hearing. Since the entry is the car owner, in this case Patrick Racing, notice was given to the owner of the hearing. King indicated also that although a call was not required, Andretti had received a phone call prior to notice being given to Patrick Racing.[37]

King pointed to the entry blank for the Indianapolis 500, which clearly gave the ruling authority of any dispute to USAC. The entry blank said, "The invitee specifically understands that its exclusive right to contest the rules or regulations of USAC and/or Indianapolis Motor Speedway Corp. is within the protest and appeal procedure of USAC and any decision reached within this procedure is final."[38] Ultimately, ACCUS chose not to hear Andretti's appeal, and Unser remained the 1981 Indianapolis 500 victor.[39]

Hoping to drive a wedge between USAC and the Pocono Raceway, CART officially banned its teams from running at the Van Scoy Diamond Mines 500 race at Pocono at a June 7, 1981, board meeting. To put teeth in the race ban, it threatened any team running at Pocono with a sixty-day suspension. CART's reasoning for this ban was that it might interfere with participation in the Kraco twin 125-mile races the following weekend in Atlanta.[40] Despite the ban by CART, seven teams chose to drive in the Van Scoy Diamond Mine 500 race. As threatened, CART suspended all seven teams and their drivers—Tom Sneva, Dick Simon, Tom Bigelow, Roger Rager, Geoff Brabham, Jim McElreath and Dean Vetrock—for sixty days, beginning with the Atlanta Kraco twin 125-mile races. At the time, Sneva was second in the point standings and the action by CART could have a significant impact upon his potential earnings.

Sneva's car owners, Dan Cotter and George Bignotti, sought an injunction in the U.S. District Court in Atlanta to set aside the suspensions so they could race not only in Atlanta but also in the other three CART races scheduled during the sixty-day period. Judge Charles A. Moye, Jr., set aside the sixty-day suspensions in a ruling on Friday afternoon. Unfortunately for Sneva, the injunction would not begin until Monday, so Sneva did not participate in the Atlanta race.[41] CART decided not to appeal Judge Moye's actions. Frasco explained the rationale: "It is our feeling that these are internal matters, best handled outside the courtroom. We have decided it is not in the best interests of racing to continue litigation in this matter."[42]

In mid–July 1981, Dr. Mattioli filed a new complaint accusing CART of antitrust action. The complaint indicated that Pocono had suffered $1.2 million in damages as a result of the CART ban and requested treble damages. The legal papers claimed that CART's action was intended "to eliminate USAC" and "to gain for CART and its members control over the entire market of United States championship racing."[43]

As the 1981 racing season was winding down, USAC rescinded all its stock-block engine specifications for the 1982 Indianapolis 500 race. In a change of direction, USAC would permit the exotic Cosworths to run, with the manifold boost power being limited to 48 inches.[44] With the preparations for the 1982 Indianapolis 500 well underway, Cooper resigned as president in order to join Crown Management Company. Joe Cloutier, a close Hulman associate, stepped back in as president of the Indianapolis Motor Speedway.[45]

In May 1982, another nail was put in the USAC coffin when Mattioli leased the Pocono International Raceway to CART for a period of five years. In return, Mattioli agreed to drop the $9.9 million antitrust lawsuit. In addition to leasing the track, CART would also promote all races at the raceway and would be the sanctioning body.[46] This left USAC with only one championship race: the Indianapolis 500.

After the conclusion of the 1982 Indianapolis 500, hope again rose for reunification of open-wheel racing. It began with news of PPG Industries, CART's primary sponsor, and the Indianapolis Motor Speedway reaching an agreement wherein PPG would provide $66,000 to increase the Indianapolis 500 purse for 1983 and $125,000 for the subsequent year.[47] PPG had originally approached Cooper; however, the proposal had been turned down. When Cloutier returned to the presidency of the Indianapolis Motor Speedway, PPG again made the proposal and it was accepted.[48] As a result of this announcement, speculation blossomed that the sanctioning of the Indianapolis 500 might be switched from USAC to CART. If this happened, CART would be the only sanctioning body for Champ Car racing, a major step in the unification of open-wheel racing.[49] More importantly, effectively the Indy car wars would have ended.

In November 1982, the top PPG Series drivers petitioned the Indianapolis Motor Speedway to drop the USAC sanctioning affiliation. The driver's petition said USAC was "too out of touch with Indy Car racing today to justify their continuance as the sole sanctioning body for the Indianapolis 500."[50] In early January, Cloutier's decision became clear—the Indianapolis 500 would continue to be sanctioned by USAC.[51]

After the 1982 racing season closed, Goodyear Tire and Rubber released its race attendance report. In a very tough economic environment, auto racing saw an uptick in attendance of about 2 percent. The good news for championship racing was that they recorded the largest gain of all racing series. Attendance at CART-USAC races increased a whopping 13.8 percent from 689,000 spectators in 1981 to 784,000. The importance of the Indianapolis 500 to championship racing? Nearly half of the spectators at championship races were at the Indianapolis 500.[52]

The Truce

After the 1982 racing season, both USAC and CART addressed the deadly events of the season. Gordon Smiley, a driver in the 1980 and 1981 Indianapolis 500, had been killed while making a qualifying run for the 1982 event. Later that year, rookie Jim Hickman lost his life at the Milwaukee race. With many racers hitting 200 miles per hour, speed seemed to be the underlying issue.[1] The increased speed of the racers was achieved through aerodynamics that increased the downforce of the cars, commonly known as "ground effects." Both leagues addressed the "ground effects" issue by eliminating the skirting from the racers, but they took different approaches, resulting in increased costs of sponsoring a racing team. While CART required the bottom of the racer be at least one inch from the race track, USAC's clearance mandate was two inches. There were also minor differences in the amount of boost permitted; however, compliance with this required only a simple action of adjusting the pop-off valve.[2] Despite the efforts by both USAC and CART to slow the racers down, the new "ground effects" regulations made no difference. As practice started for the 1983 Indianapolis 500, seven drivers took laps at over 200 miles per hour.[3]

In the midst of the 1983 racing season, talks were held between CART's John Frasco, Indianapolis Motor Speedway officials, and representatives from Chevrolet and Buick about the configuration of the CART engine specifications for the 1984 racing season. The Detroit contingency wanted their V-6 engines to have an 8-inch boost advantage over the Cosworth engines in the new rules configuration. Having made a significant investment in their engines, the CART contingency wanted to keep the current configuration of their Cosworth engines for the next cycle. In September 1983, CART released its engine specifications for the 1984 through 1987 racing seasons. They had listened to their stakeholders, which were dominated by those with interests in the Cosworth engine. If a team ran with a stock-block production engine, it would be limited to 209.3 cubic inches of displacement. Significantly, CART required the cars to race on both ovals and road courses. They also permitted the stock-block cars from the 1982 and 1983 racing seasons to continue to race in the series with the proviso that they would need to participate in qualifications for at least 50 percent of the CART races.[4]

Attendance at its CART-sponsored racings was increasing. Meanwhile, Formula One races were experiencing a decline in race attendance. One of the strategies bandied about by Formula One was to enter the robust United States market. This represented a potential danger to CART, as Frasco feared that if Formula One made big inroads into championship racing in the United States, it would push the smaller independent teams out of open-wheel racing due to the cost of fielding a team. Formula One teams normally had an investment of $20 million per year per racer, while the cost of fielding a CART team was estimated at $8 million per year.[5]

One of the motivations for CART's split from USAC was a desire to increase the payout to the racing teams. This initiative appeared to be successful, as they announced that the total prize money for the 1984 season would be $10 million. Of this amount, $5.95 million would be in purse and appearance money for the 15 CART-sanctioned races, $2.5 million for the Indianapolis 500 race, and $41,000 in points funds. With accessory prizes and other special postings, the estimated purse was anticipated to exceed $10 million.[6]

Another issue leading to the formation of CART was the escalating cost of fielding a team. CART had not been able to contain these costs. In fact, costs had grown exponentially and were crowding out many smaller independent teams. Underlying the rising costs was the changing technology. Gone were the days when a car could be used for several seasons. To field a competitive team, it was necessary to buy a new car annually. A new March racer without the engine would run $135,000 and a Cosworth engine would cost an additional $45,000. This didn't include the costs for the tires, replacement engines and other parts as well as the costs of fielding the team.[7]

The constant replacement of cars resulted in a glut of used cars on the market. This was exacerbated after the 1984 Indianapolis 500, which had 117 cars entered but had slots for only 33 in the race. With a limited market for the cars, used racers could be sold for approximately $25,000. With the continued escalation of the cost of fielding a racing team, the necessary annual replacement of equipment if a team was to remain competitive, and a glut of used equipment, there was a growing sentiment to form a new racing league to race on ovals with stock-block production engines. Also underlying the movement to form a new racing league was CART's move away from Champ Car traditional racing on ovals. With an influx of Formula One drivers from

Europe participating in the CART races, another league would provide American drivers, who had grown up on midget, dirt races and sprints, more opportunity to transition to championship racing.[8]

One of the promoters interested in a second series was Dennis Wood of the Phoenix International Raceway. He said, "It's time for a second circuit. I would love to see it. I don't think it really matters whether you spend $60,000 or $15,000 for 700 horsepower, which is what you can get with either a Cosworth or a stock-block engine." What was needed for a second racing circuit was a series sponsor and a television contract.

USAC saw this as an opportunity to reestablish itself in the Champ Car arena. For the past year, USAC had made several proposals for a series sponsor. And rumor had it that there was at least one potential sponsor interested willing to invest up to $2.5 million in the new series. If this new league could be formed, it would breathe life back into USAC.[9] Despite the growing sentiment to form a new racing league, it would be several years before this occurred.

CART and USAC/Indianapolis 500 kept an uneasy peace for several years. By 1984, there was some working together by CART and USAC/Indianapolis 500 particularly in the area of safety. CART chief Frasco met with Indianapolis 500 head Cloutier to discuss maintaining the turbocharge boost settings for the 1986 Indianapolis 500. Both sanctioning bodies wanted to reduce the speeds, but they took different approaches. CART wanted to reduce the speeds on the super-speedways through minor changes to the engines and chassis.[10] USAC's approach was to reduce the speeds by changing the engine size and boost parameters.

Although CART had seized control of championship racing, there were internal dissensions centering on the entry fees and the prize money paid. Mario Andretti, the 1984 Michigan 500 winner, was paid $76,205 out of a total purse of $485,000. As a comparison, when A. J. Foyt won the Pocono 500 race nine years earlier in 1973, he received $94,808. After the Michigan 500, Johnny Rutherford expressed the frustration many drivers were feeling with the purses. "My car took in $5,640 which I had to split with A. J. I could have made $3,000 just for driving the PPG Pace Cars and not have risked my butt. Prize money was paid years ago down the line that was more than paid at Michigan to win this year."[11]

With road racing dominating the CART circuit, Patrick was urging his fellow car owners to return to oval racing. "Our heritage is speed on oval tracks. Whether we like it or not, our heritage is the Indianapolis 500. We are not Formula 1. We should not prostitute ourselves and our sport by going to places where speeds are of a routine highway variety." Patrick also expressed concern over the long-term viability of the sport: "With our posture today, there is no development at the grass roots level. The fan at the half mile track in Bryan, Ohio, has no hope of watching a future star in action. We have taken our sport away from him."[12] With concern about the lack of a pipeline for up-and-coming race car drivers, CART cofounder Patrick started the Indy Lights series.[13]

The addition of three new events on the CART schedule during 1984 boosted attendance 13.8 percent at championship racing events, to 972,000 spectators. This outpaced the growth in U.S. racing of 5.1 percent. Leo Mehl of Goodyear commented on the growth in racing: "The increasing spectator interest in auto racing parallels increasing sales of automobiles in general and high-performance automobiles in particular."[14] For 1985, the number of races were reduced by one, but the series sponsor, PPG, announced a 15 percent growth in prize monies to $11.5 million.[15]

The entries to the 1985 Indianapolis 500 dropped to 77 from a record high of 117 in 1984. This was attributed to an increase in the entry fees to $3,000 from $1,000. With 62 new cars out of a total of 77 entries being new,[16] many teams felt they needed a new car to be competitive in the race, increasing the cost of fielding a race team.[17] Of the entries in the race, 69 were powered by a turbocharged Cosworth V-8, five were Buick turbocharged V-6s, two were normally aspirated V-8s, and one was a Chevrolet turbocharged V-6.[18]

Despite attempts by CART and USAC to slow down the super-speedway speeds, this was the fastest field ever. The 33 starters had an average speed of 208.138 miles per hour, an increase of 4.452 miles per hour over the average qualifying speed for the 1984 Indianapolis 500. The pole setter, Pancho Carter, had a speed of 212.583.[19] Although the field was dominated by the Cosworth engine, the pole and number-two-position cars were powered by a turbocharged Buick V-6 and a turbocharged Chevrolet V-6. The double overhead Cosworth engines were permitted 47 inches of boost, while the Chevrolet and Buick engines were allowed 57 inches of boost, giving 50 more horsepower to the Chevrolet and Buick engines. Needless to say, there was an uproar by the Cosworth crowd that the boost permitted to the stock-block engines put them at a competitive disadvantage.[20]

When the new CART rules for engines emerged for 1986, it allowed 48 inches of boost pressure for all engines, giving a racing edge to the Cosworth and Ilmor engines. The boost parity was obviously disappointing for the stock-block engine proponents. Ron Kociba, one of the developers of the Buick V-6, said, "We would have liked a vote of confidence from CART in some form of boost difference. CART has a vested interest in the Cosworth and the new Ilmor engines certainly, I can understand why they would want to outlaw the stock block."[21]

For the 1986 racing season, a common set of rules by both USAC and CART was anticipated in an effort to limit the speeds at the super-speedways. Roger McCluskey of USAC and J. Kirk Russell of CART hoped to find common ground and reduce the impact of the ground effects by 25 to 30 percent. This would mean a reduction of speeds of 5 to 8 miles per hour. Although both sides wanted to reduce the racing speeds, their approaches were different, making one set of rules impossible. USAC favored flat-bottomed cars. CART, which had tested scale models, felt the flat-bottomed cars would not reduce the speeds and wanted to restrict the venturi tunnels underneath the cars.[22]

When the 1986 CART rules were released, they focused on aerodynamic changes to the cars. Applying pressure on the Indianapolis Motor Speedway management, CART chairman Frasco said "While IMS hasn't indicated it will follow these rules at Indianapolis, certainly our approach to the rules format has been the most comprehensive ever in the sport. We hope because of this approach and cost considerations that IMS and USAC elect not to have a separate set of rules."[23] With a commitment to domestic car manufacturers' participation in the Indianapolis 500 and CART's decision to have parity in the engine boost, it was unlikely that USAC would agree with all of the CART specifications. USAC's McCluskey directly addressed the boost issue; "The stock block engine needs some difference in boost to make it competitive at the speedway. If they [CART] don't think that way, that's their business."[24] His sentiment was echoed by Kociba: "We will focus our efforts on Indy. The 1–2 start for Buicks at Indy brought more interest to this year's 500 than anything else during May."[25]

Taking a play from the NASCAR playbook, which had its first live broadcast of an auto race in 1981, CART negotiated live broadcasts of eleven races during 1985. For 1986, fourteen CART races were scheduled for broadcast.[26] Having fallen behind the curve in live broadcasting, the Indianapolis 500 negotiated a three-year deal with ABC for its first live broadcast beginning in 1986.[27]

For the 1987 racing season, CART and USAC once again collaborated on the rules. Both sides wanted to cut the speed on the tracks. This time, the focus was on having a restrictor plate similar to what is used in NASCAR. The restrictor plate could reduce the engine power by 10 percent. Significantly, CART and USAC agreed to work together on a testing program on the method for cutting engine power.[28]

In January 1987, Tony George, Tony Hulman's grandson, joined the

USAC board. At the time he was an executive vice president at the Indianapolis Motor Speedway and was being groomed by Cloutier to step into the leadership role at the Speedway. Growing up, George had participated in Super Vee racing.[29]

CART announced that their 1987 race season would be the richest in auto racing. The PPG series had total prizes estimated at $15.5 million, including $4 million from the Indianapolis 500. The other races on the CART schedule had an aggregate payout of $7.6 million.[30]

When CART and USAC announced the car configuration requirements for the 1988 season, the focus was on driver safety. Following a rash of foot and leg injuries, the new specifications required a high- energy-absorbing front as well as rollover bars and strengthened side panels. J. Kirk Russell, operations director for CART, said, "We have, for each of the last three years, avoided differences in rules that would make it difficult to compete. We have been very conscious of trying to work with the same structural Indy Car rather than to force a complete re-design."[31] The truce seemed to be holding.

In November 1987, a new open-wheel racing series was announced with the aim to bring down the cost of championship racing. The American Indy Car Series, with headquarters in Colorado, announced an eight-race series. The car's technical specifications would parallel those used at the Indianapolis 500 and all participants in the American Indy Car Series would be encouraged to participate in the Indianapolis 500. Walt Gatthaar, executive director for American Indy Car Series, said, "The concept of a stock-block Indy Car series has been discussed for some time now. The abundance of used Indy Cars and the affordable nature of stock block motors will bring Indy Car racing to more than those with large budgets."[32]

In 1987, there were nearly a million more spectators at auto racing events in the United States—an increase of 11 percent. NASCAR's attendance at Winston Cup events was up nearly 16 percent in 1987. Although CART/USAC had two fewer events in 1987, their attendance was up a whopping 24 percent. Leo Mehl of Goodyear said, "The automobile industry is probably most responsible for the current interest in auto racing in the United States." He explained: "Never has industry competition been more fierce. The auto manufacturers, tire makers and all companies are all trying to out-engineer one another, resulting in a steady stream of ever more functional, more efficient, better performing products for the consumer. Racing has benefited tremendously from this competitive spiral. Not only are companies using racing to develop better consumer products but also they are spending a lot of money to advertise their efforts, which has served to heighten the public's awareness of auto racing."[33]

As CART began discussions of the car configurations for the 1989 racing season, the focus again turned to reducing the racing speeds. There were a number of ways this could be done, including decreasing the ground effects, changing the wing size, and altering the engine components. One of the people favoring eliminating turbocharged engines was Johnny Capels, a former racing mechanic and part of the CART management team. He said, "We are in the entertainment business, and we need to dwell on what appeals to the fan who buys tickets and not make technology advances our number one priority. People don't care what fuel system is being used by a particular car, but they do care how close the competition is. We need to Americanize our series. I want to ban turbocharging and go to a normally aspirated set of engine rules. This certainly isn't a new concept as other series have already begun this change. Why should we lag behind NASCAR, Formula One and others?"[34]

In September 1988, CART got more welcomed news. They had been accepted as members of ACCUS. This would enable foreign drivers to participate in CART events without jeopardizing their Formula One licenses. CART's Frasco said, "This is a welcomed and very important step for the Indy Car series and the CART organization. With CART and ACCUS joining forces, we feel it is a big step in solidifying our international efforts and plays a key role in the continued growth of the series."[35] It turns out that CART had more in mind than just having Formula One drivers participate in their races. They were planning to expand their races internationally. They had already run races in Mexico and Canada before their acceptance into ACCUS. This was in direct conflict with FIA regulations, which prohibited racing series from expanding beyond U.S. borders. If they were to run races without the blessing of FIA, sanctions could be placed on all participants.[36] Despite the restrictions on out-of-country races imposed by FIA, CART's 1989 schedule included a race in Japan.[37] Five days after releasing the schedule, ACCUS president Bruce Martin denied having approved the Japanese race: "At no time could we, or would we, give permission for something we have no control over outside the boundaries of the United States." CART maintained that they had written approval from ACCUS and said they intended to proceed with the Japan race.[38] By the end of the year, this race had been scratched from the schedule.[39]

Despite the elimination of the race in Japan, CART kept its eye on international racing, including in Europe and Japan. Frasco said, "We have to look at Europe. We want to race two or three times outside this continent and we have to pick the sites very carefully. European television channels will soon double and we intend to position ourselves to supply high-quality sports events to this market."[40]

With a desire to race in Europe, CART entered into negotiations with Bernie Ecclestone, the head of the Formula One Constructors Association (FOCA). Although there were five conditions for running races in Europe, the most difficult to resolve was over the television rights. Ecclestone wanted CART to assign the television rights for the races to FOCA. This condition was clearly not acceptable to CART. CART president John Caponigro expressed optimism that an agreement could be reached: "They [FISA] want to own the TV rights and we won't give them up, but, there is a good chance to work out the difference."[41]

The CART rule changes adopted for 1990 focused on reducing speeds by changing the ground effect tunnels underneath the cars and moving the rear wings forward. These changes were approved by the CART membership with a 13-to-8 vote. The rules changes would technically disqualify the 1989 and older cars from the 1990 racing season. This obviously was distressing to the less well-financed teams,

Bernie Ecclestone is the head of Formula 1.

as they would need to buy new cars or reconfigure their existing ones. A. J. Foyt, owner of one of the affected teams, said, "If they want to slow down the cars why not put a 30 cent ring in the turbo inlet instead of making me pay $30,000 to change the aerodynamics. It's not going to hurt the big teams. The little guys are the ones it's going to hurt. What are they going to do, run races with six or seven cars?"[42]

Adding to the 1990 CART rules controversy was a decision by USAC and the Indianapolis Motor Speedway allowing 1988 and 1989 racers to participate in the 1990 Indianapolis 500 race. Penske said of USAC's decision, "I think it would be a big mistake for Indianapolis and USAC not to go along with the rules which will be adopted by CART. There has not been any technical evaluation done by USAC or the Speedway of our rules package."[43]

Unhappiness over the car specifications to be implemented for the 1990–1994 racing seasons and the escalating costs of fielding a team, rumored to be $4.5 million a year, led to an unofficial meeting of the CART membership. The concerns were centered on the cost of maintaining an Indy car team and the structure of CART. The twenty owners who attended were also concerned about television coverage, which focused on the top-running teams. Those teams that ran fifth or farther back in a race didn't receive the television coverage they desired; this also impacted their ability to attract sponsors.[44] Within a month, the board was expanded at CART's annual meeting from eleven members to twenty-four members in order to give voice to the smaller teams. Also at the annual meeting, the CART membership voted to give some financial support to the teams, approving a $7,000 guarantee per race entered for all franchise teams that entered two-thirds of the races.

In an interesting turn of events, CART chairman John Frasco was not re-elected despite a five-year contract with the organization. This would have financial implications for CART, as Frasco had a golden parachute with an estimated value of $2 million to $5 million if the contract were broken.[45] At the annual meeting, comments by CART's president John Caponigro were critical of their primary sponsor, PPG Industries. He told the membership that PPG had failed to adequately support the series with advertising on the CART-sponsored television shows. In response to these charges, PPG sent a letter to all CART members strongly denying the charges made by Caponigro. PPG went further to say that communications between CART and PPG had deteriorated during Caponigro's tenure.[46]

A New Era Begins

On December 11, 1989, Joseph Cloutier, who had been at Tony Hulman's side since the purchase of the track in 1945 and had been the leader of the Indianapolis Motor Speedway on two occasions since Hulman's death in 1977, died.[1] Within a week of Cloutier's death, John Caponigro's management contract with CART was terminated due to the controversy with PPG over PPG's support of the series. Stepping into the role of acting president for CART was Johnny Capels.[2] On January 8, 1990, Anton (Tony) Hulman George, grandson of Tony Hulman, was named president of the Indianapolis Motor Speedway.[3] A new era in Champ Car racing was beginning.

Attendance at auto racing events continued to soar in 1989, passing the 11 million spectators mark. Goodyear's Leo Mehl explained the interest in racing: "The popularity of auto racing has climbed steadily through the decade of the '80s. The catalyst for this unprecedented growth has been the dramatic increase in television coverage of racing." Driving the growth in auto racing telecasts was the growth of cable channels, especially newcomer ESPN, which televised 92 races in 1986, increasing to 241 races in four years. Also carrying selected events were cable channels WTBS, TNN and Univision. The behemoths of television, ABC, CBS and NBC, also carried selected events such as the Indianapolis 500 and the Daytona 500.[4]

Mehl also pointed to the impact of sponsorships on open-wheel racing: "The real fuel for racing's growth has been dollars—sponsor dollars. This huge influx of cash has benefited not only the racing teams but also the race tracks and sanctioning bodies as well. The result has been better promoted race weekends with larger and larger crowds for supporting races on Friday and Saturday and many more sold-out houses on race day." While the overall growth in auto racing was 6.5 percent in 1989, championship racing's growth led the pack at 7.4 percent. Significantly championship racing surpassed Formula One racing for the average attendance per race for the first time. The growth in NASCAR was only 2.7 percent; however, most of the NASCAR tracks were running at over 90 percent capacity. The NASCAR growth was due to 60,000 new seats being added.[5]

In January 1990, an agreement was reached between CART, USAC and Indianapolis Motor Speedway allowing modifications to the 1988 and 1989 racers to be competitive with the 1990 racing models for the season. Despite having reached this agreement, Carl Haas and Roger Penske, both of whom built their own cars, believed the approved modifications would give an unfair advantage to the older racers on the super-speedway tracks, including Indianapolis and Michigan.[6] Shortly thereafter, USAC agreed that their specifications for 1991 would be the same as CART's specifications.[7]

Ultimately, CART's modifications to the older racers for the 1990 season didn't please its ownership group. The implementation of the

Tony George, grandson of Tony Hulman, was the long-term CEO of the Indianapolis Motor Speedway and founded the Indy Racing League.

requirement to reduce the diffuser outlets, which restrict the amount of air traveling underneath the car, was the issue. Some of the teams attached the diffuser to the outside of the racer while others went to the expense of redesigning the sidepods to accommodate the required diffuser outlet. During the first three days of racing there were three accidents believed to be caused by the diffuser outlet being attached to the side of the car.[8]

In April 1990, CART hired William Stokkan as its president. Stokkan had a marketing background, having previously served as the president of merchandising and licensing for Playboy Enterprises.[9] Not surprisingly, Stokkan's vision for CART was a reorientation of the business from sanctioning to entertaining. Stokkan told 300 CART members gathered at a meeting in January 1991, "Racing is a sport with entertainment dimensions. Drivers are athletes, but they are also celebrities. We are looking to add to the locker room dimension and include the dressing room dimension."[10]

Early in his tenure as the head of the Indianapolis Motor Speedway, Tony George traveled to Europe and attended some Formula One races. Impressed by what he saw, George commented, "The Formula One races I saw were much more competitive than what I've seen with Indy Cars lately. The technology in Formula One is quite a bit advanced over what it is here." While in Europe, George told Jean-Marie Balestre, the head of the FIA, that he envisioned an international oval-racing circuit that would include the Indianapolis Motor Speedway. To accomplish this, Europe needed several oval tracks, including the restoration of several oval courses including the Monza track in Italy, two in France and one in Spain. The Indianapolis Motor Speedway was already involved in the construction of a 2.5-mile track, similar in design to the famed Speedway, in Japan.[11]

The 1990 Indianapolis 500 wasn't much of a race. By the twentieth lap, some of the slower cars were already being lapped by the front runners. This, combined with Speedway management's involvement in the construction of a racing facility in Japan and increased participation in rule setting, led to speculation that the Indianapolis 500 would soon drop its USAC affiliation. One racing insider said, "The Indy folk aren't going to be led around by the nose again the way they were this year."[12]

The racing community was surprised when CART announced that the Detroit Valvoline Grand Prix, their second most important race financially, would be dropped from the 1991 racing schedule. The underlying issue was the condition of the street track, which needed approximately $700,000 in paving improvements. Anticipating new commercial construction in the area where the race was to be run, Detroit didn't want to spend the money on the improvements. People critical of CART speculated that the decision was an attempt to pry the sponsorship away from PPG Industries in favor of a new sponsor, Marlboro.[13]

This action surprised and angered not only the organizers of the Detroit Valvoline Grand Prix but also the series sponsor, PPG Industries, and the race sponsor, Valvoline. This race was a major entertainment event for many of the customers of these two companies.[14] Not surprisingly, the dropping of the race spurred Detroit Renaissance (the organizing committee), several members of CART, and PPG Industries to action to have the race restored to the schedule. James P. Chapman, head of racing activities for PPG Industries, said, "A package to save the race will be in place to present to CART directors at their Sept. 11 Chicago meeting. Other than the Indy 500, it's the most important race for us."[15] After Stokkan received approval at the September CART board meeting for negotiations with Detroit Renaissance, another issue surfaced that could derail the race—the $1.5 million sanctioning fee, which was $350,000 higher than any other sanctioning fee on the CART schedule.[16] Key to getting the negotiations back on track was CART's agreeing to lower the sanctioning fee to $1.15 million. The tripartite agreement reached between CART, Detroit Renaissance and the City of Detroit also addressed the issue of the racing surface. Detroit Renaissance agreed to pay for improvements estimated at $400,000, with the remainder funded by the city of Detroit.[17] With the agreement in place, the Detroit Grand Prix was returned to the racing schedule.

CART continued to push the expansion of its racing schedule to an international basis, proposing races in Europe, a direct conflict with Grand Prix racing, then a billion-dollar business. The tension between CART and FISA (Federation Internationale du Sport Automobile, a subset of FIA) was renewed, with Jean-Marie Balestre threatening a "war" with CART. Part of the war plans involved FISA introducing an oval international championship. With Indianapolis Motor Speedway's George having previously indicated an interest in an international oval circuit, this would bring the Formula One racers into CART's backyard. FISA also threatened a lifetime ban of any teams participating in the foreign CART races.[18]

Many believed that if George decided to have the Indianapolis 500 run under FISA rules, which included a 3.5-liter engine, participation would be limited to factory-sponsored teams. This would put George in a difficult position, as he might be forced to rely upon the Formula One racers to fill the thirty-three slots at Indianapolis 500.[19] George also did not support the potential lifetime ban of racers who participated in CART's international races and would permit those teams and drivers to participate in the Indianapolis 500. In a prepared statement, George said, "I don't see us getting into a losing situation, similar to that of 1979. We can't deny the drivers the right to earn a living, we know that. I doubt seriously we would honor any sanctions against sponsors who went to Australia who also spend money with us in one form or another. Obviously that wouldn't be in our best interests."[20]

Actions at the November 1990 CART board meeting did not sit well with the drivers. The board, reflecting the ownership of CART by the team owners, agreed to a $10,000 per car, per race, reduction in the payments made to CART Properties, the franchise arm of CART. This would reduce the funds available for payments to the drivers. The car owners saw the benefit of this plan as more money in their pockets to support operating costs, a vision that the drivers did not share.[21]

At the Indianapolis Motor Speedway headquarters, George was concerned not only with the reduction in entries to the Indianapolis 500 but also with the dominance of the Chevrolet Ilmor engine, the power-plant for the last three winning Indianapolis 500 cars and the last twenty-two victories in open-wheel racing. With an obvious advantage over the other available engines, Chevrolet made this engine available only to twelve racers. George believed the playing field needed to be leveled in order to make the races more competitive and exciting for the spectators.[22]

George was also concerned about the speeds at the track, which had reached 220 miles per hour. In an interview with the *Indianapolis Star* George signaled that a change might be coming: "Maybe it's time to establish new engine and chassis rules so we can make them more affordable, more available and try to slow them down."[23] Others in the racing community shared George's concerns. Veteran racer Mario Andretti said, "The engine formula in Indy-car racing needs to be changed. I think the turbo-charged formula has run its course. Getting rid of the popoff valves would abolish the stupid arguments and mechanical failures that come with them. I'd love to see the 3.5-litre engine happen here because I think it would be appealing to a lot of manufacturers."[24]

While the 1980s had been a decade of growth in open-wheel racing, by 1991, CART was experiencing a decline in the number of car owners and out-of-control costs, which impacted not only the CART-sanctioned races but also the Indianapolis 500. In 1991, the Indianapolis 500 had only 41 entries, the smallest in the track's history, while the Michigan 500 had only 21 cars participate. Stokkan expressed frustration at the lack of interest of ownership of a CART team: "The NFL has several cities seeking franchises and there are any number of individuals seeking to obtain an NBA franchise. But when I open my office door, there's no one in the hall waiting to buy a CART franchise."[25] A part of the cost structure was the different requirements for the racing cars imposed by USAC and CART. This meant to run at the Indianapolis 500, the CART teams needed to have a car dedicated only to that race. The cost for a race car on average had soared to $350,000.[26]

After the running of the 1991 Indianapolis 500, George announced that the Indianapolis 500 and USAC were considering making the 3.5-liter, normally aspirated engine the standard, possibly beginning as early as the 1993 race. In a prepared statement, George said, "After discussing this with several manufacturers, Indy Car owners, drivers and others, it is time to make a commitment with regard to engine conformity which will allow a greater number of manufacturers to participate in the Indy 500. It is also up to us to provide chassis builders with rules stability through the end of this decade."[27]

CART's Stokkan also recognized that the escalating costs were having an adverse impact upon championship racing. In a speech to the International Motor Press Association, Stokkan said, "We obviously would like to see more manufacturers come in, since this has now almost become a total dominance of the Chevrolet engine."[28]

With both George and CART wanting to address the cost of fielding an auto racing team and an acknowledgment that both sides were dependent upon the other, discussions about reunification of championship racing began. Although CART expressed a willingness to use Indy in its name, and offered to move its headquarters to Indianapolis and give the Indianapolis 500 more of a say in the running of the CART series, there were big issues to overcome. In return, they wanted the Indianapolis 500 to take its $7 million purse and spread it around to the remaining races in the series. CART also wanted the television revenues generated by the Indianapolis 500. Since the Indy car war was about control of the Indianapolis 500, this was an obvious non-starter. George, however, expressed a willingness to negotiate the television contract for the entire CART series.[29] The rules were another roadblock to reunification. George's consideration of instituting a 3.5-liter, normally-aspirated engine could reduce the overall cost of racing, as the various versions of the Chevrolet Ilmor engine required different chassis.

Believing there were structural issues impeding CART's progress, several CART members approached George about developing a restructuring plan for that organization. They hoped George would come in as a white knight with a restructuring plan including the elimination of CART's twenty-four-member managing board and some of its professional staff. George spent the summer talking with team owners, sponsors and accessory companies. Among the team owners talking with George was Rick Galles, the owner of the cars driven by Al Unser, Jr., and Bobby Rahal. Galles reported, "Tony is concerned about the overall picture of Indy-car racing, not just Indianapolis. He thinks Indy-car racing needs to get stronger and become more visible, and I agree. He also thinks Indianapolis should have more to do with the day-to-day operation of things. And it should."[30]

One of the big challenges for CART was that every member of the organization had one vote. On major issues confronting the organization, this often resulted in gridlock. Galles said, "It's tough because there's too many self-interest things. We've got to cut the cost of racing, but how can you do it with 24 people on the board? I've sat in board meetings lately from 8 a.m. to 9 p.m., and nothing got decided." CART's chairman Stokkan put his finger on the problems underlying CART's board meetings: "Competition goes on at the board meetings and therein lies the problem of ever being able to agree on a problem. My idea was to streamline the CART board, not because they are bad people but because it's just too cumbersome."[31]

Behind the scenes, Stokkan and George had been meeting since the spring. Stokkan said, "My initial approach to Tony was to find some common ground with emphasis upon a win-win situation for CART and the Indianapolis Motor Speedway. There was no doubt both parties could benefit and we're both concerned with the issues that are in the best interest of the sport."[32]

George presented a reorganizational plan to the CART membership at a meeting in Houston in November. The board would be reduced to six members including major sponsor PPG's Kears Pollack, USAC's Tom Binford, team owners Penske, Galles and a yet-to-be-named individual from a small team, and George. The commissioner would be Leo Mehl, former head of racing for Goodyear.

Rick Galles. Photograph courtesy Indianapolis Motor Speedway.

Not surprisingly, the proposed structure of the new board came under fire. The CART contingent wanted Stokkan to be the chairman and wanted to insure team owner representation on the board. George was willing to do the later, but not the former.[33] Indy-car owner Dick Simon said, "Tony had better take a real close look at the board, because that will make the difference of whether this thing flies or doesn't fly. I agree it's time for a new structure, but I don't think a board composed of car owners, car manufacturers and promoters is the answer."[34]

As George's plan was presented to the CART owners at their board meeting in Houston, the big question was would they … could they … abandon the organization after 13 years. The simple answer was no. One sticking point for some CART owners was the presentation itself. One CART member said, "Their proposal never gave details and never showed us how revenue would be generated. When Bernie Ecclestone took over FOCA [Formula One Constructors Association], [he] showed the car owners how he was going to make them money and they were impressed because that's what they wanted to hear." Additionally, the proposal for the at-large member to be appointed by

George and Mehl as the chairman was not acceptable to a majority of the CART members. One CART member, Dick Simon, said, "Tony would have had a signed deal that day if he'd drop the driver and the at-large positions. His proposal was to make Indy-car racing level and that's all we want." A third issue was CART's organizational structure, requiring 100 percent concurrence of the ownership to dissolve the corporation.[35]

CART assured George it would review his proposal and get back to him with a response. But the follow-up was slow, and the CART board continued to show support for Stokkan. After nearly a month, George took this as a rejection of his proposal: "CART agreed to respond with the issues of our proposal that were acceptable and unacceptable, but they didn't. As far as I'm concerned, it's over. They came back with a proposal to continue to dance. They had the ball in their court and they dropped it. So, I see no reason to waste any more of my time."[36] So the opportunity to reunite CART and the Indianapolis Motor Speedway/USAC died. George had threatened that if his proposal wasn't accepted, he would walk away.[37] Which is exactly what he did.

After the rejection of George's plan, speculation grew in the championship racing community that George might form his own racing league to be sanctioned by USAC, or join forces with either Formula One or NASCAR. George fanned the flames of this speculation when he said, "It's no secret, I've been talking to Bill France, Bernie Ecclestone and Max Mosley. CART can run its 16 races and who knows, one day that race in New York City might be the biggest one on their schedule. No matter what we do, I don't think CART is going to like the alternatives."[38]

Despite the growing tension between CART and USAC/Indianapolis Motor Speedway, auto racing continued to experience an increase in attendance in 1991, with a growth of 3.2 percent. Happily for members of CART and the Indianapolis Motor Speedway, attendance at open-wheel races increased 7.2 percent for the year. Most of the growth in open-wheel racing was attributed to the Indianapolis Motor Speedway's adding a new infield bleacher section on the backstretch and the addition of the Surfers Paradise race promoted by CART in Australia.[39]

In January 1992, CART changed its status from a non-profit to a for-profit corporation. In order to do this, CART had to disperse $1.2 million, providing each of the twenty-four franchise owners a one-time payment. More significantly, they addressed the dissatisfaction of the middle and lower echelon teams by changing the purse, points and appearance fund payments. Under the new plan, each racing team would commit to fielding a car (or cars) throughout the season. In return the car owners would receive monies rumored to be in the $25,000 to $30,000 range for each race per car. They also agreed that only the top twelve teams at each race would receive prize money and the championship points would go to the top ten finishers of each race.[40]

George, bitterly disappointed by the rejection of his plan at the November CART board meeting, filed Articles of Incorporation for Indy Car, Inc., with the Indiana secretary of state on February 11, 1992. George explained, "The formation of Indy Car, Inc. means that we're following through with what we wanted to accomplish at the November Indy Car owners meeting in Houston. Our purpose is to generate discussions in order to pursue options and explore alternatives that will maximize the competitiveness and stability of Indy Car racing. Our objectives have not changed." Those objectives included cost containment, driver development, improving marketing and changing the rules governing the sport. George hoped to address the issues plaguing the Indianapolis 500 as well as the sport as a whole.[41]

While Valvoline was in negotiations over the television package for the 200-mile Valvoline race held at the Phoenix International Raceway, CART, which in March 1992 changed its moniker to IndyCar,[42] sold the television rights to Ford Motor Company. The race would be called the Ford/Phoenix 200. Valvoline, who had been the sponsor of this race for numerous years, was upset. Reacting, Carl Frey, Valvoline vice president, sent a sharply worded letter to Stokkan that in part said, "We were somewhat shocked and quite dismayed over CART's decision to sell the TV entitlement for the Valvoline 200 at Phoenix to Ford Motor Company. Clearly the action was not in the best interest of the promoter, the true entitlement sponsor or the fans who will be thoroughly confused as to what the name of the event is. We have spoken to Buddy Jobe and this action will cause him considerable embarrassment since the track has well-known ties to a competing manufacturer [Chevrolet]."[43] Stokkan defended CART's action, saying that Valvoline had an opportunity to pay the $220,000 television entitlement fee prior to its sale to Ford Motor Company.

Frey's letter to Stokkan also put into play Valvoline's providing lubricants and racing fuel for the series. Frey wrote, "Valvoline's out-of-pocket subsidy of the fueling program each year is substantially more than the difference between your asking price and our offer for the TV entitlement package, but as you yourself have pointed out many times, Valvoline never gets the credit it deserves for providing this service." Frey went on to indicate that this action might endanger Valvoline's relationship with CART: "In view of all these things, we must go on record as indicating we feel we have been forced to re-evaluate our involvement with CART for 1992 and beyond. This re-evaluation naturally includes our refueling program."[44]

At the June 1992 CART board meeting, a revised George plan was presented by Galles and Penske. This proposal called for the board to be composed of Kears Pollack, three elected car owners, the Speedway chief steward Tom Binford, and Phoenix promoter Buddy Jobe. Wanting effective control of the series, George reserved the right to appoint the chairman.[45] One of the CART owners said, "I didn't see much difference between the two proposals because the bottom line is that Tony George and his people are still trying to take over our business without showing us any good reasons." A smaller team owner talked about another problem with the proposal: "Tony's new proposal still doesn't address money and that's obviously a big concern since we all own a piece of IndyCar. We've got a lot invested and we all got a dividend last winter." This proposal, although reviewed by the board, was never voted on.[46] As CART rejected the revised George plan, Penske expressed his opinion that the two sides needed to bury the hatchet. "Personally, I think it would be a tragedy if we didn't get together with the Speedway. Forget the commercial side of this business, we need one organization for continuity in safety, rules and officiating."[47]

After the 1992 Indianapolis 500, the Indianapolis Motor Speedway started replacing all of the outside fencing with 42-inch-high, steel-reinforced walls with catch-fencing on top. This action fueled speculation that Indianapolis was considering adding other racing events to the track's schedule. George's comments neither confirmed nor denied: "Our primary consideration in renovating the walls is to increase the level of safety for the fans. In fact, that was our only discussion point when the decision was made. It is of secondary and coincidental consideration that the new walls opens up our options with regard to other racing events, but nothing has been decided along those lines."[48]

Mario Andretti.

In late June 1992, a group of NASCAR teams showed up at the Indianapolis Motor Speedway to run tests on the track. Also showing up to watch the trials were approximately 100,000 fans. The reaction by NASCAR management was very positive: "The cars looked good out there, they sounded good, the fans liked them and the drivers liked being out there. To my knowledge we haven't seen any negatives. From NASCAR's standpoint, it would be a neat deal to run here someday. It would be one of our great events." George's response was also positive but also more guarded: "Obviously, this is a decision that is going to take some thought and nothing is going to happen overnight. I don't know NASCAR's reaction, and we've got to huddle here. Like everyone else, I thought it was great." Perhaps it was the estimated purse of $7 million necessary to attract NASCAR to the Speedway that gave George pause.[49]

Although neither of the two proposals to restructure CART's board were acceptable to 100 percent of the CART membership, in July 1992 there was an announcement that CART and the Indianapolis Motor Speedway had reached a working agreement through 1993. The agreement had five car owners (Roger Penske, Derrick Walker, Jim Hall, Carl Haas and Dale Coyne), William Stokkan and George to govern Indy car racing. The owners would have voting privileges, while Stokkan and George would be there on an advisory basis. George said, "The last eight months we haven't been talking, there's been lots of negative press and it's not been a healthy situation. I think this is the first step into bringing some sanity to this sport and I feel we can work together with the common goals of making the series and Indianapolis 500 better."[50]

George felt strongly that open-wheel racing needed to become more affordable: "I think everyone agrees we've got to cut costs because otherwise there won't be an Indy-car series after 1993. If you hadn't noticed, people aren't lining up to get into this sport and I think everyone realizes things aren't as good as they're cracked up to be."[51] The *Indianapolis Star* journalist Robin Miller predicted that at the end of agreement period, if costs had not come down for open-wheel racing, George would grab the bull by the horns and make the Indianapolis 500 more affordable.[52]

One of the initiatives to reign in escalating costs driven by technology was to significantly increase fines for rules infractions, which historically had been nominal. Another action taken by the IndyCar board was to limit testing to ten days per car after June 1 and to eliminate Friday from the races at Nazareth, Phoenix and Cleveland. This meant all qualifying and racing would be held on Saturday and Sunday.[53]

For several seasons, Chevrolet's Ilmor engine had dominated the championship racing circuit. One of the ideas George had to bring down the cost of racing was to encourage participation from more engine builders. Both

Honda and Nissan were interested in developing engines for IndyCar races. Honda was ready to announce its participation in the 1994 IndyCar series. Unfortunately, CART's new engine specifications included a proviso requiring any engine supplier to furnish engines for four cars on two separate teams in its first year of participation, increasing to six cars for three different teams in the second year. With the average car using fifteen to twenty engines a season, this was a huge investment being imposed by IndyCar on new engine participants.[54]

Honda America found this requirement to be both financially and technically difficult and decided to reevaluate their engine program. Kurt Antonius, senior manager of corporate public relations, said, "American Honda is very disappointed by the decision of the board of directors of CART to maintain its restrictive policy on engine suppliers wishing to enter Indy Car racing. No engine manufacturer has been asked to meet such requirements in the prior history of the series."[55] Nissan also announced they weren't going to continue with their engine development program for championship racing. Frank Honsowetz, Nissan's manager of motorsports, said, "We are continuing to support our defending champion IMSA, GTS and GTU teams. But in the current business climate, we can't justify the financial requirement to field the type of Indy Car program befitting Nissan's racing heritage."[56]

Responding to the engine specifications that had caused American Honda to re-evaluate and Nissan to withdraw their championship racing engine efforts, USAC issued a policy allowing new engine manufacturers to enter championship racing at less cost, effectively driving another wedge between the two sides. The year after an engine passed a "race proven" milestone, the engine supplier would be required to provide engines for four car/driver entrants with two different teams and six car/driver combinations among four teams in subsequent years.[57]

After being absent from participating in championship racing for twenty years, Firestone decided to reenter the fray. According to Sunil Kumar, EVP of Bridgestone/Firestone, this decision was based upon research: "Statistics indicate that sponsors get the biggest brand recognition from auto racing. Based on a study by Joyce Julius & Associates, which analyzed 1,100 sporting events, eight of the 10 best promotional bargains are motorsports events, with the Indy 500 leading the way."[58]

In September 1993, Honda America announced it would be supplying engines for the IndyCar (CART) series. Former driver and current team owner Bobby Rahal was behind this initiative. As a Honda dealer, he pushed the initiative from its inception.[59] Needless to say, the Rahal racing team was the first to adopt the Honda engine.

After nearly a year and a half of CART's operating with a small, seven-member board, sixteen of the twenty-four franchise owners were dissatisfied with the structure. Underlying this feeling of discontent was the perception that the seven-member board frequently had a conflict of interest in making decisions that impacted all of the franchise holders. At a November 1993 board meeting, CART decided to return to the "one-man, one-vote" principle and disbanded the seven-member board. In its place, each member was given one vote for each team sponsored, with a total limit of two votes per member. Although George was to continue in his advisory role on the board,[60] his dissatisfaction with the board was growing. He left the November board meeting halfway through, and his participation at the December meeting was reportedly lukewarm.[61]

Armageddon

On January 7, 1994, George resigned from the IndyCar (CART) board. In a prepared statement, he explained: "I have personally made every effort the past 2 years to work with the car owner organization currently governing the series in order to hear and be heard with regard to the direction the series is heading. I have come to the conclusion that the Speedway and the current car owner organization are simply going in different directions."[1]

Concurrent with the announcement of his departure from the CART board, George alluded to the founding of a new racing league when he said the purpose was "to maximize the tremendous growth potential of the series surrounding the Indianapolis 500 for the added benefit of the fans, sponsors, promoters and participants." George wouldn't give any details and said none would be forthcoming until after the Indianapolis 500.[2]

Anticipating George's intention to establish a new racing series in direct competition with CART, Andrew Craig, CART's new president,[3] indicated they were preparing for the conflict. Two of the keys for a viable series were the top drivers and racetracks. CART already had all of the top drivers. By early June, after securing a commitment from thirteen racetracks, Craig announced, "At our Milwaukee board meeting, it was felt we had to do something in light of Tony George's intentions. Consequently, we contacted our tracks and made yesterday's long-term announcement."[4]

Despite having taken action to insulate CART from any possible strategy by George, Craig continued to express his desire for reunification of the series: "Our intentions are still to try to find a practical method of working with Tony George. The last thing in the world we want is a split. It's not good for motorsports, it's not good for us, and actually I don't think it is good for the Speedway at all. I think they, too, would be severely damaged. We're better off together than apart. But I will tell you the one thing we don't want is a quick fix. That is, get things patched up, only to have the same problems next year and the next year."[5]

The cost of open-wheel racing had not decreased, and Robin Miller's speculation that if costs were not contained, George would grab the bull by the horns, was prophetic. In March 1994, when the majority of CART owners were flying to Australia for a race, George announced the formation of a new racing league by USAC and the Indianapolis Motor Speedway. The press release said the two organizations were in "the process of establishing a schedule and rules for a new series of automobile races which will include the world-famous Indianapolis 500-Mile Race." The new series would use the same cars as currently competed in the Indy 500. The gauntlet had been thrown.[6]

Trying to make a connection with the world-famous Indianapolis 500, George announced the new league would be called the Indy Racing League (IRL). Responding to an information void, rumors swirled around championship racing that George was going to sell race cars, including the chassis, engine and electronic components with a total cost of $2 million, to participating teams.[7]

In June, the Indy Racing League announced its engine configuration, with a 2.2-liter power-plant. They also addressed the Mercedes-Benz 209-

cubic-inch pushrod engine, which had been secretly developed and had dominated the 1994 Indianapolis 500 by Al Unser, Jr., who started on the pole and took the checkered flag. In order to achieve parity within the teams, the Indy Racing League announced the lowering of the manifold pressure on the Mercedes-Benz engine from 55 inches to 52 inches.[8]

George dropped another bombshell with the announcement in July 1994 that participants in the new organization would be financially rewarded, including incentives for being an IRL member. These incentives included having a number of designated starting spots based upon championship points. With the top drivers being members of CART, this meant the Indianapolis 500 might not have the fastest teams on the

Andrew Craig became CART's CEO in 1994.

track.[9] George explained his actions:

"The primary purpose of the new series is to maximize the tremendous growth potential of the series surrounding the Indianapolis 500 for the added benefit of the fans, sponsors, promoters and participants."[10] Compared to the prior 16 years of relative peace, George's action would reignite the war between the CART members and the Indy 500.

In July 1994, George revealed the plans for the Indy Racing League. Not surprisingly, the league would be based in Indianapolis and would have the Indianapolis 500 as its cornerstone event. The five-member board of governors consisted of George, Dick King (president and CEO of USAC), John Cooper (vice president and director of International Speedway Corporation), Daniel A. Cotter (president and CEO of Cotter and Co., a hardware co-op that would become better known as True Value) and Don Smith (president and CEO of First Financial and Terre Haute National Bank).[11] Cotter was a team owner who had won the 1983 Indianapolis 500 with Tom Sneva at the wheel. Smith was a promoter of racing events for numerous years in Terre Haute and was George's cousin.

When USAC announced in August 1994 the further reduction of the engine boost for the Mercedes-Benz 209-cubic-inch engine to 48 inches for the 1995 Indianapolis 500 and outlawed this engine configuration for the 1996 Indianapolis 500, Penske was outraged. Ilmor Engineering, in which Penske had a major ownership stake, had built the engine which had dominated the 1994 Indianapolis 500 and was highly sought after by other racing teams. Penske called the decision "politically motivated" and told *National Speed Sport News*, "When they made their announcement on June 13 that the boost on the Mercedes-Benz would be cut from 55 to 52, we immediately began development on next year's package and took orders from some of our customers who wanted to use the engine package next season. We had 30 engine blocks and 30 heads cast and ready to go. Now, those engine blocks and heads are useless and we have to absorb the loss because USAC decided to change its mind after telling us the 52-inch boost reduction was their final decision on the 209 pushrod."[12]

In August 1994, the Indianapolis Motor Speedway broke with tradition of holding one race a year when it hosted the inaugural Brickyard 400, featuring various NASCAR teams.[13] With historic ties to ABC Sports, which broadcast the Indianapolis 500, IMS Properties, the marketing arm of the Indianapolis Motor Speedway, negotiated for ABC Sports to also televise the Brickyard 400. In a departure from how Indianapolis 500 races were broadcast, the Speedway, not ABC, would assume the risks for selling the commercials. Historically, a television network would have paid the Speedway for the broadcast of the race.[14] IMS Properties also negotiated for ABC Sports to broadcast the Indy Racing League's races, with the IRL assuming the financial risks of the broadcast.[15]

Behind the scenes, George was negotiating with Disney World to hold one of the IRL races. The agreement was announced in January 1995 not only for the race but also for an innovative oval racing track. Utilizing techniques used in Formula One races, the two-mile asphalt racing oval would not be a permanent structure but rather would have temporary seats, retaining walls and fencing. This would permit Disney World to utilize the space for parking when the facility wasn't being used for racing. With a guaranteed purse of $1 million, the inaugural Disney World 200 would be the kick-off event for the Indy Racing League's inaugural season. Behind the scenes, the Indianapolis Motor Speedway would be the promoter, taking care of the promotion, ticket sales and advertising. The Speedway was also responsible for the construction of the facility.[16]

As the IRL continued with their plans to develop the inaugural racing season, behind the scenes, George and Craig were in discussions about reuniting open-wheel racing. Publicly, Craig said his goal was to reunite open-wheel racing within the next four to six weeks. Craig also recognized the underlying issue: "In the end, it really does come down to one absolutely central issue, and that is control of the sport. The Speedway and Tony [George] take the view that the sport should not be controlled by the race teams, and Tony's always been very consistent on that point. Our teams, I think with justification, are very proud of what they've achieved in the past 15 years and have made a very significant contribution to developing the sport. They, for their part, would be very reluctant to see what they've built handed over to another organization and be relegated to a secondary role."[17]

Earlier, USAC had announced the engine and chassis specifications for the 1996 racing season. Engines were to be reduced from the 2.65 liters (161.65 cubic inches) utilized by both USAC and CART to 2.2 liters (135 cubic inches) for all IRL races. In March 1995, the implementation of the downsized engine was put on hold by USAC. In making the announcement, George said, "Due to the inability of IRL and Championship Auto Racing Teams to reach common ground at this point in time on the subject of rules specifications, USAC has agreed with IRL's concern for putting undue cost and timing hardship on racing teams which are already in the midst of a new PPG Cup series."[18]

The IRL scored a third racing venue when promoter Buddy Jobe aligned the Phoenix International Raceway with the series for the 1996 season. Combined with the Indianapolis 500 and the Walt Disney World 200, the IRL would have a minimum three-race series for the inaugural season. The IRL also had a verbal commitment from promoters interested in building a track at Las Vegas.[19]

As the IRL continued to make progress in arranging its inaugural season, tensions between the two camps intensified. An article by Mike Kiley of the *Chicago Tribune* laid bare the animosity between George and Craig. Craig told Kiley, "Tony George has no experience whatsoever in running a racing series. He runs the simplest business there is. Opens the Speedway doors in May and closes them on Memorial Day. His only view of racing is self-serving and not in the best interests of all." George took aim at Craig's difficulty in managing his board of directors. "When we have negotiated, Craig has told us before every meeting. 'Now I can't promise you that anything we agree to, I can get the owners to agree to.' He's not empowered to cut a deal and qualifies everything he says, so what's the point of talking to him?"[20]

The war between the two sides escalated when in June 1995, CART announced some races that would directly conflict with some races being run by the IRL. In reaction, George said, "CART's action could diminish the opportunities for some drivers and teams to compete in the greatest motorsports event in the world, the Indianapolis 500."[21] That statement signaled George's next move. In early July 1995, George stunned the racing world when he announced that 25 of the 33 racing slots of the Indianapolis 500 field would be guaranteed to drivers who participated in the IRL series.[22] An unnamed Indianapolis Motor Speedway source explained the action: "What we are trying to do is to treat the Indianapolis 500 as a business. For the longest time, the owners have looked at us as a charity. We have provided them with the race and have tried to stay out of the way. What we are doing in regards to running our race is no different than what Carl Haas does as track promoter at The Milwaukee Mile or Road America or what Roger Penske does as the track promoter at Michigan Int'l Speedway or Nazareth Speedway. And remember, for the last 79 races, the Indianapolis 500 has been an invitational. Tradition sometimes has to give way to business sense."[23]

The CART team owners didn't care about being largely excluded from the Indy Racing League. What they cared about was being participants in the premier open-wheel racing event of the year. Craig said, "We wouldn't even be talking about it if one of those races wasn't the Indy 500. That's the real issue, whether they are going to put qualifying impediments in the way of high quality drivers who might not race in other races in that league."[24]

George's announcement had the participants in the CART series up in arms. CART team owner Tony Bettenhausen said, "Tony George is trying to put CART out of business, which means he is trying to put people like me out of business." He continued, "This is unfortunate, it's unnecessary and it will cause the sport of Indy car racing some serious damage. The fans are going to be disgusted with the sport. There are already fans who are disenchanted with what they are seeing for qualification rules at the Indianapolis 500 next year." Carl Haas hinted that CART might pursue antitrust litigation against the Speedway and the Indy Racing League. Jim Hall said, "What is most important is that we get on with the business of improving the series which we have developed quite successfully to date. I don't believe we should throw away all the work we have done through the years. That seems to be what Tony George is proposing. From that viewpoint, I view that as a threat to our series."[25]

George later wrote an open letter published in *National Speed Sport News* giving his rationale for the guarantee of spaces to the IRL participants:

> That was when CART announced its 1996 schedule. The components of our modest, five-race IRL schedule had been announced in January, April and late May, and each announcement was accompanied by an IRL promise not to create conflict with what we understood would be CART's schedule. We obviously hoped they would enter our races.
>
> On June 10, CART announced its 15-race schedule. Ultimately, four of its dates appeared to us to have been put deliberately in conflict with three important IRL dates: CART's Brazil and Australia races were placed one week before and one week after the IRL's announced Phoenix date of March 24, 1996; CART's Nazareth race was listed on April 28 against USAC's important Indy Rookie Orientation Program; and inexplicably CART chose to schedule Elkhart Lake directly opposite the IRL's Aug. 18 New Hampshire race.

Not surprisingly, this move was not well received in the CART camp. Rumors of a CART boycott of the Indianapolis 500 swirled around the racing fraternity. These rumors were heightened by Carl Haas' statement, "It's not a boycott, we are just going somewhere else to race. The boycott is the other way around. The Speedway has excluded us from coming there by only leaving us eight positions. We decided if we can't get some compromise on their part, then we were going to race at Michigan on the same date."[26] Despite this statement, Carl Haas and Penske tried to tamp down the rumors that CART would be running a competing race at Michigan.[27] Despite these protestations, CART responded in October 1995 by announcing they might run a race in direct competition with the Indianapolis 500. Craig, IndyCar (CART) chairman, said, "We've stated many times we want to compete in the Indianapolis 500, but under its present format, the Indy Car board of directors cannot justify the expense and risk of a race in which the fastest 33 cars will not necessarily qualify."[28] Chip Ganassi, a CART team owner, said, "Let me be clear; Target/Chip Ganassi Racing wants to race at Indianapolis. However, business requirements, sporting tradition and plain common sense make us want to be there competing under the traditional, open, qualifying rules which help create a level playing field. The new qualifying rules established by the Speedway make this impossible."[29]

Both George and Craig knew this hardening of positions would thwart reunification of the sport. In competing teleconferences, the two leaders laid out their positions. George said, "We view the IRL and the Speedway as something that is important and necessary to ensuring that the 500 is preserved for the future. We certainly hope that all the teams that have participated, especially in seasons past, are welcome to come back and join us at Indianapolis as well as all the other IRL events." CART's Craig said, "Our objection, as you all know, is very specific, related to restrictions being imposed upon the Indy 500, which we think are repugnant and just go against the very essence of fair competition and open sport."[30]

Finally, on December 18, 1995, CART announced they would be running a race at Penske's Michigan International Speedway on Memorial Day in direct competition with the Indianapolis 500. In making the announcement, Craig said "We believe, at the end of the day, the underlying objective [of the IRL] is to put us out of business, and we don't find that an enchanting prospect."[31]

George retorted in *National Speed Sport News*, "In response, we can only say we are disappointed by the action because of its negative impact on automobile racing in North America. CART's action could diminish the opportunities for some drivers and teams to compete in the greatest motor sports event in the world, the Indianapolis 500." George continued, "However, it does not change or influence any of the plans for the 1996 Indianapolis 500 or the launching of the Indy Racing League, the series of oval track races which is designed to provide growth and long-term stability for the sport. If anything, CART's action underscores the need for our new league."[32]

The battle lines had been drawn. The decision by CART to have a competing race on Memorial Day in many cases forced sponsors to choose sides. Not only did the Indianapolis 500 and CART series have major sponsors, but the racing teams also had sponsors. Would the racing teams' sponsors continue to back them, even though a large amount of their support was based on the exposure the sponsors would get through the running of the Indianapolis 500? Many of the CART sponsors chose to back the inaugural U.S. 500 race at the Michigan International Speedway. Others chose to split their corporate sponsorship monies between the two races. This was not a surprise to George, who said, "I think sponsors are going to honor existing commitments and evaluate both series this year and in the future. I don't think they're going to make an emotional decision."[33]

With the huge chasm between the two sides, out poured details of a series of meetings in the spring that could have reunited open-wheel racing. But as with other issues, the perception was radically different by both sides. Craig told *National Speed Sport News* that a compromise was at hand, with a nine-man, independent governing body. To be based in Indianapolis, the board would have three members from IndyCar (CART), three directors appointed by the Indianapolis Motor Speedway and three independent directors mutually agreed to by CART and the Speedway. Craig also indicated that they had agreed to at least half of the races being on ovals. Haas wasn't comfortable with this structure but agreed to it in hope of restoring stability to open-wheel racing. According to unnamed sources, Penske was against the structure, as he believed IndyCar (CART) gave up too much power.[34] The Indy Racing League's executive director Jack Long also believed the reunification discussions had been fruitful and was hopeful that a solution could be worked out after the second meeting. Long conveyed the idea that the sanctioning of the races would be split between the two organizations with CART running the street and road races and the IRL running the oval races.

The third meeting, held in New York City, changed everything from the IRL's perspective. According to IRL's Long, "There was a fairly tightly structured presentation made to the IRL by CART, and looked nothing like the prior discussions we had. The heart was a nine-man board, and involved several things, including tossing the Indianapolis Motor Speedway rules, control, technical enforcement—several issues that were not included before—into the package which made it unacceptable." The bottom line was that the IRL perceived this as an attempt by the CART contingent to seize control of the Indianapolis Motor Speedway.[35]

Things were on an uptick going into the 1996 open-wheel racing season for both IndyCar (CART) and the Indy Racing League. Record crowds had shown up for several races, and television ratings were improving. Additionally, some new companies were becoming sponsors.[36]

Behind the scenes, officials at the IRL and the Speedway felt that Penske had used his influence to thwart their efforts at gaining sponsors for the fledgling series. One anonymous IRL source told *National Speed Sport News*, "There hasn't been one sponsorship proposal we have discussed with prospective sponsors that hasn't been sabotaged by Roger Penske. Motorola was interested in becoming a major sponsor with the IRL before Penske got hold of them. Roger told Motorola all of his Penske Leasing trucks have Motorola two-way radios on board and if they get involved in sponsoring the IRL, they could kiss that deal goodbye." The IRL official also said, "The latest we've heard is that Roger Penske plans on meeting with all the major oil companies involved in auto racing in an attempt to keep them from an involvement in the IRL. All we are trying to do is run our series, which includes the Indianapolis 500. We are not shutting any CART teams out of our races. In fact, we would like them to join us."[37]

The Indianapolis Motor Speedway received more bad news when Valvoline, a major Indianapolis 500 sponsor since 1964 and provider of all of the oil products, pulled its sponsorship. IMS was quickly able to line up a replacement, Pennzoil. Despite having pulled out as a sponsor of the Indianapolis 500, Valvoline continued as a sponsor of ABC's television coverage of the event.[38]

As the New Year began, the pressure mounted for George to prove the IRL was viable. There were many skeptics among sportscasters and fans of championship racing. While covering CART's 1995 opener at Miami, Robin Miller of the *Indianapolis Star* had predicted that the IRL would "never turn a wheel." Respected racing journalist Gordon Kirby had proclaimed at the 1995 New Hampshire race that the IRL "lives only in the pages of *National Speed Sport News.*"[39] Despite the skeptics' proclamations, the IRL opened with a 200-mile event at Walt Disney World in January 1996. With only two lead changes in the 200 miles and the sixth place finisher being five miles behind the race's winner, the race didn't have much excitement. Robin Miller of the *Indianapolis Star* wrote, "The IRL debut looked like a late 70s USAC race, with a big disparity in speed, shallow field and overall uncompetitiveness."[40]

Meanwhile, CART's 16 race schedule would open in March with 28 drivers. The equipment was all 1996 models. This promised to be the most competitive season in CART's 17-year history.[41]

Rumors, fed by a meeting between George and Penske in late February 1996, began to circulate throughout the open-wheel racing world that there might just possibly be some sort of movement towards reconciliation. In the meeting, George offered to increase the field for the Indianapolis 500 to 42 cars, which would allow more CART teams to participate in the race but did not drop the guaranteed slots for 25 IRL cars.[42]

One of the main philosophical differences between CART and the IRL lay in how to lower the cost of fielding a race team. Costs had become prohibitive unless a team had strong financial backing. The biggest component of the cost was the engines. A CART 2.65-liter engine with a turbocharger cost two times as much as an IRL 4.0-liter engine. The larger sized IRL engine meant the chassis was also redesigned. To be able to race at Indianapolis, a CART team would need to have two separate cars. In the meeting with George, Penske urged the elimination of the 4.0-liter engine and allowing

1996 CART models to participate in the 1997 Indianapolis 500.[43] The discussions between Penske and George were not successful in resolving the chasm between the two sides. IRL's Long said, "They would have to run their 1995 cars and equipment. I'm sure you've seen the horsepower figures between 1995 and 1996 engines, and the IRL is about parity."[44]

In the war of words played out in the press, Adam Saal, spokesman for CART, said,

> The Speedway is looking for a band-aid, but we are looking for a long-term solution that will address the gamut of issues between our organizations. In reality, what was offered was an attempt by IMS to get through 1996. It was not an olive branch that was offered by the Speedway. It was an arm reaching from a sinking pit, and it's truly sad that this is what the Indianapolis 500 has come down to. We are not responsible for bailing out the Speedway to save them from their folly. We are interested in a comprehensive settlement that will take into account all the issues between our organizations, but to achieve that before Memorial Day is impossible.[45]

The comments by Saal did not necessarily reflect the view by the entire CART membership. Although CART members had rejected the Penske overture, reports of a CART meeting varied; some said all of the members had rejected the move to reunite while others indicated a willingness by a good number of CART members to seek a compromise. Among those CART team owners wanting to see a compromise between the two sides was Barry Green, owner of the 1995 Indianapolis 500 winning car driven by Jacques Villeneuve. Green said, "I would go back to Indianapolis in a heartbeat. All we ask Tony is to go back to his open qualifying like he has in the past and I would go back right now. I don't want to go to Michigan, but under the current rules I don't think we have a choice."[46]

After rejection of the Penske efforts, both sides recognized they were going separate ways for the 1996 racing season. Penske said, "We would all like to have a solution that we can have one Indy car series. I guess we will all have to play out our own game here in 1996 and see what takes place." But Penske still held out hope of a reconciliation on a long-term basis: "I think once we have some miles on both sides, we can sit back and say where are we? Then, there certainly can be dialogue. I don't think Tony George or anybody else doesn't want to talk. It is a matter of having more facts in our hands based on the results. At this point, the IRL feels very strong about how good their series is. They will have to run venues to find out what level of competition they have, the quality of the fields. And most important is what happens at the gate. That will be an important factor because a series can't sustain itself if you don't have the following of the fans."[47]

In mid–March, the war between the two sides once again escalated when IMS revoked the licensing agreement with CART for the use of the trademark "IndyCar." Bill Donaldson, IMS's vice president for marketing, said the revocation was based upon the agreement's "language that they can't put the Indianapolis Motor Speedway or the sport in an unfavorable light. Remarks they've been making about the Speedway, the event and about Tony himself have been violations."[48] George also pointed to the planned U.S. 500's being in direct competition with the Indianapolis 500 as a significant factor in their decision: "The agreement was entered into based on the premise we were going to try to keep this sport somewhat unified. It has become obvious we have different philosophies, different principles and we are going in different directions. Indianapolis, Indy and Indy cars are all terms in racing that suggest Indianapolis. If those cars and competitors aren't going to be competing there, it doesn't make much sense for them to be calling themselves Indy Car."[49]

Not surprisingly, CART wanted to maintain control of the moniker "IndyCar." Believing that they had not violated the licensing agreement, CART filed legal action in the United States District Court for Eastern Michigan. Citing the Lanham Act, the primary trademark legislation, CART fought to keep their right to the name.[50] The IRL responded with a lawsuit filed in United States District Court of Southern Indiana against CART, Penske, Penske Corporation, Penske Motorsports, Penske Racing and Fittipaldi USA. The suit alleged that CART and its principals had intentionally interfered with the IRL's attempts to gain sponsors. It also alleged that CART had violated both the Lanham Act as well as the Sherman Antitrust Act. Of the filing, George said, "It is unfortunate CART has decided neither to cooperate nor to adhere to the terms of its contract with us. Indeed, CART continues to trade on our good name at the same time it maligns us and the Indy Racing League, and boycotts our race. Their conduct has left us with no other choice than to file this suit."[51]

Fittipaldi USA was added to the suit against CART et al. upon its filing legal action against the Indianapolis Motor Speedway. Fittipaldi USA had the broadcast rights for the Indianapolis 500 in Brazil, which were expanded to include the other IRL races. When the IRL races in Orlando and Phoenix were broadcast at 1:30 a.m., the Indianapolis Motor Speedway rescinded the rights to the broadcast. This resulted in Fittipaldi's filing suit in Miami against the Indianapolis Motor Speedway. At the hearing for this suit, the court ruled in favor of the Indianapolis Motor Speedway.[52]

Behind the scenes, as the Speedway prepared for the Indianapolis 500, the IRL was busy developing its engine and chassis specifications with a focus on making racing more affordable. The chassis needed to be redesigned to accommodate the larger stock-block engine. The IRL selected three compa-nies to build the new chassis—Dallara of Italy, G Force of Great Britain and Riley and Scott, based in Indianapolis.[53] With a maximum price in the $250,000 range, the cost was significantly below the $400,000+ cost of a CART chassis. Helping to lower the cost was a standardized gearbox and fuel tank. To further trim costs, the cars would be sold factory-direct rather than through an intermediary.[54]

Indianapolis has a vibrant cottage industry related to race cars. One of IRL's focuses was to bring auto racing back to its American roots. With the selection of Dallara and G Force as chassis constructors, some of the seventy-one companies just south of the Speedway, involved in the industry, were upset that the involvement of American firms was limited to Riley and Scott. USAC technical director Mike Devin explained the lack of American partic-ipation: "The American chassis companies have been all but put out of busi-ness. As for Gasoline Alley, there are a few people over there who will see a benefit from this and there are several who already do a lot of business the way things are now."[55]

The dispute also spilled into pop culture. Indianapolis native and late night comedian David Letterman had an ownership interest in the Bobby Rahal racing team. He invited movie star Paul Newman, who had an own-ership interest in the Newman-Haas racing team, to his show. On the show, Newman said, "The fans deserve to see a blue-ribbon event. The tradition is there, the spectacle is there. It's just too bad that this year the best competition will not be … this really takes the wind out of me." Not surprisingly, with a financial interest in CART racing teams, both Letterman and Newman pro-claimed that they would not be attending the Indianapolis 500.[56]

As the Memorial Day holiday approached, both sides of this split were looking for sponsors. The Indianapolis 500 anticipated little turnover of their sponsorship ranks. CART announced the landing of Miller Brewing Com-pany, Toyota Motor Company, Mercedes-Benz, Mobil Oil Company, and No Fear (a line of clothing), which would each pay $200,000 for their sponsorship deal. In return, the sponsors would get 1,000 tickets to the race and two 30-second ads during the ESPN telecast event.[57]

Despite CART's running a race in direct competition with the Indi-anapolis 500, the Speedway received 77 entries for the race. Although most casual observers think the drivers enter the race, entries for the race are always the cars. The Speedway revealed in mid–April that only 35 drivers had been assigned to the cars.[58] In a continuation of the very public war of words between the two factions, CART drivers pointed to the lack of expe-rience of the IRL drivers and claimed it was an accident waiting to happen.

On the first day of qualifying for the Indianapolis 500, Arie Luyendyk ran 239.2 miles per hour to take the pole. CART driver Michael Andretti quipped, "They're throwing horsepower at [teams] and adding more and more boost. But [Indy] is not designed to run those speeds and, let's face it, they're running older equipment, with cars that are not as safe as the cars we're running today. I think it's totally ridiculous. It's unconscionable. If you ask me, someone's going to get hurt. I hope to God I'm wrong and they get through it, but if they do get through it, they're lucky."[59]

With 17 of the 33 drivers in the Indianapolis 500 field being rookies, George responded to the CART stance: "There's no magic to competing at this level. They've competed and won at other levels and they're race drivers." Former CART racer and 1998 Indianapolis 500 winner Eddie Cheever said, "Everybody's been saying that these rookies that were going to be here were going to cause hideous accidents and there were going to be all sorts of problems. USAC will not let anybody onto the track that they do not believe is competent enough to be there. That's a policy they have had for the past 30 years and it hasn't changed."[60]

The race for both the Indianapolis 500 and the U.S. 500 held at the Michigan International Speedway wasn't what the promoters would have wanted. The U.S. 500, which boasted of the superiority of their drivers, including Michael Andretti as well as former Indianapolis 500 winners Emerson Fittipaldi, Bobby Rahal and Al Unser, Jr., had a wreck on the pace lap, damaging twelve of the twenty-seven cars and closing the track for nearly an hour to allow cleanup of the debris. When the field was restarted, all but one of the racers returned, nine in back-up cars and two in cars that had been repaired. The Indianapolis 500 was also filled with crashes, including one coming out of the fourth turn on the final lap. A quarter of the race was run under yellow. Thankfully, with three injuries, the carnage that Michael Andretti had predicted had not come to pass.[61] For the folks at the Indianapolis Motor Speedway, the ending of the Indianapolis 500 couldn't have been better scripted by Hollywood. Buddy Lazier beat the second place finisher by just 0.695 seconds. The ending at the Michigan 500 wasn't nearly as thrilling as Jimmy Vasser's margin of victory of 10.95 seconds.[62]

The big winner in the race for sponsors was NASCAR, which had lined up $405 million for its thirty-one-race schedule. This dwarfed that arranged by CART, with total sponsorships of $331 million, and the upstart IRL, with ten sponsors valued at $26 million for a three-race schedule. The effect upon the Indianapolis 500 and the city of Indianapolis was fewer dollars being spent. As an example, Mercedes-Benz attended the U.S. 500, entertaining approximately 1,200 prospective customers and spending an estimated

$250,000, which in prior years would have been spent in Indianapolis. While they also provided housing for dealers, executives and foreign journalists in Michigan, they had no presence at the Indianapolis 500. Also benefiting from the split was NASCAR. Texaco historically based its motorsport entertainment around the Indianapolis 500. But in 1996, their biggest corporate event was the Coca-Cola 600, NASCAR's race run on Memorial Day. Texaco also had a presence at the U.S. 500, with approximately 300 corporate guests, and the Indianapolis 500, with approximately 150 corporate guests.[63]

Very telling was the television viewership, as television ratings ultimately impact the value of the sponsorships. NASCAR's season opener and their biggest race, the Daytona 500, telecast over CBS, had a television rating of 9.2 in 1996.[64] The television ratings for the Indianapolis 500, open-wheel racing's largest race, was 8.4 in 1995. In 1996 it declined 21.4 percent to 6.6. The inaugural U.S. 500 race, shown on cable channel ESPN, drew a cable rating of 2.8, which is roughly the equivalent to a 2.0 rating on a major network.[65] Despite the lower ratings, the Indianapolis 500 was the second-most-watched sporting event for Memorial Day weekend. The Eastern Region NBA finals between the Chicago Bulls and the Orlando Magic garnered 8,740,000 households. Of the three big racing events, the Indianapolis 500 had 8,290,000 viewers, outpacing the 3,104,000 viewers for NASCAR's Charlotte 600 and CART's U.S. 500 viewership of 1,935,000.[66]

A New Normal

After the running of the U.S. 500 on Memorial Day, CART officials were very pleased with the results of the race. As with everything in CART, there were multiple opinions about when the race would be run in 1997. But one thing was very clear: CART intended to run a race on Memorial Day weekend. Rick Galles, a CART team owner who also ran a team at the Indianapolis 500, said, "I don't see any benefits of going head to head with the Indianapolis 500. Why split the television audience? If we ran on a different day, it would create more interest in our race." Bobby Rahal, who was both a CART team owner and driver, had a different opinion: "I think we have to stick with Sunday. I think the TV ratings show our race had an effect and it was the most people we've ever drawn to Michigan."[1]

A month after the Memorial Day head-to-head confrontation, Penske told the *Indianapolis Star*, "My focus would be to see everyone get together in a way the sport wins, and not one side or the other."[2] Was this a signal that perhaps next year's Indianapolis 500 would have both IRL and CART teams?

As the summer continued, CART's intentions became clearer, with the announcement of their 1997 race schedule. On the opening day for qualifications for the Indianapolis 500, CART scheduled a race on the Nelson Piquet Raceway oval in Brazil. They also planned a race for Memorial Day weekend but not in direct competition with the Indianapolis 500. Carl Haas, owner of cars driven by Michael Andretti and Christian Fittipaldi, said, "It's important we run that weekend, but not necessarily on the same day."[3]

In July 1996, the seriousness of the split was underscored when the Indianapolis Motor Speedway sent notices to CART participants that they could not renew the suites at the fabled track for the upcoming year. Car owners such as Penske, Patrick and Mario Andretti, and major sponsors such as Marlboro, paid the Indianapolis Motor Speedway from $60,000 to $80,000 for the use of the suite.[4]

During the summer, companies were beginning to look at the sponsorship opportunities for both the IRL/Indianapolis 500 and CART for the 1997 racing campaign. It would be the first time the sponsors would set their budgets with the knowledge of the depth of the split between the two sides. William Dyer, Jr., chairman of Barnes Dyer Marketing, Inc., said, "There is probably not room from a sponsor's perspective for two of these series."[5] Corporations don't pay millions of dollars to sponsor a race or a racing team without anticipating that they will benefit from the exposure. In the evaluation of sponsorship opportunities, corporations evaluate the viewership of the races broadcasted. For both the IRL and CART, this was not good news, as low television ratings did not indicate strong exposure. In 1996, both CART and the IRL had average ratings of less than 2 percent of the national television audience. Meanwhile, NASCAR's ratings were twice those of either of the open-wheel racing leagues.[6] Why would a corporation sponsor an IRL or CART team when they could have better exposure at the NASCAR races?

CART's schedule continued to take shape when in September, they announced they would not be running a race at the new Texas International Raceway, giving the IRL control of the Dallas–Fort Worth market, the fourth largest in the nation. Craig, CART's CEO, attributed the decision to safety concerns. Eddie Gossage, general manager of the track, protested that nothing had arisen in discussions with CART until he signed a contract to host an IRL race.[7] By October 1996 CART had decided not to run a race in direct competition with the Indianapolis 500. Since Memorial Day weekend was well established for auto racing, they announced the Gateway 500, to be run on a new track being built outside of St. Louis, Missouri, the day before the Indianapolis 500.[8]

After months of legal wrangling, CART agreed to drop the moniker of "IndyCar" for their races in December 1996. George said, "It will be clear to sponsors, fans and the general public that Indy cars are the cars that participate at the Indianapolis 500."[9] Prohibited from using the moniker IndyCars, in December CART announced they would be known as Champ Cars.[10]

In February 1997 Roger Penske, who had ten prior Indianapolis 500 winners, signaled his desire to participate in the Indianapolis 500: "Every race is important to win, but there is no question there are some with higher worldwide visibility. The Indianapolis 500 falls into that category. A lot of us have run in the Indianapolis 500 when we didn't run the other races in their series." Although Penske wanted to run in the Indianapolis 500, he made it clear that his participation in the race was subject to being able to bring his own chassis and a Mercedes or comparable engine to the race. Although this wasn't within the specifications of approved IRL equipment, George signaled a willingness to bend the rules when he said, "I think in regards to rules, we can get it sorted out to the point where there won't be an issue if he wants to come back." One of the issues needing to be resolved before Penske could run his own equipment at the Indianapolis 500 was the IRL mandate that a chassis maker must make the same equipment available to other teams. Penske felt this wouldn't be an obstacle since he had a chassis operation in England.[11]

Not surprisingly, Penske's consideration of participating in the Indianapolis 500 was met with mixed reactions from fellow CART team owners. Penske, after all, had been one of the founders of CART and one of the leaders in the multiple skirmishes. Team owner Carl Haas said, "If Tony George had opened the Indianapolis 500 up rather than reserving places for the IRL teams, we would have all been there last year. But to return there under their rules with their cars, I have no interest in returning." Fellow team owner Barry Green said, "Some of my fellow team owners may feel Roger is betraying CART, but I'm taking a very open mind and we are going to monitor the situation to see if it is feasible to return. I think we all want to return to the Indianapolis 500."[12]

Although the 1997 race continued with the 25 set-aside slots for participants in the IRL, there was some softening of the position. Perhaps this was due to recognition that the action had not only caused a great chasm in the world of open-wheel racing but was also damaging the sport and the Indianapolis 500. Undoubtedly part of the softening was that only 23 IRL teams qualified for a guaranteed slot for the Indianapolis 500.[13] George recognized the necessity of having more CART teams involved if he wanted the race to have a full contingent of 33 racers. In recognition of this, Leo Mehl, who had been hired as the IRL's CEO, announced before the running of the 1997 Indianapolis 500 that they would drop the 25/8 rule for the 1998 race.[14] Although the softening of the 25/8 rule would permit more CART drivers to participate in the race, the differences in the engines—with CART's being higher tech while the IRL's were bigger requiring a separate chassis—continued to be an issue. The cost of maintaining two separate cars would prohibit many teams from running both CART and IRL races. George acknowledged the two different specifications for the race cars was an issue and did not anticipate that the dropping of the 25/8 rule would create an influx of participants in IRL races or the Indianapolis 500.[15]

In response to the dropping of the set-aside for IRL participants, CART's CEO, Andrew Craig, commented, "The elimination of the 25/8 rule is a positive first step toward resolving the differences that exist between the Indianapolis Motor Speedway, IRL and CART. We believe these changes signal that the Speedway and IRL recognize the importance of having the teams and drivers that race in the CART/PPG series as a part of the Indy 500." Then Craig sounded an ominous note: "There remain many major issues that separate CART and the Speedway. We hope motor racing fans everywhere are not misled into believing this announcement guarantees the teams and drivers that comprise CART will be racing at Indianapolis in 1998."[16] George responded, "Now they're saying that if we accept their technical regulations, they'll come. That's not going to happen. Basically, they're saying they're not coming back."[17]

On the final day of qualifications, USAC officials, concerned that some of the fastest racers had been excluded because of the guaranteed slots for the IRL racers, allowed Lyn St. James and Johnny Unser, who had been bumped from the field by slower racers from the IRL league, to join the race. To accommodate St. James and Unser, the field was increased to 35 starters. IRL executive director Leo Mehl said "In my opinion, this is the fair thing to do, to start the fastest 33 cars. To do that we'll end up starting with 35."[18] After having been criticized by the public for initially not having the fastest 33 in the race, Indianapolis Motor Speedway officials were hopeful of a good race. That was not to be.

Just like in 1973, the race was postponed two days due to rain. Unfortunately, the conclusion of the 1997 Indianapolis 500 plunged into controversy after a wreck on the next to final lap required a restart of the race. As the two leading racers, Arie Luyendyk and Scott Goodyear, roared down the main straightaway, chief steward Keith Ward called for the green flag. However, Claude Fischer, the Indianapolis 500's chief observer, not hearing the call, failed to change the yellow lights on the field. Although Luyendyk took the checkered flag, some believed this prevented Goodyear from passing Luyendyk.[19]

Leo Mehl was the head of racing for Goodyear Tire & Rubber. Tony Gerge appointed him as the executive director of the Indy Racing League.

Two weeks later more controversy hit the IRL with the finish of the True Value 500 race at the Texas International Raceway. On the next to final lap, Tony Stewart's engine blew and he lost control of the car, spinning into turn one. Race officials declared Billy Boat the winner of the True Value 500 and awarded him the trophy. The Luyendyk team, however, believed he had won the race. Review of the tapes showed that Luyendyk and other racers had used pit row to drive around the wreckage and their laps had not been properly counted. USAC officials changed direction, awarding the race to Luyendyk.[20] The scoring and technical errors at the 1997 Indianapolis 500 and the Fort Worth True Value race led the IRL to drop USAC as the sanctioning body after a forty-three-year affiliation. The IRL executive director, Leo Mehl, promised that the IRL would begin sanctioning their races, beginning with the next scheduled race in less than two weeks.[21]

Although the Indianapolis 500 continued to be a sold-out affair, there had been a noticeable reduction in the spectators attending the practices and qualifying. In December 1997, George announced the end to the second week of qualifications and practice. He said, "If you could plot a trend, I think that you would see the crowds, for whatever reason, were beginning to drop off even when the CART teams were here. It kind of went up and down, but even when they were here in the early '90s, and up until '95, the trend started going down. I attribute that as much [to] competition for people's time and money as anything."[22] The CART teams had been agitating for this change for several years prior to the split. The change was applauded by both drivers and team owners. Rick Galles, who had run teams both at CART races as well as at the Indianapolis 500, said, "It's like signing a $200,000 sponsor, because you have people back there all month and run your cars into the ground. To be honest, we all find our optimal speed on the third day and then we just run. The more miles you run, the more chance there is for something to happen."[23] The change also financially benefited the Speedway, as it cost approximately $25,000 per day for track operations including ticket takers, firemen, nurses, doctors, and guards. Eliminating eight days of practice and qualifying would save the Speedway approximately $200,000.[24]

The shortening of the activities at the Brickyard led to speculation of another race being held at the track in May. George had discussed with Penske, Jay Signore and Les Richter, the principals of the International Race of Champions (IROC), the possibility of holding a race at the track. George also continued to be interested in bringing a Formula One race to Indianapolis. He commented, "It's no big secret that I am interested in a Formula One race here. I have been interested in it the last 7 years, and it might take another 7 years for me to be successful. I would not be opposed to having another race here."[25] After the successes of the Brickyard 400, George acted on his desire to hold a Formula One race at the Speedway, traveling with Leo Mehl to Europe to meet with Bernie Ecclestone, head of the Formula One racers. To hold a race at the track would require significant modification. The Speedway would continue to use the main straightaway and turn one as part of the road course.[26]

The off-season, which also is the time most corporations are setting their budgets for the next fiscal year, is when many sponsorships are lined up. In December 1997, CART announced a change in the sponsorship of the series to FedEx, bringing an estimated $8 million to $10 million into their coffers.[27]

CART wasn't the only group trolling for sponsors. Reports circulated that the IRL was close to signing a multi-year deal with Reebok. Mehl, the IRL commissioner, would neither confirm nor deny this. In January 1998, the IRL announced that Reebok would sponsor a team. Although Reebok had hoped to sponsor a team as well as the series, the IRL ultimately decided against that due to the potential conflict-of-interest issues.[28] Towards the end of January, the IRL announced Pep Boys as the series sponsor for a five-year term. In making the sponsorship announcement George said, "Attracting a series sponsor is something we knew would take some time. It took some time to where corporate America would recognize the Indy Racing League. This is right on my schedule, according to my watch. I thought it would take three years."[29] For the first three years of the IRL's existence, they had garnered an estimated 10 percent of the sponsorships of CART. The IEG sponsorship report for 1998 estimated the Speedway would have $101 million in sponsorships. This represented approximately 25 percent of the estimated $419 million in sponsorships for CART.[30] Progress was slow but steady for the IRL.

Over the years, Patrick had been pushing Craig to take CART public.[31] This became reality when in March 1998, CART issued an initial public offering (IPO). The sale of 4.1 million shares of stock, valued from $16 to $18 per share at the initial public offering, was anticipated. Although the team owners would retain approximately 65 to 68 percent of the business,[32] the sale of stock would result in a market capitalization of $275 million. On its first day of trading, CART's stock roared out of the starting gate and increased approximately 24 percent, ending at $19.9375 per share.[33] The proceeds from the initial public offering were used to buy the Indy Lights series from Patrick for $10 million and to pay the current CART members $9.5 million in aggregate for "accrued points awards." It also provided a nice war chest to promote its own races.[34]

The CART board of directors included Gerry Forsythe, Chip Ganassi, Carl Haas, Bruce McCaw, Pat Patrick, Bobby Rahal and Derrick Walker. Obviously missing from the list was Penske, fueling speculation he would leave the series. This was vehemently denied by Penske Corporation Communications vice president Dan Luginbuhl: "It's the most ludicrous thing I've ever heard. Roger has been a champion of CART from its inception and will continue to be so."[35]

Having been shut out of the lucrative Dallas–Fort Worth market, CART scored with the announcement of a race in the nation's third-largest market, Chicago. Chip Ganassi announced he was joining with Charles Bidwell of Sportsman's Paradise to expand this traditional horse racing facility with a 1.1-mile auto racing oval. Following the example of Dover Downs, the facility, when completed, could be used for both horse and automobile races. The initial phase costing $50 million would increase the seating capacity from 11,000 to 67,000 in addition to building the asphalt track. A couple of years earlier, Ganassi and CART had been excluded from an alliance including the Indianapolis Motor Speedway to build a proposed track in DuPage County, Illinois, outside of Chicago.[36]

As the 1998 open-wheel racing season came to a conclusion, there were three things that were abundantly clear. First was the continued fall of television ratings for both CART and the IRL, which paled in comparison to the television ratings for NASCAR. Before the CART/IRL split in 1996, the television ratings for the IRL's premier event, the Indianapolis 500, had been equal to or greater than those for NASCAR's premier event, the Daytona 500. In 1998, the cumulative television viewership for CART was 9.169 million people. By way of comparison, the Daytona 500 had 8.428 million viewers. The Nielsen ratings for CART included a 1.1 rating for a race in Japan, a 0.8 rating for the Long Beach race and a 1.9 rating for the opener in Miami. As bad as those numbers were, the IRL numbers were worse.[37]

The second issue was the lack of stars in the open-wheel racing circuits. In the early 1990s, household names such as Mario Andretti, Emerson Fittipaldi, Al Unser, A. J. Foyt, Rick Mears and Johnny Rutherford retired from the sport. While enjoying the success these racers brought to the open-wheel circuit, CART failed to groom the next generation of drivers. By outlawing rear-engine racers and eliminating the dirt races from the championship circuit, CART inadvertently eliminated the pipeline of drivers who would become the next generation of stars. Dennis Wood, the promoter of the Phoenix International Speedway, lamented, "There hasn't been an American driver cultivated in 20 years."[38]

A third item to be resolved prior to any reunification of open-wheel racing was the engine and chassis configuration used in the cars. CART teams utilized turbocharged engines while the IRL series used normally aspirated engines. The engine specifications for the IRL were under review, and George was expected to release the new specifications in November 1998. If the two sides could resolve the differences between the engine specifications, it might help in reunification of the series.

In the fall of 1998, representatives from Honda, Ford, Mercedes and Toyota provided George an engine formula that could ultimately result in a reunification of the two warring sides. The manufacturers are believed to have proposed either a 3.0- or 3.5-liter V-8 engine with no pushrods, stock blocks or rev limiters. Bobby Rahal said, "I know there is a proposal and a willingness on the part of our engine manufacturers to create a solution and create a spec that satisfies what they [IMS] want. There's been a lot of talk and some momentum for this, and everyone [all four engine suppliers and CART] is involved. And they all want to come back to Indianapolis like we do."[39]

A secondary but very important issue related to the engines and the reunification of the two racing leagues was the ownership of technology. Honda, Ford, Mercedes and Toyota produced turbocharged engines that were then leased to the racing teams. In order to protect their technology, these four manufacturers were insistent upon the lease structure's including the maintenance and rebuilding of the engines. On the other hand, the suppliers of the IRL engines sold the engines to the teams, and the teams assumed all maintenance and rebuilding tasks. Bobby Rahal commented, "It's the biggest single issue the keeps the sides apart, the ownership of technology. We're not going to turn over our technology to anybody on the street so he can immediately sell it off to Toyota or Honda or whoever." CART chairman Craig explained, "Our [engine] manufacturers aren't married to turbocharged engines. They're very straightforward; they don't have a bias to any particular type of engine, providing it's a technical challenge and they can keep that proprietary information intact." Penske added, "If Tony wants to get together, give us an engine rule we can all take a look at that would be realistic for the next four or five years."[40]

George made his decision about the engine specifications for IRL races in 2000 through 2004 in mid–November, and it dashed any hope of reunification. The specifications called for a 3.5-liter, non-turbocharged engine with rev limiters. He also continued with the IRL teams owning their engines rather than leasing them, which the CART engine manufacturers considered essential.[41] Leo Mehl, executive director of the IRL, said, "We've got a series, and we want additional competitors, but we're going to stay with the principles developed by our founder, Tony George. My feeling is that the owners in CART will like this rule." But the CART owners didn't like the rule. Patrick said, "I understand what they've done. They've decided they don't want to cooperate with us. I think they do want us there, but under their terms." Dan Gurney, who was also a CART car owner, said, "It looks like [George is] still playing games and doesn't care about the sport, other than the Indy 500. He had a chance to unify the sport, but he chose to be a spoiled brat."[42]

Those involved in the manufacturing of racing engines were not impressed by the direction the Indy Racing League was taking, either. Robert Clarke, general manager of Honda Performance Development, said, "I can tell you rev limiters are not a direction we want to go. We're interested in challenging technology, not using artificial means to restrict engines." Paul Ray, a vice president with Ilmor Engineering, which provided the engines for Mercedes, said, "They moved a little closer to what we would consider a racing type engine. But many of the rules are still restrictive on the core technology." The response of Kevin Kennedy, public affairs manager for Ford's Special Vehicle Operations, was more balanced: "The positives are long-term stability, which helps defray costs, and a 3.5-litre engine. On the downside is the IRL's stance on the lease and rev limiters."[43]

At the end of 1998, the IRL and Indianapolis Motor Speedway announced a one-year contract with FOX and the FOX Sports Network to broadcast nine of the eleven IRL races. They also announced that the season-opening TransWorld Diversified Services 200, held at Disney World, and the Indianapolis 500, including qualifications, would be broadcast by ABC.[44]

By 1999, the war between CART and the IRL had impacted the level of sponsorships and television ratings for both organizations. With lower levels of revenue, it was inevitable that financial difficulties would follow. At the time, CART was on strong financial footing with nearly $100 million in liquidity. The underlying question was what would the rates be when renewals came up for the sponsorships and the television rights. Predicting the potential for long-term financial difficulties, Forrest Bond wrote in racefax.com, "We have it on good authority that CART and NASCAR's Bill France are at least feeling each other out, with an eye toward France acquiring the series." Not surprisingly, NASCAR officials denied this possibility."[45]

A combination of CART and NASCAR in some ways would have made sense. Many of the oval tracks on which CART ran were also used for NASCAR races. CART team owners Chip Ganassi (Chicago Motor Speedway) and Carl Haas (Milwaukee Mile) both owned speedways upon which both CART and NASCAR ran. And Bill France's International Speedway Corporation had tracks where five CART races were run.[46]

The CART team owners who also owned speedways understood the necessity to stop the downward spiral in terms of revenues. Besides the cars, they had significant investment of up to $150 million in each speedway. The owner of the Fontana racetrack, Carl Hogan, thought the merger of NASCAR and CART made sense. He said, "With their marketing and organizational might, and his guidance, it's something I think would be good for the sport. And I also believe it would likely lead to both CART and IRL joining."[47]

When George was the featured speaker at the Rotary Club of Indianapolis in April 1999, he acknowledged the two sides must "get together at some point in the future." He also indicated there had been some limited conversations between the two groups. When George showed up at a CART race in Homestead, Florida, the rumors of a pending merger of the two sides intensified. In an attempt to set expectations, George commented, "There are many complicated issues that have to be addressed."[48]

The 1999 IRL season had strong attendance at races at the Texas Motor Speedway and over 400,000 at the Indianapolis 500, which remained the largest one-day sporting event in the world. But the races at Dover Downs in Delaware had only an estimated 8,000 in attendance. The IRL made the decision to drop the Dover Downs race and the Pikes Peak International. Following a wreck in which three spectators were killed, the promoter of the race at the Charlotte Motor Speedway dropped the IRL race from the schedule.[49]

In mid–April, CART filed a "Registration Statement" allowing CART team owners to sell their stock on an orderly basis. The blockbuster news came a week later when Penske announced he was selling 700,000 shares of his total holdings of 800,000 shares of CART stock. Dan Luginbuhl, one of Penske's associates, intimated to the *Indianapolis Star* that the sale of stock was to avoid a conflict of interest. Among his many investments were not only the racing teams but also the ownership of several race tracks on which four CART races were held.[50] A month after selling his CART stock, Penske Motorsports, owner of the Michigan International Speedway and California Speedway, was sold to International Speedway Corporation, controlled by NASCAR's France family. With the contract between CART and Penske Motorsports for the Michigan International Speedway ending in 2001 and the contract for the California Speedway ending at the conclusion of the 1999 racing season, CART was potentially left exposed to losing these two venues if International Speedway Corporation chose not to renew the contract.[51] At the time of the Penske sale, various racing venues owned by International Speedway Corporation hosted five of the eleven IRL races.

At the conclusion of the 1999 racing season, corporate sponsors urged CART not to run a race in direct competition with the Indianapolis 500.[52] In late October 1999, CART CEO Craig released a statement to the press that brought cheers and hope from the open-wheel racing community: "It is widely known we made significant efforts to secure a resolution to the issues that have divided CART and the Indy Racing League. When it became apparent in early October that our efforts were not going to result in a resolution of those issues, CART and its team owners examined whether it would be feasible to compete in the Indy 500. Many of the specific issues relative to Indy which have precluded CART teams from participating in recent years have been resolved." He concluded his remarks, stating, "Our teams have decided it is in their best interests, as well as that of the sport, to return to the Speedway to compete for the title of Indianapolis 500 champion."[53]

In late January, the IRL announced the signing of Northern Light Technology, an Internet search engine firm, to a five-year sponsorship.[54] The IRL also garnered a five-year contract with ABC for the live broadcast of their races on ABC, ESPN or ESPN2.[55]

More good news for the IRL was the defection of popular driver Al Unser, Jr., from the CART circuit to the IRL. When Penske failed to renew Unser's contract as part of the Penske Racing team, Unser was picked up by Galles Racing, whose teams raced at Indianapolis. The move to Galles Racing reunited the winning team from the 1992 Indianapolis 500. Unser, a two-time Indianapolis 500 winner, was clearly pleased to be once again racing at Indianapolis. He said, "All I know is I don't have to convince anybody of my reasoning to come to the IRL, because I simply don't give a [bleep] what they think. My heart lies in the middle of Indiana, not at Mid-Ohio. I'm a race car driver risking my life at all these other races so I can run in the Indianapolis 500, not so I can run in St. Louis on Memorial Day Weekend because of some political battle like I had to the last three years."[56]

When the Indianapolis Motor Speedway opened for practice in May 2000, not only was Al Unser, Jr., at the track; another stalwart CART team also returned to the Speedway. The Target–Chip Ganassi Racing team brought two top drivers—1996 CART champion Jimmy Vasser and the defending champion, Juan Montoya. Speculation abounded that this was the beginning of many CART teams' returning to Indianapolis in future years.[57] When the 2000 Indianapolis 500 race began, IRL driver Greg Ray sat on the pole.[58] He was joined on the front row by Montoya from the Chip Ganassi Racing Team and Eleiso Salazar of A. J. Foyt Enterprises. Montoya won the race.[59]

Penske also dipped his toe into the waters at the Indianapolis 500 in 2000. His foray to the Speedway was as a sponsor for Treadway Racing and its driver, Jason Lefler.[60] In early June, Penske announced he was exploring a return to the Indianapolis 500 with a team for the 2001 race. He had arranged to lease a G-Force Aurora Oldsmobile from Treadway Racing and planned to bring his two team drivers, Gil de Ferran and Helio Castroneves, to the Speedway for tests. Penske said, "What we would like to do is rent the track at Indianapolis later in the summer and give both drivers a full day at the track. That way, they can get used to it and run rather than us just showing up there next spring and running without any track time."[61]

After four years, things were looking up for the IRL. They had a series sponsor and a television contract with one of the big three networks, and CART teams were beginning to return to the Indianapolis 500. Although the CART teams didn't participate in the rest of the IRL schedule, this was potentially a glimpse of things to come.

Things were not looking up for CART. Attendance at their races was down. Television ratings were down. And with significant exposure in Europe and many foreign drivers participating in CART, they were perceived by many as having abandoned their American roots. There was also the residual impact of running the U.S. 500 in direct competition with the Indianapolis 500 in 1996. Rick Galles said, "Roger Penske knew how important it was to try to save the Indianapolis 500 for CART. He actually put an effort together with some other team owners to meet with Tony George and came up with a way to save the Indy 500 and not do the U.S. 500. Andrew Craig caught wind of this and got several team owners together and undermined Roger's effort to try to keep Indy." As a result of all these factors, the CEO, Andrew Craig, was fired six months before the end of his contract.[62] CART turned to a familiar face to lead the series on an interim basis—Bobby Rahal, winner of the 1986 Indianapolis 500.

In July, George announced that the Indianapolis 500 would return to two full weeks of practice and two weeks of qualifications. Underlying the decision was an increase in open testing at the track. During March and April 2000, various teams ran 21,000 miles of testing, an increase of roughly 10 percent from the 19,000 miles run during 1999.[63]

In August 2000, Mercedes-Benz, a longtime engine supplier to CART, announced its decision to withdraw. Mercedes spokesman Jurgen Hubbert attributed this action to their increasing focus on Formula One racing and participation in the rejuvenated Deutsche Tourenwagen Masters (DTM) Touring Car Series in Europe.[64]

With some racing teams having deeper pockets than others, enabling them to invest in the newest equipment, open-wheel racing was losing some of its spectator interest, as the races tended to be boring. Unlike the tight racing featured at many NASCAR races, CART racing didn't have much action during the races. In an effort to make the races more competitive, interim CEO Bobby Rahal wanted to decrease the power of the engines by 150–200 horsepower. His strategy included reducing the turbo-boost and possibly decreasing the inlet area. The auto manufacturers, who were interested in pushing the technological envelope, were not on board with the plan.[65]

Rahal's tenure as the head of CART was brief. Hired upon the resignation of Andrew Craig in June 2000, Rahal announced he was joining the Formula One Jaguar team in September.[66] He would honor the remainder of his contract, through the end of the year. CART was once again in search of a leader.

The top contender to lead CART was Chris Pook, the founder of the Long Beach Grand Prix. After reviewing the situation, Pook took himself out of consideration. Concerned about the domination of the board by team owners, Pook felt it would not give him the flexibility to institute the changes he felt were necessary.[67]

CART Implodes

CART announced its new leader, Joseph Heitzler, in December. Previously the CEO of National Mobile Television Productions, Inc., Heitzler identified the issues with the declining attendance at races and viewership: "The main weakness is a lack of visibility to the public, but it comes down to a major tweaking of a successful product." Heitzler then laid out the key to turning things around: "Our drivers are a commodity and we need to enhance their visibility, and acknowledge the great drivers that built the sport."[1] Heitzler identified this as a dream job, but his tenure at the head of CART would be anything but a dream.

For 2001, the IRL announced a 13-race season. Even more importantly, it acknowledged the need for new fans at its races and bulked up its marketing staff from 3 people to 30. It also developed 30-minute infomercials to be shown in race markets and purchased additional air time, increasing its television exposure from 88 hours in 2000 to 500 hours in 2001. The new television contract with ABC had all races to be shown live on ABC, ESPN or ESPN2.[2] Also providing good news for the IRL was Penske's decision to run two teams in the league's races, including the Indianapolis 500, beginning in 2001.[3]

Although CART team owners initially had management control of the company, with the sale of stock to the public, things began to change as the team owners sold stock to diversify their portfolios. By June 2001, a Securities and Exchange Commission filing revealed that James Grosfeld had more than 5 percent of the stock. Through his company, Grosfeld and Associates, Grosfeld had the reputation of being an activist shareholder, and forcing change on management of companies in which he had an ownership interest.[4]

The simmering discontent by the engine companies came to a boil when CART announced the immediate adoption of a modified pop-off valve during the middle of the racing season. Honda and Ford, using aerodynamic testing, had discovered they could lower the pressure around the pop-off valve, effectively allowing them to run with more boost. An engineer from Honda revealed this insider secret to Toyota when he went to work for the latter company. Toyota then went to CART, protesting they were at a competitive disadvantage. The end result was a ¾-inch space at the bottom of the pop-off valve to eliminate the additional boost.[5] Ford and Honda were very unhappy with this mid-season change in the rules. Their engine designs had been approved by CART's technical committee. The new spacer requirements had received very little testing. More significantly, Ford and Honda believed Toyota had been given advance notice of the change in the standard, allowing their competitor to test the new requirement.

This change and the resulting uproar caused Honda to reevaluate its participation in CART as an engine builder. Honda decided to appeal the required change; CART denied the appeal within three days. Honda then filed legal action with the appellate court. By mid–July, a three-member appellate panel had ruled in favor of Honda. As part of the ruling, CART was required to go back to the engine configuration initially approved by their technical committee for three weeks. Additionally, the appellate court instructed Honda, Toyota, Ford and CART to work together to find a mutually acceptable solution.[6]

The successful appeal by Honda of the pop-off valve spacer requirement was not well received by the folks at Toyota. They responded with an angry letter to CART CEO Heitzler. In the letter, Lee White, president of Toyota Racing Development, threatened to protest the upcoming Toronto race if the pop-off valve spacer was not part of the engine requirements. Toyota proposed running the Toronto and Michigan races without the awarding of points. This was a non-starter, as point standings are very important in the overall scheme of auto racing. Needless to say, Toyota's proposal was quickly dismissed.[7]

Within days, the solution to the pop-off valve spacer seemed to have been found. CART announced it would continue with the requirements for the spacer; however, the maximum amount of turbocharger boost would be limited to 36 inches for the races at Michigan and California and 37 inches elsewhere.

But the situation was much more dire than just one engine manufacturer reevaluating its position. With Toyota already announcing they were going to be supplying engines to the IRL, what would Ford do? Would they remain as an engine supplier to CART?[8]

By July 2001, Heitzler had been the CEO of CART for a mere six months. When hired, he had promoted the hope of better days ahead. Instead, CART was faced with a growing list of issues and his leadership was being questioned.

In fact, there were some who believed CART was imploding and its days were numbered.

In addition to the pop-off valve controversy, CART was in a dispute with marketing firm ISL Worldwide. The two firms had entered into a nine-year marketing agreement with an aggregate value of $235 million in July 1998. The marketing agreement was prematurely terminated by ISL Worldwide on February 28, 2001. CART immediately filed a lawsuit seeking damages of $100 million, claiming ISL Worldwide had deceived CART. They maintained that ISL Worldwide had used CART as a vehicle into the North American market and then failed to deliver. Among the broken promises was a marketing guarantee of $20 million; ISL Worldwide had delivered only $14 million and had not paid the differential.

Of course, there are always two sides to every story. In ISL Worldwide's $150 million countersuit, the filing states, "CART's management fraudulently induced ISL to enter the agreement in order to create the illusion of ever-increasing value for shareholders and the stock market." The ISL suit continued, "The announcement of the deal was delayed by CART until after [its] initial public offering. Based upon these representations, ISL invested more than $30 million between June 1998 and the present in marketing, promotion, and the sale of CART corporate sponsorship. ISL has received no return on that investment."[9]

Subsequently, CART received a $25 million judgment against ISL Worldwide. Rather than accepting a $5.5 million cash offer from ISL Worldwide, CART pushed for the payment of the judgment. This decision was costly, as ISL Worldwide filed Chapter 7 bankruptcy and CART ultimately received no compensation.[10] Obviously, Heitzler wasn't at the helm of CART when the agreement was reached with ISL for marketing services (it was Andrew Craig), but he was in the leadership role when the deal unraveled.

The ISL Worldwide lawsuits and counter-suits weren't the end of the issues for CART. Heitzler was also dealing with a lawsuit filed by Bruton Smith of Speedway Motorsports, Inc., for $20 million. This followed the cancellation of the inaugural Firestone Firehawk 600 race at the Texas Motor Speedway a couple of hours before the start of the race. CART pulled out of the race after multiple drivers complained of dizziness while driving the 1.5-mile circular track at high speeds.[11] The suit was filed after Smith was unable to get a refund of the sanctioning fee by CART.

Although a lawsuit wasn't involved, there was also the near-cancellation of a race in Rockingham, England, due to the condition of the track. J. Kirk Russell, CART's vice president of competition, had visited the track fifteen times in preparation for the race, yet there were significant issues with water seeping through the track.[12] Additionally, CART under Heitzler's leadership was unable to renew races at three tracks owned by International Speedway Corporation, which is owned by NASCAR's France family.[13]

The troubles for Heitzler didn't end with the two lawsuits and the pop-off-valve controversy. There were also severance payments totaling $1.2 million to three previous members of the CART leadership team and the demise of the Indy Lights series, which CART bought for $10 million in 1998. CART also lost its primary sponsor, FedEx. Heitzler had assured investors in March 2001 that the renewal of this long-term sponsorship would be inked shortly, but it wasn't. By June, FedEx was saying they were not involved in negotiations for the renewal of the sponsorship.

If that was not enough, Heitzler didn't have a television contract and Fox Sports Network announced there wasn't going to be one. That would be devastating to this company and its future. They had already gone down the path of self-production and paying a broadcaster to carry the telecast.[14] As negotiations were continuing with ESPN for a television package, in early August 2001 Heitzler tried to reassure CART's sponsors that a television deal was all but inked and an announcement would be made in mid–September.[15] Heitzler delivered on his commitment to the sponsors when in late August, an announcement was made of a deal with CBS and Speedvision. In the three-year deal, CBS would broadcast seven events per year and the remainder of the races would be telecast on Speedvision. CART would buy television time at a rate of $235,000 per hour and would pay its producer, Fox Sports, $325,000 per broadcast. The deal struck with CBS reflected CART's diminished power. In the 1999 broadcasting deal with ABC, the agreement called for the broadcasting of thirteen events. Additionally, Speedvision viewership was only about 50 percent of the viewership of ABC affiliate ESPN.[16] The sponsors couldn't have been happy about this deal.

Shortly after the announcement of the CART broadcast deal, the Indianapolis Motor Speedway announced a five-year partnership with ABC/ESPN, a much stronger package than that negotiated by CART. The IMS-ABC/ESPN contract also included the exclusive coverage of IRL races. In making the announcement, Mark Shapiro, senior vice president and general manager of ESPN, explained their rationale for the long-term contract: "The Indy Racing League is the leading American open-wheel racing circuit, based upon the programming heritage of the Indianapolis 500. ESPN has chosen to partner with the Indianapolis Motor Speedway and the Indy Racing League as the future of open-wheel racing is in the United States."[17]

Heitzler's headaches weren't limited to those at CART. He was also dealing with the residue of issues of his defunct business, Sports Communications,

Inc. This marketing firm represented 17 of the 33 sponsors of the 1984 Olympic Games held in Los Angeles. Founded in 1981, the firm ceased operations in 1985 and moved out of its facilities. Heitzler claimed that the landlord had agreed to the termination of the lease with no contractual liability. Unfortunately for Heitzler, he didn't have this agreement in writing. Sports Communication, Inc., filed Chapter 7 bankruptcy in 1989 when the landlord filed for the back rent, in the amount of $91,000.[18]

With the difficulties at CART, Derrick Walker, the only car owner to have teams in both CART and IRL, prophetically told the *Indianapolis Star*, "I think by 2005 or 2006 open-wheel racing is going to look a lot different than it does now. A lot of things are going to shake out in the next four or five years. Open-wheel racing has a unique opportunity to reshape itself— and it needs to. We need to put behind all the dogfights and get down to the big picture."[19] Barry Green, a CART owner who was in discussions with George for the reunification of the two series, said, "It's not time to panic because I truly believe there are a lot of exciting things on the horizon. But I will say, and I underline it, that open-wheel racing in this country has been badly hurt because of the two series. It's very sad that we, CART and the IRL, are not good enough to resolve the differences."[20]

Another shoe dropped for CART when Toyota announced it would not be in the engine supplier mix for the 2003 season. Toyota spokesman J. Davis Illingworth, Jr., explained the rationale: "From a financial perspective, it is not prudent for Toyota to supply two different engine specs for U.S.-based open-wheel racing while also in the early stages of a Formula One program internationally." But he left the door open for Toyota to rejoin Honda and Ford as an engine supplier: "If CART adopts the same engine specifications as the IRL, and it makes good business sense from both a financial and marketing standpoint, Toyota would consider again participating in the series."[21]

There was also unhappiness in the ranks of the "independent" promoters, whose tracks were not owned by others affiliated with CART. They sent a letter demanding a reduction in the sanction fees, which averaged between $1.5 million and $2 million, to hold a race. They contended that with the loss of major race teams, such as the Penske Marlboro team and the Mo Nunn Hollywood team, the loss of sponsorships, the disappointing TV contract, and the loss of manufacturers promoting the race, the race was no longer worth the sanctioning fee. Some industry insiders believed it would be cheaper for the promoters to pay the cost of a lawsuit rather than to absorb the cost of the race.[22]

When the owners of CART took the firm public, they retained control of the company by owning 65 percent of the stock. This control was diluted when various team owning stockholders sold their stock to rebalance their portfolios or to provide working capital to support their team's operations. In October 2001, a Securities and Exchange Commission disclosure revealed that Jonathan P. Vannini had purchased 8 percent of the stock. Over an eight-day period from October 17 until October 25, Vannini increased his holdings in CART by 439,400 shares at a price of $5.7 million, putting his total holdings in CART at 1,189,700 shares with a market value of $15.5 million. Vannini, an activist shareholder, wanted changes made.

In a letter sent to the board of directors, Vannini wrote, "Team owners may have economic relationship with industry suppliers that have interest and objectives that are contrary to those of the Company." He continued, "Certain team owners have positions on various committees of the Board, which gives them an influence with management that may be contrary to the Company's interests."[23] Chief among Vannini's desired changes was the composition of the board of directors, many of whom had conflicts of interest resulting from owning the teams that raced as part of the CART series, while some also owned tracks upon which CART raced. Additionally, he wanted to change "internal procedures, policies and governance." If the board did not respond, he was willing to wage a proxy fight if his desired changes were not implemented.

Initial reports also indicated that Vannini wanted a change in the leadership to someone with more experience in the motorsport industry. Within two days, Vannini denied his desire to oust Heitzler.[24] When the CART board of directors met about a month later, Grosfeld and Vannini had filed statements indicating they wanted a change in senior management. Grosfeld, who was the second largest CART stockholder, was very pointed about his desires. He wanted Chris Pook, who organized and ran the Long Beach Grand Prix, to replace Heitzler. Just like the initial indications of Vannini's desire to oust Heitzler, within two days, Grosfeld dropped the reference to Pook but remained adamant that Heitzler needed to go.[25]

Gerry Forsythe became CART's largest stockholder in mid–December, with 13 percent of the stock. He supported Heitzler and felt Heitzler should be able to choose his own management team. Forsythe also was in favor of CART's retaining the turbocharged engine configuration, a differentiating point with the IRL.[26] At the board meeting in mid–December 2001, Heitzler stepped down as CEO but remained as CART's chairman of the board. With Heitzler's ouster as CEO, Forsythe, a board member since 1998, stepped down from the board of directors.[27] The announcement of Heitzler's departure had a positive impact upon CART's stock, as it rose 8 percent after the announcement.[28]

The leading candidate for the job was Pook, who was under a lifetime contract with Dover Downs Entertainment, the Delaware-based racing track.[29] Behind the scenes, Pook reportedly had been talking with various sponsors who were thinking of leaving the CART series. Vannini was very confident Pook would be the next head of CART and told ESPN, "Trust me, Mr. Pook is interested and has the ability to come work for us."[30]

It didn't take long for Pook to come on board. His vision for CART was not as a sanctioning body, but rather as a "marketing company that will position its open-wheel motor racing series as a 'delivery' mechanism for national and multi-national corporations in which to conduct business." CART was well positioned with races in Mexico, Canada and the United States to take advantage of the recently enacted North American Free Trade Agreement (NAFTA). They were one of the few sports-oriented companies with an appeal to international companies.[31]

As part of the plan to become a marketing-oriented company, Pook also wanted to increase the number of domestic races under the CART banner. Before leaving Dover Downs Entertainment, he formulated a plan for Dover Downs to be the sponsor of a road race in St. Petersburg, Florida.[32] To turn

CART's focus towards promotion, CART announced the Grand Prix of the Americas street race in Miami, Florida, would be added to their schedule in mid–March. Pook had negotiated the purchase of the majority of RaceWorks, the promoter of the race in 2001, from Peter Yanowitch. Pook also arranged for CART to be the co-promoter with IMG Motorsports of the Cleveland Grand Prix. After the Chicago Motor Speedway announced it was going to cease auto racing operations, Pook was able to save the Chicago Grand Prix on the CART calendar by leasing the facility. By taking on the responsibilities as the promoter—the ticket sales, the promotion, interfacing with sponsors and the actual running of the race— CART was assuming the financial risk of the race.[33]

Gerry Forsythe was a member of CART, one of the founders of Champ Car and an owner of Forsythe Racing.

The structure of the CART board, which was dominated by insiders with their own agendas, had historically made it a challenge for the CART CEO to initiate change. Pook was able to negotiate with the CART Franchise Board, composed of CART team owners, to agree to a simple majority rule on any item not related to the bylaws. This was seen as a positive step forward in improving CART's speed in dealing with issues such as rule changes. Pook also took steps to streamline CART's management structure by establishing seven key management positions as his executive management committee.[34] Dennis McAlpine, the principal of McAlpine and Associates, one of the investment firms actively following CART, said, "What Chris Pook has done, in a very short period, has changed the very nature of the company. It is no longer a passive, contract-driven sanctioning body. It is now very actively participating in the promotion of its events."[35]

All of the changes instituted by Pook were received positively by Wall Street. Despite a diminishment of earnings estimates from $0.50–$0.80 per share to $0.01–$0.15 per share and the specter of an operating loss, the expected downward impact upon the stock price didn't happen.

As Pook finished his third month as the CART CEO, CART wanted to sever the relationship with Heitzler, who was still the chairman of the board. On March 25, 2002, Pook sent Heitzler a letter outlining the reasons why he was being "terminated for cause" including "gross dereliction of duties." It also asserted Heitzler's "failure to properly manage the relationships with the company's promoters, sponsors, and other strategically important entities." Heitzler, whose contract had an additional two years to run, didn't want to forego the pay totaling $2 million. So CART became embroiled in another lawsuit. CART fired the initial salvo, accusing Heitzler of "Breach of Contract," "Breach of Fiduciary Duty," and "Fraud" in a filing in Detroit's Federal Court on March 26. Just two days later, Heitzler responded with his own lawsuit seeking $2 million in damages plus compensatory damages, filed in California's Superior Court. Heitzler's suit accused CART among other things of "Breach of Contract" and "Fraud." Heitzler's lawsuit alleged that many of the failures of his administration could be traced to failures by the CART board. He alleged that CART members had failed to disclose multiple things that impacted his administration, such as the sale of $5.1 million worth of CART stock by CART members Chip Ganassi, Barry Green, Pat Patrick, and Carl Haas prior to the announcement of the switch from the turbocharged engines, the purchase of the Indy Lights program from Patrick and the imminent failure of the ISL WorldWide contract.[36]

After the defection of Al Unser, Jr., to an IRL team and Penske's announcement of the fielding of two teams to run in the IRL series, the IRL continued to gain steam. More defections included CART team owner Ganassi with a trio of popular and successful drivers, Michael Andretti, Dario Franchitti and Kenny Brack. There were other CART drivers who defected to Formula One racing, including Cristiano da Matta, Juan Montoya, Alex Zanardi and Jacques Villeneuve.[37]

During the 2001 racing season, the IRL averaged 24.5 cars at its thirteen races. Officials at the IRL were hopeful that there could be 32 teams at the 2002 opening race at Homestead, Florida. Meanwhile, the rival CART series was facing the possibility of fielding only 19 teams. This could be a huge issue for them, as some tracks required the series to field 18 cars and at least two called for 20 cars. John Lopes, the senior vice president of racing operations, confirmed the series was subsidizing several teams and would have to have "a drastic reduction in cost" for 2003.[38]

When Honda announced in October 2001 that they would not be building engines for CART, they had strongly indicated they would not be participating in open-wheel racing engine production in the next year. Tom Elliott, American Honda's president, told *National Speed Sport News*, "We want to have an American racing program. Certainly in 2004, for sure we want to be racing again. With CART's rules for next year, neither series really meets our goals of racing in a technological challenging environment. Of course, it would take 18 months to design and build and engine for either series and at the moment we have nothing on paper, let alone ready for development."[39]

After Tony George and a contingent of IRL and Indianapolis Motor Speedway staffers traveled to CART's Bridgestone Potenza 500, held at the Honda Twin Ring race track in Motegi, Japan, in May 2002, speculation circulated that Honda would be building engines for the IRL. This was flatly denied by Elliott, who said, "It's no secret that Tony is talking to Motegi about holding an IRL race here and that's no surprise. The track needs more races to become profitable. But Honda won't have an engine for any American racing series in 2003." The speculation turned out to be true. In June 2002, Honda announced they would be building engines for the IRL.[40]

Perhaps it was just a coincidence, but in the week Honda announced it would be building engines for the IRL, CART's stock price took a swan dive, plummeting to under $9 from $13.30 the week before.[41] The next week, the stock continued its downward trend, declining an additional 4.9 percent to $8.79 per share. Despite the fact that Bear Stearns had downgraded the stock to "neutral" and A. G. Edwards had issued a "sell," indicating the stock was speculative in nature, rumors circulated throughout the racing community that behind the scenes, Bernie Ecclestone, head of Formula One, was manipulating the price. He was allegedly artificially lowering the price so he could have a "front" purchase it at a discount. This accusation was vehemently denied by Ecclestone.[42]

After adopting the normally aspirated engine in an attempt to find common ground with the IRL, CART reversed its decision and reverted to the 2.6-liter turbocharged engine for the 2003 and 2004 racing seasons. With the loss of their three historical engine suppliers, Honda, Toyota and Ford, CART struck a deal with Cosworth to be the engine supplier for the next two years. The deal with Cosworth placed additional financial stress upon CART, as the company became an intermediary between the engine supplier and the teams. CART agreed to buy 100 engines from Cosworth at a total cost of $40 million (or $400,000 per engine), which they would then lease to the racing teams at a cost of $100,000 per year per car for a two year period. Additionally, CART would provide at-track assistance to the teams, for which the teams would pay $750,000 per racing season. The savings of about $1.25 million per year to the teams was significant.[43] This decision was championed by Gerald Forsythe, who had been relentless in politicking against the normally aspirated engine. The engines, including the electronics and turbo ancillary packages, would cost each team $1 million per season.[44]

The decision also signaled a return to the deep freeze between CART and the IRL. Pook said bitterly, "My administration decided to create a common chassis with the IRL to try and give our teams flexibility and good economics to be able to run in both series, and to give manufacturers involved a greater quantity of clients, so that in turn would bring the cost down. We were summarily rejected on that. We put it out as an olive branch to try to form some type of compatibility with the other side to bring us closer together to see if we could merge the two together. But the olive branch was broken off in two pieces and we were slapped around the face with it and told to get out of town."[45] George found Pook's comments about trying to make bridges with the IRL mystifying. George retorted, "Somehow, they are trying to make us responsible for their success, or lack thereof. They can only be responsible and should take responsibility for their own success or failure."[46]

With the excessive cost of supporting a racing team in CART and concern over being able to field a full contingent of racers, Pook announced an expansion of the Entrant Support Program to help defray expenses associated with the racing program. This program would provide up to $1.5 million to assist twenty teams with the cost of engine leases, freight and travel, and tires.[47] Two months later, the support to the teams would increase from $10,000 per race to $22,500 per race.[48]

Trying to keep the series together, Pook took a page from the NASCAR playbook by announcing a second phase of the Entrant Support Program in which teams could earn up to $400,000 annually by displaying CART-mandated decals on the car. Pook explained, "This unprecedented program is being launched to assure that CART continues to be the preeminent open-wheel racing series in America. It is designed to retain current racing teams and attract new participants for the CART series in 2003."[49] In making the announcement, Pook explained, "Over the last three to five years, there has been a lot of money put into the CART series, and the cost of racing has escalated to a level that it is really very high. We need to bring back under control the cost of automobile racing in this series, but we need to maintain the level of competition and sophistication that the series has enjoyed."[50]

When the second quarter 2002 financial results were announced, CART was hemorrhaging cash. There were many reasons behind the loss of $4.7 million on revenues of $25.3 million.[51] After cancellation of the Lausitzring, Germany, race, the cost of racing at the other European venue, the Rockingham Motor Speedway in England, escalated, as travel costs could not be prorated to two races. To help the teams with the travel costs, CART picked up an estimated $900,000 in team travel costs to the Rockingham race. Additionally, Rockingham Motor Speedway's management used the cancellation of the race at Lausitzring to renegotiate the sanctioning fee from $4.2 million to $2.8 million, a decrease of 33 percent, claiming their race had been damaged by the cancellation.[52]

The financial woes didn't stop there. In order to ensure it had teams to participate in the series, CART provided the teams with $667,100 in financial assistance in the second quarter in addition to the travel costs to England. Not surprisingly, CART's stock price continued its downward spiral, dropping from $7.47 per share to $4.50 per share, a whopping 40 percent decline.[53] When the CART stock price reached $4.50 per share, it was below the book value of CART's assets, which were particularly easy to evaluate since a majority consisted of cash and investments. It also meant CART's market capitalization was below its liquidation value, leading LaGrange Johnson of LaGrange Capital, an institutional investor, to call for the liquidation of the firm. Johnson explained, "When you start trading below your liquidation value you lose control of your destiny."[54]

Johnson was very frustrated with the lack of communication from the company. "The business has challenges, but I think the lack of communication by the Company [to Wall Street] has driven the stock down below its liquidation value. There have been negative events. But with a clearer communication with its investors, the stock price would be closer to its book value of $7 or $8." Given the company's lack of financial guidance to investors, Johnson suspected that the company's actions were part of a plan to depress the stock price so that insiders could buy the company cheaply.[55]

As the stock price plummeted, former board member James Grosfeld, the second largest stockholder, sold his shares over a fifty-day period at a loss of $2.5 million. The buyer of the 1,172,400 shares was Gerry Forsythe. This purchase put Forsythe's holdings above the 15 percent limitation. Forsythe had been wanting to buy the stock and worked with the board of directors to approve his purchase while not invoking CART's "poison pill" provision of their bylaws. In approving Forsythe's request to purchase the shares, the board mandated that he vote the shares acquired from Grosfeld in concert with the board directives for a period of three years.

Why would the board approve the purchase of the stock from Grosfeld, which clearly put Forsythe into a position of increased influence? As a team owner, he had recently added two additional cars for the CART circuit. Was the approval by CART tied to his additional racing teams? But the bigger question was probably Forsythe's motivation. With this purchase, Forsythe owned 22.95 percent of CART's outstanding stock. And he was significantly upside down in his CART holdings. His cost basis was approximately $36 million, resulting in a paper loss of $19.4 million. Why was he so anxious to increase his holdings? Was Forsythe trying to take control of the series, in accord with the speculation of LaGrange Johnson? His latest stock purchase from Grosfeld had been at $5 per share, which was below the liquidation value of the firm.[56]

As CART's largest stockholder, Forsythe insisted the final race of the season be the Telmex Gigante Gran Premio Mexico, held at his Mexico City venue. Although the race was successful, it was at a financial cost to CART. Not only did Forsythe pay a rock-bottom sanctioning fee of $125,000, but also CART had to pay International Speedway Corporation a $250,000 cancellation fee for the race at the California Speedway, which had been scheduled as the season finale. In an interesting twist, Forsythe, who had resigned from the CART board over the firing of Heitzler, hired Heitzler to help him in the running of the Gigante Gran Premio Mexico. Effectively, Forsythe was helping Heitzler in his legal battles with CART and CART directors Carl Haas and Pat Patrick.

Despite increasing the payments in the Entrant Support Program to the teams, Pook was unable to stop the move of teams to the IRL. In September 2002, Michael Andretti announced that his three-car team would be moving to the IRL. Andretti said of the move, "The main thing we wanted going back to April was a guarantee of 18 cars next year. Everybody can say whatever they want that there's going to be 18 cars but the reality of the situation is we don't see it. There's no guarantee that there's going to be a field next year. We feel that really hasn't changed at this point. If anything, it's worse." The move of the Andretti team to the IRL resulted not only in the loss of three cars on the race track; it also resulted in the series only having one American driver, Jimmy Vasser, for the 2003 races.

Despite having $90 million in liquidity, Andretti believed CART was running out of money not only to support the racing teams through the Entrant Support Program but also to pay for the broadcast of the races: "It takes a lot of money to do it and even if they spend the $90 million they have, that's not enough to do it with the television package that they have to buy and everything else. They're running out of money. Is Forsythe going to pay for the whole field? Nobody's got that much money."[57]

LaGrange Johnson's suspicions of a plan by some of the CART insiders to take the racing series private gathered credibility when an anonymous but informed source told *National Sport Speed News* that Pook, Ecclestone (the head of Formula One) and Forsythe had been discussing how to make CART a viable series, potentially with ties to Formula One, and take it back to being privately owned. At the time, Forsythe and Craig Pollock owned the British American Racing Formula One team. Although Pollock did not confirm the informed source, he felt that CART's joining forces with Formula One made sense: "F-1 needs to be promoted in North America. It needs to open up the North American market, not just for the series but for the sponsorship for the series and on the media and TV side. Everything needs to be improved. And vice versa: the CART series needs to be promoted in Asia and in Europe. And the link between F-1 and CART makes sense."[58] After the *Toronto Sun* published reports that Bernie Ecclestone, the Formula One chief, was buying shares of CART stock, Pook finally acknowledged he had been talking with Bernie Ecclestone about collaboration efforts but strongly denied that merger talks were in progress: "There are no formal discussions going on about our relationship with Formula One."[59]

As Pook struggled to turn CART around, the board approved using up to $30 million of CART's liquidity to support the FedEx series operations.[60] FedEx had still not renewed their contract to be the primary sponsor of the race.[61]

In frustration, Pook told Steve Mayer of the *Indianapolis Star* that he believed forces on West 16th Street in Indianapolis, an allusion to the location of the Indianapolis Motor Speedway, were actively trying to destroy CART. CART's media chief, Adam Saal, said, "There is no question that there is an effort within Indianapolis that is focused upon CART's demise. In many ways, the IRL gauges their success upon CART's failure. This is a battle. One of

CART's failings in recent years was its inability to see that the conflict with the IRL is a battle for survival. Under Chris Pook's administration, there is no question that this is a war." These accusations were, of course, denied by the Indianapolis Motor Speedway. Fred Nation told the *Indianapolis Star*, "The only activity which we are engage in is building our series. We're not engaged in any kind of covert or other activity against CART. We wish them well in solving their problems. All of our energies are devoted to building our series. We're looking forward not backward."[62]

There was finally some good news emanating from CART headquarters when it announced that its tire sponsor, Bridgestone, was not only going to continue for the 2003 racing season but had also agreed to be the sponsor for the racing series.[63] Within a month, CART would announce that Ford had also signed on as a sponsor. Instead of being known as the FedEx series, the new name would be the "Bridgestone Presents the Champ Car World Series Powered by Ford."[64]

When CART released its third quarter 2002 earnings, reflecting an $8.3 million loss, the share price dropped 16 percent to close at $4.01 per share. The loss was partly attributable to a $5.4 million charge for the Miami Grand Prix race even though the race had not yet occurred. CART's auditors required this charge to go into the third quarter since the loss was already known. The financials also reflected a revenue decline of 37.2 percent. A portion of the decline in revenues can be attributed to the series running one fewer race and a decline in the average sanction free from $2.4 million in 2001 to $1.8 million for the 2002 racing year. The decline in the average sanction fee reflects the loss of the Lausitzing (Germany) fee of $2.4 million and a decline in the Rockingham Motor Speedway (England) fee by $1.4 million. In order to have races at some tracks, CART had also agreed to "sharing of the net revenues" with four promoters, resulting in a reduction of these fees by 35 percent. For the 2003 racing season, the net revenue sharing agreement would be expanded to six promoters. CART was burning through its cash. It had agreed to support its racing teams to the extent of $57 million for the 2003 racing season as compared to $15 million for the 2002 racing season.[65] Pook didn't have long to turn around the racing series.

Activist shareholder Jon Vannini was contemplating filing legal action against some of the biggest names in auto racing. Although not naming names, in public forums Vannini had stated that Roger Penske, Tony George, International Speedway Corporation (owned by NASCAR's France family), Chip Ganassi, Honda, Toyota and ABC Sports had contributed to CART's woes. Vannini also said that the Indianapolis Motor Speedway and the IRL had induced track owners, team owners and engine manufacturers to switch sides.[66] Isn't that what the team owners who owned CART did when it originally formed? Induced track owners to switch sides and actively pursued sponsorships? But it does add substantiation to Pook's assertions that the Speedway and IRL were actively working to defeat CART.

When the race at the Rockingham Motor Speedway in England brought only 40,000 fans and did not break even for the promoters, despite a lowering of the sanctioning fee, they wanted the sanction fee lowered further for the 2003 race. Unable to reach an agreement with CART, the racing series would not be returning to Rockingham, England, in 2003.[67] Believing Europe was part of their strategic plan and having lost the races at the Rockingham Motor Speedway and Lausitring, Germany, CART announced in January 2003 that they would race at the Eurospeedway and Brands Hatch facilities. In both of these races, CART would serve as the promoter at an estimated cost of $7.5 million.[68]

Not only were the European races expensive for CART, they also lost money on the Chicago and Miami races. The Chicago Grand Prix had a mere 26,000 in attendance and lost $2 million. The Grand Prix of the Americas in Miami, which was recorded in the third quarter financial results, ended up with a loss of $5.45 million. Only 12,037 tickets were sold to the event.[69]

In December 2002, CART announced that they would no longer provide financial guidance to Wall Street and its investors. With increasing doubts about their ability to field an eighteen-car roster for the 2003 racing season, rumors were circulating of an impending bankruptcy.[70] Despite all of the setbacks, Pook remained positive and saw 2003 and 2004 as rebuilding years for CART. His goal was to make CART into "the most efficient automotive-technology sports-marketing delivery system in North America." As part of the rebuilding effort, CART unveiled a new logo. Pook also announced they had eighteen teams on the roster for the 2003 racing season.[71] In an effort to re-energize the Chicago and Milwaukee races, they would be run under the lights for the 2003 season.[72] Pook also indicated that they were looking at adding two additional races in major North American markets. Utilizing the example of the Houston street race, he served notice that the races would not be "40 miles outside of town."[73]

At a January 15, 2003, press conference, Pook announced that the 2002 racing season had seen a record attendance, with 2.6 million attendees at the various CART racing events. This number soon was questioned. While grandstand seating at the Grand Prix of Long Beach provided room for only 63,000 spectators, CART proclaimed there were 250,000 spectators. Likewise, CART's pronouncement of the attendance at the Grand Prix of the Americas of 85,000 was questioned. An internal memo to the assistant city manager of

Miami revealed the sale of only 16,205 tickets and an additional 12,175 complimentary tickets being distributed. Pook tried to reassure the public of the validity of the spectator numbers. He explained their numbers were from media reports, an independent third party. The numbers also included all spectators in any race-related event, so they did not reflect only the attendance at the race itself. As a comparison, during 2002, the IRL events drew 1,160,000 fans, which included the Indianapolis 500. The IRL only reported attendance on race day, so the methodology in reporting attendance at CART events was not the same as at IRL events.[74]

Despite having significant liquidity, CART was showing increasing signs of stress. CART reported a 23 percent decline in sponsorship revenues in 2003.[75] Another significant contributor to the lower level of revenues was a 32 percent decline in sanctioning fees, one of the primary components of race promotions. In 2002, CART had run 19 races, of which 17 were sanctioned. In 2003, the number of sanctioned races dropped to 13. Instead, CART increased the number of races they ran directly. Television ads decreased by a whopping 58 percent, or $2.6 million. A part of this was attributable to a lower number of ads being sold; however, the greater portion of the decline was a decreased value of the ads because of the lower television ratings.

With an eye to the calendar, when the December 1996 agreement prohibiting either side from using IndyCar as a moniker expired, it was quickly adopted by the Indy Racing League.[76] The series would become known as the IndyCar series. Three-time Indianapolis 500 winner Johnny Rutherford commented on the name change: "The change to IndyCar series depicts very clearly what the series is—an auto-racing championship based upon the rich traditions and heritage of the Indianapolis 500-Mile race."[77]

Although CART received good news when Stefan Johansson announced he was bringing two cars to the series, and Ernie Bachelart, an IRL team sponsor since 2001, also announced he would be bringing a team with the car driven by Mario Haberfeld,[78] the bad news outweighed the positive. In mid–February, CART sued Road America, Inc., which was among the longest-running venues and was partially owned by CART director Carl Haas. The dispute was over the failure of Road America to pay the sanctioning fees for the 2002 race and also to make the initial payment for the August 2003 event. CART had agreed to a modification of the Road America sanctioning fee originally negotiated in 1999. The fee for 2002 was to have been $1.65 million, an amount the promoter believed was unrealistic given the decline in sponsorship and attendance at the CART races. The renegotiated fee was a reduction of $75,000, which included $375,000 to be placed into escrow to be paid out depending upon the profitability of the event. The failure of Road

America to pay the first installment of the 2003 sanctioning fee of $262,500 and the quickness of CART to sue for the $375,000 in arrears for the 2002 race led to speculation that negotiations were taking place between Road America and the IRL to host an event in 2003. Of course, the rumors of negotiations were quickly denied by both parties.[79]

The talks between CART and Road America to resolve the sanctioning fee issue were unproductive. In mid–March, CART announced it was dropping Road America from its 2003 schedule, ending a 20-year relationship. The CART press release said, "The balance of last year's sanctioning money remained unpaid at the close of business March 7, and Road America was also unwilling to adhere to the current sanctioning agreement and failed to pay initial installments of this season's sanctioning fee. Furthermore, the Road America race organizers rejected a reduced and revised financial arrangement that was offered by Champ Car management as a settlement of the lawsuit. As a result, the series was forced to remove this year's race from its schedule in order to give its teams, sponsors, and broadcast partners proper time to adjust travel and logistics schedules."[80]

Prior to the release of the 2002 financial statements, CART stock hit a new low, breaking through the $3 per share barrier. Stock analyst Dennis McAlpine of McAlpine and Associates said, "They're creating their self-fulfilling prophecy. There's a rumor that they're driving the stock down, so that team owner Gerry Forsythe (the largest CART shareholder) can take the company private."[81] When the financials were released a week later, they reported a loss of $14.5 million. More concerning was the operating loss of $24.7 million.[82] At this rate, CART was burning through its cash very quickly. Dennis McAlpine was the only investment analyst still following CART. After the release of the financials, he commented, "Without a turnaround in income, we expect that the company could be close to going through its cash by the end of 2003."[83]

As Pook attempted to revive the moribund firm, he had multiple challenges. In an effort to help its racing teams and to have television coverage, CART had made significant financial commitments which would continue to burn through its cash. To support the race teams CART had committed $44.5 million of its cash during the 2003 racing season. The Entrant Support Program had gone from a total cost of $3.5 million in 2002 to a projected $14.5 million in 2003. Then there was a Team Assistance Program, through which CART leased space on the race cars where CART-related logos were placed. The total estimated cost for this program was $30 million. Approved by the board of directors, three directors/car owners would receive $9.3 million in benefits from this program.[84] CART had also assumed the role of promoter for six of its races (Miami, Hatch Brand, Lausitzing, Cleveland, Portland and Mid-America). It had also entered into revenue-sharing agreements for an additional five races.[85]

Bad news continued to plague CART. In May 2003, it released the first-quarter financials. The good news was it actually had increased revenues, but that was driven primarily by the change in its operating model to being a promoter. The bad news, which outpaced the good news, was that expenses continued to soar. For the first quarter of FY 2003, the company lost $9 million. Even more ominously, its cash reserves in the first quarter had continued to shrink and now stood at $70.6 million. Another piece of bad news was that it had been unable to sell any sponsorships in the Team Assistance Program. More bad news followed when the television audience for the Grand Prix at Long Beach, one of CART's premier races, sank to an all-time low. Only 68,000 people watched the telecast. There were more people watching the race live.[86]

As CART's financial position condition continued to worsen, Pook spent more of his time trying to reassure the public of CART's future. He had become frustrated with the naysayers: "I find it fascinating that once again we're hearing statements out of Indianapolis (mainly from Roger Penske) saying there should be one series. That's like a red rag to a bull for the shareholders because the shareholder community is now in an uproar and it's not a sensible thing to do to get the shareholders upset by this talk of becoming one."[87]

Despite the constant negative chatter, Pook continued to lay out his vision for CART. It would become a "powerful 'marketing delivery vehicle' for international automotive manufacturers seeking to penetrate the US & Mexico markets."[88] To accomplish this vision, Pook had a three-point plan. First, CART would have an international racing schedule. Second, it would bring in additional engine manufacturers, who traditionally were a backbone of support for the teams, as well as sponsors. As part of this strategy, he was in favor of having a normally aspirated engine, similar to what was used in Formula One. Lastly, Pook acknowledged that CART needed to attract more American drivers for the league's long-term success. To do that, he focused on improving CART's ladder system for young drivers. In USAC days, drivers would go from the Midgets to Sprints and finally, as their skill set developed, on to Champ Cars. With the complexity of driving Champ Cars, the bottom rungs of the ladder needed to be solidified.[89]

By mid–June, the long-awaited move towards privatizing the company was announced. CART hired Wall Street investment firm Bear Stearns and Company in an effort to find private investors. Most people believed Gerry

Forysthe, owner of 25 percent of the stock, was behind the effort. It was also believed the most likely private investors would be Bernie Ecclestone, the head of Formula One, and Kevin Kalkhoven and Craig Pollock, the principals of the PK Racing Team.[90]

Penske, one of the lynchpins in the formation of CART, was now predicting that the IRL would be the survivor in the battle with CART for the dominance of open-wheel racing: "As we appraise the current situation in the IRL, 18 months ago we didn't have Michael Andretti's team, we didn't have Bobby Rahal's team, we didn't have Adrian Fernandez's team so some good teams have migrated to the IRL. These teams came on their own. The real crunch time will come at the end of 2003 when CART has to make a decision about their future." His analysis of CART continued: "Right now, they have elected to be a series that has mostly international venues with road races. They had also been supporting the teams through the capital base of CART and that can only go on so long. One of the worst things we found is any business that is subsidized can't stand on its own two feet. At some point, you end up hitting the wall."[91]

Phoenix Rising?

When CART gathered in Toronto for a board meeting and the running of the Molson Indy Toronto race in mid–July, the primary topic of speculation was who would be the investors in privatizing CART. Craig Pollock, one of the potential investors in CART, told the *Toronto Sun*, "There are three groups that I understand are interested in putting cash into CART. There's the Ecclestone group, the Forsythe group and the Kalkhoven group. CART has an opportunity to start with a blank sheet of paper with its efforts to get a cash infusion. But it must be done quickly, because of the pressures of competition."[1]

These three groups were very intertwined through friendship and business relationships. Ecclestone had a business relationship with Forythe and Pollock. He also, however, was a close personal friend of CART CEO Pook. Kalkhoven and Pollock own PK Racing. Another name thrown into the mix was Paul Gentilozzi. While in Toronto, Pook, Pollock, Kalkhoven and Gentilozzi met over the racing weekend to discuss how to privatize CART. Although Forsythe was not at meeting, he sent a representative.[2]

For the first half of the 2003 season, CART lost $43.5 million. Total revenues for the six-month period of $20.6 million didn't even cover the race distributions of $29 million. Cash and short-term investments had dropped by $34 million in the past six months. The 10-K report bluntly stated, "The cash reserves remaining at the end of 2003, if any, will not be sufficient to fund anticipated operating losses and contractual commitments for 2004."[3] A report issued by CART said of the first six months, "Recognizing that its current business structure needs to be altered in light of financial challenges and a generally down global economy, CART has begun to implement changes."[4] The changes included a reduction in the support for the racing teams beyond the standard Entrant Support Program and some races. Without the additional support, some of the race teams might not have the financial wherewithal to participate in the races in 2004.[5]

Kevin Kalkhoven (l), principal in PK Racing and one of the owners of Champ Car, and Mark Cipilloni, president of AutoRacing1.com.

Although CART was on the ropes, some aspects of the racing league continued. After the July board meeting in Toronto, CART announced that it was working with CBS to broadcast up to ten of its races. Without a television deal, it was unlikely the racing series would be purchased. It also discussed extending the deal with Cosworth racing to provide engines for the series through 2005.[6]

Three weeks later at the Mid-America race, the investor pool became clearer. The core consisted of Gentilozzi, Kalkhoven and Forsythe. Discussions were continuing with Ecclestone and Carl Russo, the owner of the RUSport racing team, about joining the group to take CART private.[7] On August 15, Open Wheel Racing Series (OWRS), a company formed by Forsythe, Gentilozzi and Kalkhoven, made an offer of $7.4 million for the assets of CART. This was equivalent to 50 cents a share. The offer was below the liquidation value of the company, leading most to believe that CART's board would make a counter-proposal. There was also the specter that CART investor Jon Vannini, who owned 9 percent of the outstanding shares, might bring a class-action suit or would make a counter-offer.[8]

Not surprisingly, CART's board rejected the opening offer. Less than a month later, a bid of 56 cents per share by OWRS was accepted by CART's board on September 10, 2003. As a public company, there were regulatory hurdles to taking the firm private, the first of which was the proxy statement. The shareholder vote was expected between Halloween and Thanksgiving. Since Forsythe owned 22.9 percent of the CART shares and had been identified as being part of the OWRS investor group, there would be two shareholder votes. The first would be by all shareholders and the second would exclude Forsythe's shares. Gentilozzi explained the rationale for the second vote: "For the second vote, we're not going to vote Gerry's shares so it doesn't appear in any way that there is a thumb on the scale trying to make this deal happen."[9]

Kalkhoven explained the focus of the series. "First of all, it's centered on North America. Second, it's multi-faceted and I would like to always see it having a mixture of different types of races. And three, the formula that we've got at the moment has led to some very competitive racing at a relatively economic price compared to Formula 1."[10]

As the process of the sale of the company was moving ahead, CART management received notification that they had been delisted from the New York Stock Exchange. The trading price had fallen below $1 per share for a 30-day period and the market value of the stock had dropped below $15 million.[11] That reflected the agreed purchase price of the company at $0.56 per share and was the least of their worries. As CART was moving toward the shareholder vote scheduled for December 18, timing was becoming critical, as CART was expected to run out of cash by mid–December.[12] It had gone through its $100-million war chest in an effort to salvage the racing series. The day before the proxy statement was to be submitted to the Securities and Exchange Commission, Open Wheel Racing Series' attorneys told CART's attorneys that they were concerned about CART's ability to meet its obligations under the agreement. The concerns included CART's ability to pay its outstanding obligations and the absence of litigation. If the transaction were not to close, the Open Wheel Racing Series reserved the right to purchase some of CART's assets in bankruptcy and to continue the racing series.[13]

Not surprisingly, on December 2 the purchase of CART by Open Wheel Racing Series was called off. Key among the issues was legal action filed by International Speedway Corporation seeking the return of its $2.5-million sanctioning fee for a race at the California Speedway. Additionally, the participation of Stefan Johansson's American Spirit racing team in the racing series was in question.[14] As an alternative to the merger, Open Wheel Racing Series suggested a prepackaged bankruptcy in which it would buy the assets for $2 million. The purchase price included a variety of assets necessary for the series, including the contracts with Cosworth for the racing engines, contracts with International Speedway Corporation for races on their tracks, sponsorship contracts with Bridgestone and Ford, television contracts, the rulebook, all trademarks and the membership in ACCUS and FIA.[15]

The prepackaged bankruptcy opened the door for a bid by the IRL's Tony George. The IRL bid $3.3 million for the assets of CART on January 23, 2004. The Open Wheel Racing Series bid was $1.6 million. Frank J. Otte, the judge presiding over the bankruptcy, would make the decision on what was best for CART and its various stakeholders. As with other skirmishes between CART and the IRL, this one quickly got nasty and personal. George wrote a letter on the IRL Web site in which, referring to the investors in Open Wheel Racing Series, he said, "None of these guys has as much appreciation for open-wheel racing as I have." Gentilozzi retorted, "Our commitment is to rebuild what he, in essence, has destroyed. His intentions have nothing to do with the future of open-wheel competition, but rather the future and profitability of his series. To challenge our appreciation and commitment to open-wheel racing is a direct assault on our integrity."[16]

By January 29, 2004, OWRS had increased their bid to $3.2 million in cash while the IRL's bid had been increased to $13.5 million. Judge Otte stunned many observers of the court battle when he ruled that CART's assets would be sold to Open Wheel Racing Series because they were willing to honor the existing contracts. Otte explained his decision: "I realize there's a difference between $13.5 million and $3.2 million but this bid must account for the assumption of these contracts. We know for certain there would be litigation, and there would be damages."[17] With the decision by Judge Otte, open-wheel racing would continue to have two series—the IRL and the CART successor, which opted for the name Champ Car World Series.

Gentilozzi, Kalkhoven and Forsythe had their work cut out for them. With the racing season to begin April 18, they had a schedule of eleven races with five more anticipated. They needed to line up series and team sponsorships and to finalize a television contract.[18] Forsythe explained why he invested in Champ Car: "I was not about to let [the Champ Car series] die and whatever it took I was prepared to do it. I was not about to let them beat CART. CART was the best racing in the world, but unfortunately we had the wrong people running it. People have tried to beat us down but we're still standing."[19]

Before the court decision Penske said, "Open-wheel racing has gone through a lot of hell the last four or five years. We don't have enough sponsors to run two open series, just like there's not enough to run two NASCAR series. To me, that's going to be an important part of this decision."[20] With the court decision resulting in there continuing to be two open-wheel racing series, Penske once again tried to broker a reunification of the two series during the summer of 2004. He succeeded in getting George to offer cash for the Champ Car series, and there was a counter-offer. But ultimately, these discussions broke down over how the series would be governed. Additionally, Champ Car was adamant that George not be involved in the series. That was an obvious non-starter.[21]

Recognizing that their decision to go with Spike network for the telecast of the 2004 season was a disaster, Champ Car management struck a deal with CBS, NBC and the Speed Channel to cover their racing events in 2005. NBC would cover one race, while CBS and the Speed Channel would broadcast four races each.[22] Within a week, Champ Car announced that it had hired sports entertainment production company Molson Sports and Entertainment, a subsidiary of the Canadian beer company, to be the producer for the telecasts. Although this was the first venture into auto racing broadcasting for Molson, they had been active in sponsoring auto races for many years. Molson was experienced in producing equestrian events, the Arena Football League, the National Hockey League and Women's Professional Tennis.[23]

The racing world was surprised when George announced he was going to field a team for the IRL and Infiniti Pro Series.[24] He and his wife, Laura, had bought the assets of Kelley Racing from Fort Wayne, Indiana, auto dealer Tom Kelley. Kelley had owned the team from 1998 through 2004, and the team had been successful with nine wins over its seven-year life.[25] George hired his stepson, Ed Carpenter, as the driver for the team in the IRL series and defending USAC Sprint Car Series champion driver Jay Drake for the Infinity Pro Series. Heading the team, the name of which was changed to Vision Racing, was veteran mechanic Larry Curry. Concerned about a conflict of interest, George had talked with three other team owners prior to buying the Kelley Racing team.[26] There was a long history stretching back to the early days of the Indianapolis Motor Speedway, when owners Carl Fisher and Jim Allison bought some race cars in 1915 and established the Prest-O-Lite and Speedway Team racing teams in order to insure enough race cars were fielded for the 1916 races. Other, more recent examples include Penske, who not only owned a team but also several race tracks, and even CART itself, which was originally owned by racing team owners.

Despite being in the driver's seat in open-wheel racing world, all was not smooth sailing in the IRL. Eddie Gossage, president of the Texas Motor Speedway, was unhappy about the continual increases in IRL sanctioning fees. He intimated to the *Dallas Morning News* that the sanctioning fees had grown faster than the revenues from sponsorships and attendance at the race. He was considering severing his relationship with the IRL: "We have great races here. But there again, if we can't afford them—and they're getting pretty dog-gone pricey—we're going to have to look hard at the future of Indy cars here at all. That's something that's really on my radar screen." Gossage continued making it clear that track profitability was essential. "We're not here to have a good time. We're here to have a good time and make a dollar or two in the process."[27]

Gossage wasn't the only one unhappy with the IRL. There was also friction with the Phoenix International Raceway, one of the tracks owned by the International Speedway Corporation, which had hosted Indy car races since opening in 1964. At the March 2004 race, Phoenix International's attendance was a mere 8,500 people, hardly enough to pay the bills for the promoter. Indy car people believed Phoenix International was much more interested in promoting NASCAR races than the Indy car race. Management at Phoenix International indicated that they would not have another Indy car race in March but would offer the IRL another date, possibly under the lights in late August. This conflicted with the IRL's push to have more races in the spring before the Indianapolis 500.[28]

As had happened so many times before, there were efforts to bring the two warring factions of open-wheel racing together. This time, Honda Performance Development led the charge. This was an interesting circumstance, as Honda Performance Development's president, Robert Clarke, had often been highly critical of George and the IRL. As an engine manufacturer, Honda was very unhappy about the IRL's micromanagement of the engine specifications. They were also dissatisfied with the growth in the IRL despite the fact that they and Toyota had poured millions of dollars annually into the series in print and television advertising as well as ticket distribution. But Clarke, like so many others in open-wheel racing, recognized that the ongoing animosity between Champ Car and the IRL was continuing to damage to the sport and that, ultimately, reunification needed to happen. As Clarke began his talks with Kalkhoven, George indicated the IRL had no interest in having a common chassis or engine with Champ Car.[29] George said of rumors of negotiations to reunite the two leagues: "I think with each day that passes, it becomes more and more obvious it would be the right thing to do."[30]

The drama of the past twenty-plus years of the split in open-wheel racing kept the racing public focused on the dissension rather than on the racing, to the benefit of NASCAR. Jim Hunter, NASCAR vice president, said, "Anytime you have a strike or anything negative in your sport that boils over into the public, it's a problem. It put open-wheel racing fans in the position of having to choose and I would say it had to help us."[31]

In a move reminiscent of the CART playbook, Champ Car took a step to ensure that their most popular race would remain in their series for years to come. Because of declining ticket sales and a lower level of sponsorship, Dover Motorsports wanted to sell the Long Beach Grand Prix, one of the top races in the CART/Champ Car Series. Kalkhoven and Forsythe purchased the rights to some of the assets of this street race for $15 million.[32]

The 2005 Indianapolis 500 brought some much-needed good news to the IRL. The race, always the top race in America and the linchpin of the IRL, had better viewership than NASCAR's Coca-Cola 600 for the first time since 2000. ABC Sport's live telecast of this event garnered a television audience that was 59 percent higher than it had been in 2004, and it was also the best viewership of the race since 1995. The television ratings for the Indianapolis 500 were 6.5/18 as compared to 4.7/11 in 2004.[33]

The Honda engines dominated IRL racing in 2004 and 2005. Disappointed by their lack of competitiveness and supporting only the Panther Racing team, Chevrolet decided it would not supply engines for the IRL for the 2006 racing year. The issue for Chevrolet was that with only one team using their engines, supplying engines was not economically viable. There had been rumors that they would stay if they could attract more teams to their stable. The dominance of the Honda engine also resulted in Toyota's pondering whether or not to continue to supply engines to the league. If Toyota joined Chevrolet in pulling out of the engine supplier ranks, only Honda would remain as an engine supplier.[34] Despite great success in dominating the IRL for the past two years, Honda desperately wanted to have other engine manufacturers in the IRL. Robert Clarke, president, explained: "Having competition is a way of challenging our engineers to develop a superior product that can win against our competition." But after reviewing its options, Honda decided to remain as an engine supplier to the IRL, whether or not any other manufacturers participated in the series. Its announcement said, "Honda originally elected to compete in the IRL because we recognize the series is the pinnacle of open-wheel racing in this country." With this, the IRL was assured of an engine manufacturer through the 2009 racing season.[35]

On the racing circuit, Champ Car had been looking forward to the Molson Indy Montreal, held on the Circuit Gilles Villeneuve. The Circuit Gilles Villeneuve also held Canada's largest sporting event, a Formula One race with an attendance of 300,000. The Molson Indy Montreal race debuted in 2002 with an attendance of 172,000. After a strong beginning, attendance slid to 143,000 in 2003 and to 93,755 in 2004. At the race in 2005, four representatives from NASCAR were spotted, including the head of Canadian development, Richard Buck, leading to speculation that the promoter of the event, Norman Legault, wanted to replace the Champ Car event. This, of course, was strongly denied by a track spokesman, who attributed the decline in attendance to rain on one day of the three-day event. But racing fans questioned why there were only 20,000 grandstand seats available when there were, clearly visible to the crowd, additional grandstand seats that had been set up for the World Aquatics Championship in July. Attendance on race day was 36,204 and the grandstands were filled to capacity.[36]

While Champ Car officials were able to secure the Long Beach Grand Prix for future races, they canceled the race penciled in for Ansan, Korea. Although the track was ready for racing, important structures such as the control tower and media center were not complete. Additionally, the race promoter in Ansan had not fully paid the sanctioning fee, and other contract terms had not been adhered to.[37]

When Champ Car rolled out the new chassis configuration for the 2007 racing season, participants in the series were delighted that the cost of racing was being reduced. The new Panoz chassis produced by Elan Technologies was 135 pounds lighter than the previous chassis, produced by Lola. This weight reduction was achieved by the chassis being one foot shorter and three inches narrower than the Lola chassis. The cost of under $300,000 was a reduction of about 35 percent from the cost of the Lola. An additional saving to the Champ Car teams with the adoption of this chassis was an estimated 50 percent reduction in the cost of the spare parts.[38] With increased nimbleness attributed to smaller wings and more ground effect tunnels, the car's design was expected it to increase the competitiveness of the racing teams on the tracks and allow more passing to delight the spectators. Tony Cotman, vice president of racing for Champ Cars, crowed about the new chassis, "The design and cost will keep our current teams in the series, but will also attract new teams to the series. Combined with the reduced cost, the new design also makes the Champ Car World Series even more of a driver's series. The lighter smaller car means teams will rely even more on the drivers to achieve maximum performance."[39]

As the first year of ownership came to a close, Kalkhoven and Forsythe were pleased with the progress they had made towards revitalizing the series. Kalkhoven explained, "The speed at which we've been able to do that is much faster than we thought. It's really succeeded way beyond our imagination. We're at least one year ahead of our plan." Central to the plan was vertically integrating the company. They had purchased Cosworth, the engine designer and manufacturer, and Pi Technologies from Ford. They also had control over two racing venues: Long Beach and Toronto. Kalkhoven said of the integration strategy, "When we have the opportunity to gain access to an asset like that, we're going to be all over it."

He also talked about their strategy for the races: "One was obviously to validate the concept that open-wheel racing is not dead. It needs to be reformatted and the three-day event is a good format. We proved that principle with San Jose and Edmonton." Another part of their race strategy was to make it more entertainment focused. Kalkhoven said, "It's not that American open-wheel racing is dead, it's that the old format is dead. You have to recognize that it's an entertainment business and you have to change the entertainment."[40]

One of the strategies employed to emphasize the entertainment scope of the business was a media tour of a dozen major American cities by some of the popular race teams. One of the drivers involved in the "Turbo Tour," Oriol Servia of PKV Racing, said, "It's the first time that anything like this has ever been done, and I think it's really good for Champ Car. I think it's great that we can go around the country and get out in front of the fans as well as the media and the sponsors."[41] Another part of the strategy employed was reestablishing a ladder for American drivers to move up to championship racing, with a focus on the Formula Atlantic series. As an incentive for Formula Atlantic teams to move up to Champ Cars, Kalkhoven and Forsythe provided a $2 million bonus to the Formula Atlantic champion. Equally importantly to the effort was a redesign of the engine and chassis for this series, which resulted in forty cars for twenty participating teams.[42]

As the fortunes of Champ Car were improving, there were some forces pushing George towards being receptive to a merger. Possibly the most important was the desire by ABC for the series to be united. British journalist Gordon Kirby reported that ABC/ESPN had told George that if an agreement was not reached for the merger with Champ Car, they would no longer broadcast the Indianapolis 500 or the IRL series. Another concern was that Honda was going to pull its financial support from the series at the end of the year. This would mean less money for the drivers and the teams. Without the continued support of Honda, George would need to dig deeper into his wallet to support the series. Reportedly, he had provided financial assistance to fourteen of the teams participating in the 2006 Indianapolis 500. Finally, Honda's top driver, Dario Franchitti, was reportedly looking for a ride in NASCAR.[43]

When Kalkhoven and George were spotted together at the Race of Champions in Paris, France, rumors once again started to fly about a possible merger of the two series. Both men summarily rejected the rumors. George told *Autoweek*, "The IRL just signed a four-year agreement with Honda, and we've got a four-year agreement with our broadcast partner. We're looking into entering long-term agreements with our promoters so all the teams, sponsors and constituents can have an idea where we're going." Kalkhoven reiterated that there were not merger talks in progress when he told the *Indianapolis Star* he didn't foresee any developments.[44]

But within a month, George confirmed that discussions with Kalkhoven had been underway since December when they met at the *AutoSport* awards in London. He confirmed to *National Speed Sport News* that he was interested in a merger if it was done right. George said, "I think everybody would like to see it happen sooner rather than later. But it's not something that you can hurry along. It's not something we can resolve in a few weeks or a couple of months. It's going to take some time, but I've considered every conversation we've had, every e-mail we've exchanged to be positive with an eye toward moving things forward. It's just a question of how long it may take to get there."[45]

Penske tried to tamp down any hopefulness of a merger with a little bit of reality. "I've sat back for the last three years trying to make it happen and it never has. Mario Andretti, he went to the wall to try to get it together [last year]. I did it the year before. What's changed? I think it's all talk. I'd like to see the facts. I've been there, that's why I'm so pessimistic that there's anything there." Despite his pessimism, Penske indicated he was in favor of the two sides joining forces: "I'd like to have it happen, but I don't see what's going to be the economic benefit today."[46]

As the racing world turned its eyes toward Indianapolis and the venerable Indianapolis 500, the rumor mill increased, with speculation that a merger would be announced, possibly on Carb Day (the last practice day before the race). George confirmed that talks were still ongoing but tried to set the expectation of no resolution in the near future: "We're making progress, but it's very slow progress, and that's just the way it should be right now. We have a lot of ground to cover, and we're not there yet. These talks are going to take time if we're going to bring this together."[47]

Penske talked about the need to bring the two sides together for the benefit of the sport. "We need to get at the table and get all the stakeholders—the team owners—we need to have some input and let rational heads come to an agreement. If we don't do that, I'm not sure you are ever going to have a satisfactory solution." Penske, who had formed a relationship with Tony George over the years, expressed his opinion: "I think Tony George wants to do it. I don't know Kevin Kalkhoven at all. I've talked to him once. He has a vision of what they want to do and from our perspective, it's so simple. People have to give a little bit to make it happen."

Penske also talked about the difficulties he had encountered when he tried to broker a deal between the two sides. "I tried a couple of years ago, and it was very apparent that Kevin Kalkhoven and Gerry Forsythe were absolutely not interested in coming together with Tony George and his organization. They really didn't want Tony to be part of it, and I think that's a mistake. Tony brings more to the party than anybody else, and that has to be understood. I'm a supporter of what Tony has done. I wasn't always that way." He also expressed a new vision for championship racing. "I also see some valuable pieces of Champ Car that could be integrated into a new series that isn't the IRL and isn't Champ Car but a new open-wheel series that could be very productive for everyone."[48]

Carb Day came and went, as did the Indianapolis 500. At the end of May, George indicated to the press that the talks were continuing but it was not going to be a fast process. He also believed that all of the rumors of the merger had been planted, but he wasn't sure why. He had been trying to lower expectations of a deal announcement.[49]

Gordon Kirby revealed there were three main items keeping the two sides apart. The first was that although George indicated he was amendable to a 50/50 split, he wanted to have the controlling vote. George was also wed to the Dallara chassis and didn't want to give consideration to using the Cosworth chassis in Champ Car. Finally, Honda wanted the league to use its normally aspirated engine rather than the 2.6-liter engine used in Champ Car.[50]

Finally, after the war had been raging for a decade, in July 2006, the two sides signed a cease-fire. George and Kalkhoven signed an ownership-sharing agreement. George said, "We've agreed conceptually [to share ownership], yes. Now we have to agree on how we would go about resolving differences that might come up."[51] Would this agreement lead to the reunification of open-wheel racing, or would it be like other apparent opportunities and fall apart over the details?

Penske said of the progress being made, "We have to put together a deal where we're more than dating, we're making a real partnership. That's how we'll get this back to where it belongs."[52]

Richard Clarke, Honda Performance Development president, underscored the urgency of making this merger work to ESPN.com: "I'm talking to team owners in both series, and I want to be able to go back to Tony and Kevin and show them there's unity within each series but also within the community as a whole on the merger issue. Sure, people have their preferences on chassis, engines, schedules and other issues, and of course they want the series to be affordable. But the real thrust of what they're telling me is that there are no deal-breakers as such. Just get the merger done."[53]

All of a sudden, the talks and the goodwill between the two sides came to a screeching halt. While at the Cleveland Grand Prix, Kalkhoven revealed to a reporter from the *Cleveland Plain Dealer* in an "off-the-record" comment that George and Champ Car had reached an agreement for joint decision-making. This infuriated George, who thought he had been negotiating in good faith. Believing Champ Car had more to gain from a merger than did IndyCar, George put the brakes on the process.[54]

So, once again, the two sides were operating in separate silos, and the opportunity to reunify open-wheel racing evaporated. Champ Car went on about its business and in November announced a five year agreement with ABC/ESPN to broadcast eleven of Champ Car's races during 2007, with the remainder being covered by existing agreements with CBS and NBC. In 2008, ESPN would broadcast all of the racing events. At least when it came to broadcasting, there would be unity—if only in terms of who carried the race, a point emphasized by Kalkhoven: "If we can't have open-wheel unification, at least we can have a common broadcast partner. For motor racing fans, it's a very good thing because now American open-wheel racing is at a place where fans can find it. Speed Channel has become so NASCAR-centric that we were just a speed bump in their day." This agreement also led to speculation that ABC/ESPN would pressure Champ Car and IndyCar to merge the two racing organizations.[55]

At the season-end Champ Car dinner, Kalkhoven looked to better days ahead for open-wheel racing when he said, "We have faced many challenges over the last three years, and it has been a difficult journey. I believe 2007 will be a transitional year—not just for Champ Car but for open-wheel racing around the world."

The beginning of 2007 brought more bad news for Champ Car. Ford Motor Company, which had been involved in open-wheel racing since the early 1960s when they started providing engines to USAC teams, announced they were withdrawing as the presenting sponsor of the Champ Car World Series. This announcement followed Bridgestone's withdrawal as the co-sponsor of the series. In making the announcement, Dan Davis, head of Ford's racing division, said, "We evaluate all of our racing programs on an annual basis and have decided that this sponsorship does not align with our current business objectives." The next day, Ford announced record losses. Without a series sponsor, Champ Car's road to recovery became much more difficult. They then looked to Mazda, the American Championship series sponsor, for support.[56]

Reunification

To encourage participants in the Atlantic Championship series, Champ Car's top training rung, to step up to the highest level of open-wheel racing, Champ Car established a $2 million incentive to compete in the Champ Car series. This strategy was effective in 2006 when Simon Pagenaud, the winner of the Atlantic Championship, used the funding to buy a seat with Team Australia. Despite being a competitive rookie during the 2007 Champ Car series, when teams were hiring drivers for the 2008 season, Pagenaud couldn't find a ride.

By January 2008, the Indy car wars had taken a toll, and Champ Car's popularity was at an all-time low. When Rafael Matos won the 2007 Atlantic Championship, he was eligible for a $2 million bonus. All he needed to do was to race in the Champ Car circuit in 2008. Matos decided to turn down the $2 million in bonus money and instead signed a multi-year agreement with the Andretti Green racing team that he would participate in both the Indy Pro Series, the top rung for driver training in IndyCar, and some American LeMans series races. The inability of Pagenaud to obtain a ride in Champ Car was the primary factor in Matos' decision. Matos explained, "I don't want to run just one year in Champ Car; I want a professional deal. What would I do in 2009 when I have no money? Be out of luck just like Simon? That's why I made this decision—it's the best for my career."[1]

Not only did Champ Car lose Matos, it also lost Tony Cotman, the vice president of racing operations, a critical role in any auto racing series. He also served as the chief steward for Champ Car.[2] After joining Champ Car in 2004, Cotman was the linchpin in the introduction of the new chassis and in the writing and implementation of competition and technical rules for the league. His expertise was well-recognized; he was a member of the FIAs circuit commission responsible for writing the safety rules for use in tracks around the world. In less than two weeks, Cotman resurfaced as the vice president of competition at the Indy Racing League and Infiniti Pro Series.

At all IndyCar events, Cotman would be an assistant to Brian Barnhart in race control. He was also named the senior race director at the Infiniti Pro Series.[3]

The Indy Racing League was clearly in the driver's seat. It was perceived by the television networks as being the driving force in open-wheel racing. It had the top drivers. It had the stronger sponsorships. And it had the Indianapolis 500 anchoring its series. The only question was how long Champ Car would hold on. As astute businessmen, Kalkhoven and Forsythe were spending millions of dollars to support the series even as it spiraled downward.

Once again, the tea leaves started to point towards a reunification of the two sides. In the fall of 2007, George made an offer to help finance equipment for those Champ Car teams migrating to IndyCar with the proviso that they participate in the series for two years. But he had no takers until December or January, which was too late for him to order equipment for the 2008 season. Like so many other times over the thirty years of hostilities, the two sides had different stories. Kalkhoven and Forsythe maintained they had not received an offer. Kalkhoven told *National Speed Sport News*, "I never, ever saw an offer from Tony George. We never received anything in writing." George steadfastly maintained he had discussed this possibility with the two Champ Car owners.[4]

For the 2008 racing season, Champ Car's season included fourteen races in seven countries on three continents.[5] Meanwhile, IndyCar's sixteen-race schedule included fifteen in the United States. The sole outlier was the Twin Ring Motegi race. Ten of the racing dates were occupied by both Champ Car and IndyCar.

As seemed to happen frequently in January and February, there was much speculation of an impending merger. But this time, things seem to be more promising. Behind the scenes, Robert Clarke, retired executive of Honda Performance Development, met with Kevin Kalkhoven and Dick Eidswick of Champ Car and Tony George of the Indy Racing League to try to broker a deal to bring the two sides together.[6] One of the things driving the potential merger was that both IndyCar and Champ Car had difficulty fielding a full field of race teams. In their agreements with broadcasters, both leagues were required to have a minimum number of participants per race.

Champ Car had already lost many of its strong teams, including Team Penske, Target/Chip Ganassi Racing and Andretti Racing, to IndyCar. When Derrick Walker, one of the stalwarts of Champ Car racing, told *USA Today* he was contemplating a change to IndyCar, it must have been devastating news to the folks at Champ Car. Walker said, "We're just a small company who is trying to sell our wares, which for us is getting sponsors and going racing. That's our business. So we had to look at the IRL and the Indy 500, which we thought had a comeback year in 2007."[7] Underlying Walker's potential defection to IndyCar were rumors of Champ Car teetering on the verge of bankruptcy. After expressing a lack of confidence in Champ Car management, Walker told the *Indianapolis Star* that his ability to move to IndyCar was dependent upon getting a sponsor. Walker's team did not participate in Champ Cars testing at Sebring, Florida, because the cost of the testing was $150,000. He said, "If I'm going to spend that kind of money, I want to be damn sure there's going to be a series and I'm not."[8] Walker believed the end of Champ Car was near. He told the Associated Press, "It has all the makings of the end of Champ Car. How it's going to be done, I don't know, but I think Champ Car is going to be shut down."[9]

By mid–February, it appeared the two sides were getting closer to a merger. *National Speed Sport News* indicated only two items remained to be resolved. First, IndyCar's Twin Ring event in Motegi, Japan was on the same weekend as Champ Car's Long Beach Grand Prix. Second, when a merger agreement was reached, those teams wanting to transition to IndyCar would need new equipment in order to participate in the series.

A delegation from IndyCar including George, Brian Barnhart (IndyCar president of commercial development), Terry Angstadt (IndyCar president of racing) and Robert Clarke flew to Japan to meet with representatives from Honda in an effort to move the date of the Twin Ring race from April until later in the year. A race in Japan was critical for IndyCar, as Honda was the sole supplier of engines to the series. And the Long Beach Grand Prix was a critical component in trying to reunify the two series. Long Beach Grand Prix's date could not be changed because of the contract with the Long Beach Convention Center. Officials at Motegi offered to move their race back a week; however, the Kansas Speedway already had a sold out double-bill race featuring both IndyCar and NASCAR on that weekend.[10] Despite their efforts, they were unable to negotiate a different date that would fit into both the IndyCar and the race track's schedule.[11]

Despite the difficulties in changing the date of the Twin Ring Motegi race, there seemed to be a growing feeling that the two leagues were on the cusp of a merger. Even George seemed encouraged. He commented, "It's as close as it's ever been to being put together, but we don't know if we can get across the goal line. But no one is giving up yet."[12]

With tightness in the IndyCar schedule to accommodate many of the races from Champ Car, IndyCar officials were reportedly exploring the possibility of having the international races scheduled after the official end of the IndyCar season. That would also resolve the issue of the Twin Ring Motegi race conflict. The league's sponsoring races in Japan, Australia at Surfers Paradise and Mexico City would also make sense logistically.[13]

Speculation of Champ Car's impending bankruptcy continued to circulate throughout the open-wheel racing community. Fearing continued talk would further damage the series, Kalkhoven emphatically told the *Toronto Sun* the talk of bankruptcy was "absolutely wrong."[14] Despite Kalkhoven's assertions, ESPN reported that Champ Car insiders believed the series was poised for bankruptcy. Speedtv.com reported that the recently hired director of public relations for Champ Car, Pat Caporali, had been urged to seek her old job with Chip Ganassi. Additionally, others at Champ Car headquarters in Indianapolis were reportedly cleaning out their desks.[15]

In a desperate attempt to reassure Champ Car's sponsors, fans and teams that they were open for business and bankruptcy was not being contemplated, David Higdon, executive vice president, said, "We've been hearing this rumor since Friday and, as we continue to say, our doors are open and people are working. We're proceeding with our plans and will keep operating as Champ Car." Champ Car also issued a statement that the merger talks had been halted because of all of the leaks to the media.[16] Despite the attempts by Champ Car to tamp down merger speculation, it would not go away.

Because Champ Car's chassis and engine specifications were different from those of IndyCar, a part of the negotiations centered around IndyCar's willingness to provide the teams agreeing to race in all IndyCar events with a Dallara chassis and a Honda engine. Robin Miller of Speedtv.com reported that the Champ Car teams were told to expect delivery of the free cars being offered by Tony George. Adding credence to this report, Paul Tracy, one of the drivers for Forsythe Racing, said, "I'm supposed to fly in Indy later this week to get fitted for a seat, and then were going to have to thrash to make it to the first test at Homestead. We don't have any experience with those Dallaras and we're going to need all the practice we can get, but this is definitely the best thing that can happen to open-wheel racing."[17]

Fred Nation, the spokesman for IndyCar, confirmed that negotiations were continuing and, more importantly, that drafts of a merger agreement were being traded. But nothing was expected in the next few days as George was attending a motorsports conference in Florida and Kalkhoven was on family business in England.[18]

The news of the merger being very close was not well received by Kalkhoven, who pleaded to the press to butt out of the coverage of a potential merger: "If people really want to see unification, the best thing to do is to leave it alone. It frustrates me because the parties are operating in good faith, and external influences prevent the transaction from taking place. You cannot do a business transaction in the public eye. When you do a normal business merger, the principals agree to the transaction then you make an announcement, and then you take it to the stakeholders for comment. When there is a leak like this, everyone and their opinions get involved and it becomes a complete stalemate. This has happened several times before; it's not helping the process."[19]

There was another elephant in the room: the beginning of the IndyCar season was a mere seven weeks away. If the two sides were to agree to merge, it would have to be in the very near future, as those teams transitioning to IndyCar needed not only the new equipment but also to have a chance to get used to the equipment. Although George and Kalkhoven tried to keep the negotiations underneath the radar, others were more open and were making plans to help those teams migrating to the IRL with their equipment needs. Penske told the *St. Petersburg Times* he would provide "an extra car or pieces in order to get them going." He was joined by Chip Ganassi of Team Green, who told ESPN, "I got a call that said if we get this thing back together, they might need a [spare] car" and pledged his support to help the teams.[20]

Finally, Champ Car admitted they were involved in merger talks, and a meeting was planned in Indianapolis between George and Kalkhoven for February 21. Kalkhoven indicated that the major issues had been resolved when he told the *Indianapolis Star*, "It's just grinding out the details."[21] Unless something unforeseen occurred, it looked like the merger was going to happen. The major topics of conversation at the meeting between George and Kalkhoven included IndyCar's desire for full rights to all Indy-style racing along with all trademarks and history. Additionally, they wanted a non-compete agreement with the principals of Champ Car.

The other major unresolved issue was how the races on the Champ Car schedule would be absorbed by the Indy Racing League. IndyCar was interested in adding races at Edmonton, Alberta, Canada, Surfer's Paradise in Australia and the Long Beach Grand Prix. It was believed the two sides would run their respective races at Long Beach and Motegi as scheduled and award points for each race. The other two races were somewhat more problematic. The Edmonton race, scheduled for July 20, conflicted with an IndyCar race at Mid-America. IndyCar officials were believed to have offered alternative dates to Edmonton for either July 27 or August 3. The Surfer's Paradise race was scheduled for October 7, an open date on the IndyCar schedule. Unfortunately, IndyCar had agreed that their season finale would be at the Chicago Speedway in early September. Either the Chicago Speedway would have to agree that the season champion would not be crowned at their race or the promoters at Surfer's Paradise would have to agree that the race in 2008 would be an exhibition race.[22]

On a cold snowy evening, Kalkhoven and George met for dinner at the Eagle's Nest restaurant in downtown Indianapolis. The United States open-wheel racing community was expecting an announcement that détente had been reached and the reunification of open-wheel racing was going to occur. As the meeting broke up, there was no indication of a deal having been struck. In fact, the press conference previously scheduled was put on hold. Indications that were there were still issues to resolve. Fred Nation, IMS director of communications, tried to reassure the open-wheel community: "I don't think there is any fatal problem, they just didn't get everything done. They stopped for the evening and they will resume in the morning."

When Kalkhoven flew out of Indianapolis after breakfast with George, many felt the talks had broken down again. Both George and Kalkhoven had unbreakable commitments in the upcoming week[23] and timing for reunification was at a critical juncture. IndyCar's testing schedule was beginning the next week and the race season would start at the end of March, barely a month away. Even if they could reach an agreement, would there be time for the Champ Car teams to participate in the 2008 racing season? Later that day, George flew to Chicago to get Forsythe's signature on the agreement. When George and Forsythe met, George extended an olive branch and invited Forsythe to have his two open-wheel racing teams participate in the IndyCar series.[24] Forsythe neither accepted nor rejected this offer.

The *Indianapolis Star's* lead story when the news of the merger broke wasn't about the reunification. In this town so closely identified with auto racing, the story was upstaged by the other major sport in the minds of most Hoosiers, basketball. The lead story was about the Indiana University basketball coach, Kelvin Sampson, accepting a $750,000 buyout of his coaching contract by the university. But the *Indianapolis Star* did have a banner at the top of the page proclaiming the news, "IRL, Champ Car Make Up."[25] The sports section shouted "UNIFICATION!" Although an agreement to merge the two open-wheel racing leagues had been reached, there were still details being worked out, including what Champ Car races would be included on the 2008 IndyCar schedule. The work to combine the two entities began immediately, although the formal announcement wasn't made until February 27 at the Homestead-Miami Speedway.

The driving forces behind the reunification were the loss of sponsorships, the loss of viewership and the need of the two series to support the racing teams. Jimmy Vasser said, "The No. 1 thing in my opinion is that the teams need to be able to sustain themselves through sponsorships. The thing that drove everyone to the bargaining table is that both sides had to subsidize teams."[26]

Kalkhoven said of the decision to merge, "Look, neither side was succeeding and nobody was winning. It was a tough, emotional, gut-wrenching decision, but somebody had to put their ego aside and do this." At the Champ Car headquarters across town, about fifty Champ Car employees were cleaning out their desks.[27]

After thirty years of conflict, the racing community was happy that open-wheel racing would be unified. Michael Andretti, an owner of the Andretti Green racing team, said, "This is a huge day for the IndyCar Series and for our sport as a whole, for sure. Over the years, whether I was in the role of a driver, team owner or promoter, I have always wanted a unified sport. This has been my only goal throughout this entire process and I applaud everyone who played a part in making this happen. So many people have worked tirelessly, both publically and behind the scenes, to get this done. Everyone can now focus on taking the IndyCar Series to new heights for the good of our sport and everyone involved in it."[28] Derrick Walker chimed in: "From a fan and a sports business point of view, one open-wheel racing series in the United States has long been recognized as what fans and sponsors want to have both series together and I'm happy to say that Walker Racing embraces the decision."[29]

Penske, along with some other long-time open-wheel racing team owners, including Michael Andretti, had worked behind the scenes for years to reunify the sport. Although Penske was one of the founders of CART, he believed that there should be one series. After the merger was announced, Penske praised George for his tenacity and vision. "I take my hat off to Tony [George], who stuck to his guns. He wanted to have one series, but you didn't want to have a combination of too many people at the top. Fortunately, Gerry Forsythe and Kevin Kalkhoven were able to come to a decision in the best interests of their investments, along with the Speedway, that Tony is the one that they should go with." Penske was also very positive about the future of open-wheel racing. "We don't need a $20 million budget to go racing open-wheel. That's going to prove successful, and we'll gain some teams and the mix of road races and ovals, I think that's important. That will draw in more people."[30]

George revealed the "behind the scenes" tale of the beginning of the merger talks. He was close to his grandfather, Tony Hulman, who had rescued the Indianapolis Motor Speedway and its famous race, the Indianapolis 500, after it was closed during World War II. George reminisced, "It was last fall on the anniversary of my grandfather's death that I was thinking to myself it really had been 30 years ago since the sport of open-wheel racing had been truly unified. Last month when the calendar turned over to 2008, I was wondering if it was possible this could ever happen? Lo and behold, I got a phone call that just made me feel really warm. I felt like this was perhaps going to be the best year of my 48 to have a chance to do something that's very important to me and very close to me and that is to help bring about the unification of open-wheel racing." The person on the other end of the phone call was Kalkhoven.[31]

As employees of Champ Car were cleaning out their desks, George told his staff of the completion of the merger around 3 p.m. on Friday. The IndyCar staff had a busy weekend, as on Monday morning they welcomed nine Champ Car teams representing a total of sixteen cars into the fold at a meeting at the Indianapolis Motor Speedway. With little time before the beginning of the racing season, Barnhart tried to ease the transition for the Champ Car teams to oval racing by pairing them with IndyCar teams as technical advisors.[32]

For those Champ Car teams joining IndyCar with the financial strength to fund operating budgets, the purchase agreement included being given two Dallara chassis from the pool of cars being donated by various teams to the extent possible and a one-year Honda engine lease. To sweeten the pot, Indy-Car offered those teams that participated in the series eligibility for the TEAMS programs, which guaranteed $1.2 million for participation in the full series in lieu of prize money.[33]

The deal struck with Kalkhoven and Forsythe included IndyCar's buying the assets of Champ Car, including all race-sanctioning contracts, the company's intellectual property, intangible assets and the mobile medical unit for $6 million. It also provided Kalkhoven and Forsythe with a "goodwill" payment of $2 million each. The agreement also required Aquarium Holdings, LLC, an entity owned by Kalkhoven and Forsythe, to run the Grand Prix of Long Beach race on a long-term basis.[34] The total cost to unify open-wheel racing was estimated at $30 million. In addition to the $10 million paid to Kalkhoven and Forsythe, additional costs included supplying all of the teams transitioning to IndyCar with both a new and old chassis and an engine lease. The chassis cost was estimated at $400,000 while the cost of the engine lease was just south of $1 million. There was also the $1.2 million per car in TEAM support for teams running in the series for a full year.[35]

After reunification of the sport, George said, "Everybody's got an opinion of what we should do. It's my hope people would view this series as a destination for those who want to [compete in] a high-profile, top-shelf form of racing. I would hope that is enough to attract, retain and even draw back some people who had been part of it in the past."[36]

George wasn't under any illusion that merging the two sides would be easy. There were the technical things to be done, including the merging of the schedules, and the equipment needs of the teams who had participated in the Champ Car series. But the most difficult thing would be healing the wounds of the past thirty years. Some participants in Champ Car, such as Forsythe, would not come back to IndyCar. And the folks at IndyCar had a mere month until the opening race.

George acknowledged the hard work ahead for the series. "We just made it to the starting line, we didn't cross the finish line. It is the beginning, now all the hard work starts. There is a lot of opportunity. We won't realize everything all at once by simply announcing this. But I know that everybody has been awaiting this day for a long time. Now we have to roll up our sleeves and get after it. It's all about the future from this point forward. There really is no time to reflect on the past. It's a tremendous opportunity, but it's going to be very challenging at the same time."[37]

IndyCar anticipated only six or seven Champ Car teams joining the series. Brian Barnhart, president of competition, told *National Speed Sport News*, "I think if we see anything in the seven- or eight-car range of new participants joining as a result of this unification is a home run."[38] By May, six teams had transitioned to the Indy Racing League, bringing ten cars and drivers. This was great news not only for the series but also for the cornerstone Indianapolis 500. As opening day approached, nearly forty car-and-driver combinations were waiting for a chance to snag one of the thirty-three starting spots. That clearly meant Bump Day, the last day of qualifying, could achieve some of the past drama when spectators filled the stands. It also meant a higher-quality field. Indianapolis 500 winner Helio Castroneves enthused, "The Champ Car guys have made the field deeper, for sure, and I think they'll be a big factor in the race."[39]

The availability of engines was not an issue for participation in the Indianapolis 500. Even though the two series had different engine and chassis configurations, the Champ Car teams racing in the Indianapolis 500 already had the necessary equipment. The IndyCar engine builder, Honda, was already preparing the engines for the Memorial Day classic.[40] The real push was for those teams who had not participated in the Indianapolis 500, as this would be a totally new race car for them.

The challenge of providing equipment for the Champ Car teams was the need for three different types of car configuration. Barnhart said, "Our biggest short-term challenge will be the equipment transition, the availability of the equipment and getting it distributed and put into the new teams' hands as quickly as possible, as expeditiously as possible. Because of the great diver-

sity of our schedule, the one thing it creates a necessity for is additional equipment. You just don't have one configuration of cars. You have a superspeedway
car, a road-course car and a short-oval car. It's not just a matter of getting
them a car. You have to get them a car in three different configurations that
they are capable of running in." Offers of help from the well-heeled IndyCar
racing teams poured in. Those teams with extra cars or extra equipment,
such as Penske Racing, Target/Chip Ganassi Racing, and Andretti Racing, all
offered help. The biggest contributor, who also happened to be the one with
the most at stake, was Tony George, the owner of Vision Racing. He had ten
spare Dallara chassis and he was willing for many of these to go to teams
joining the unified series.[41]

Some teams failed to migrate from Champ Car to IndyCar. Some, such
as Walker Racing, were unable to find sponsors. But others, such as Forsythe
Racing, made the determination not to join.[42] Immediately after the merger,
it was believed that Forsythe Racing would bring two teams to IndyCar. But
by Monday it was one team, and within days, the decision was made not to
participate in the series. Forsythe Racing would continue to participate in
the Atlantic Championship, the former training league for Champ Car, with
a two-car team.[43]

Paul Tracy, one of Champ Car's star drivers and a member of the
Forsythe Racing team, was one of the drivers unable to find a ride in the
series. Initially, it was believed he would join Vision Racing, owned by George.
But Tracy wasn't interested in being part of a second-tier team, one that had
never won a race. Rather, he wanted to join one of the top teams, such as
Penske or Ganassi, but they weren't in need of a driver. Many teams were
unable to meet his salary requirement of $1 million per year. Tracy com-
mented about his salary requirements: "[Oval racing] is pretty dangerous,
and I'm not going to drive for hamburgers and hot dogs."[44] Ultimately, Tracy
was unable to find a ride with a new team because he was contractually obligated to drive for Forsythe Racing, owned by Gerry Forsythe. The contract
prohibited Tracy from driving for any other team, but he would earn $2 mil-
lion for the 2008 season while sitting on the sidelines. Despite his salary
demands, as a driver, he really wanted to be involved in the on-the-track
action. Within a couple of months, Paul Tracy was testing for Germain Racing
at the Chicagoland Speedway for the NASCAR Craftsman Truck series.[45]
Tracy's attorneys maintained that Forsythe Racing's failure to participate in
the IndyCar's opening race at the Homestead-Miami Speedway invalidated
the contract. There were teams interested in signing Tracy as a driver, including Vision Racing.[46]

Paul Tracy wasn't the only one left scrambling in the new world of open-wheel racing. With sixteen races scheduled prior to the merger, there were limited opportunities for the promoters of Champ Car's fourteen-race schedule to become an IndyCar race. IndyCar added the Grand Prix of Long Beach, the Grand Prix of Edmonton and the Gold Coast 300 at Surfer's Paradise. The other promoters were left vying for a limited number of slots. Estimates of the total number of potential IndyCar races ranged from a low of twenty races to a high of twenty-two races, and after adding the three of the races to the schedule, IndyCar had a total of nineteen races scheduled.

After purchasing the assets of the Grand Prix Association Toronto Corporation, Andretti Green Toronto, a subsidiary of Andretti Green Promotions, struck a deal with IndyCar to be the promoter for the Toronto Road race beginning in 2009. CART/Champ Car had hosted a road race event in Toronto from 1986 until 2007. But over the years and with the loss of its primary sponsor, Molson, interest had waned. Reportedly, the race lost $2 million toward the end of its run. Andretti Green Promotions, the promotional arm of Andretti Green Racing, was an experienced promoter. In 2004, it began the Honda Grand Prix of St. Petersburg, which had become a mainstay of IndyCar racing, Firestone Indy Lights and American LeMans series.[47]

With promoters vying for a limited number of slots in the Indy Racing League schedule, one long-time partner wasn't pleased with his relationship. Eddie Gossage, president and general manager of the Texas Motor Speedway, had seen attendance at the race drop by 20 percent since 2005. When the Indy Racing League was formed, Gossage secured the first race scheduled following the Indianapolis 500. In 1997, IndyCar's first race at Texas Motor Speedway had 129,000 spectators. On the advice of television partners ABC/ESPN, in 2006 the Indy Racing League returned to the format that had been successful for AAA, USAC and CART by having a race the weekend immediately following the Indianapolis 500 at Watkins Glen. By 2008, attendance at the Texas Motor Speedway was only 70,000—disappointing to Gossage but still the second-largest open-wheel race in the series. Since attendance had declined significantly, Gossage wanted IndyCar to cut the sanctioning fees. With the Texas Motor Speedway paying the highest sanctioning fees, Gossage maintained that he was being penalized for promoting the most successful IndyCar race outside of the Indianapolis 500. What he failed to mention was that the Texas Motor Speedway had added a second NASCAR race, which some believed cut into the attendance of the IndyCar race.[48]

After the merger, news came of the Champ Car's board of managers (Forsythe, Kalkhoven, Gentilozzi and Dan Pettit) voting on February 14, a week before the merger agreement with George, to put Champ Car into bankruptcy. The bankruptcy filing on March 5 included a statement by Gene Cottingham, the chief financial officer, indicating that the four-man board of managers had "determined that it is no longer economically feasible to sustain an open-wheel series and that [Champ Car] did not have the funds to operate the series in 2008." Champ Car's assets were estimated to be between $10 million and $50 million while the liabilities were estimated at less than $10 million, the largest of which was $1.825 million owed to Cosworth, Inc., the provider of engines to Champ Car owned by Kalkhoven and Forsythe.[49] The filing of Chapter 11 bankruptcy enabled Champ Car to run the Grand Prix of Long Beach in the middle of April while in a debtor-in-possession status. After the conclusion of the race, Kalkhoven and Forsythe planned to sell the remaining Champ Car assets, pay the company's expenses and then liquidate the company.

Realizing the toll the war had taken over the past twelve years, George began reaching out to ticketholders of the Indianapolis 500 who hadn't seen the race in several years. Paul Newman, an owner of the Newman Haas Lanigan Racing team and a long-time critic of George, wrote a letter to five hundred former ticketholders imploring them to join him at the Indianapolis 500. Also signing the letter was Roger Penske, the captain of open-wheel racing's most successful team. The letter said in part, "Unification has created a new level of enthusiasm but the hard work is just beginning. A major part of our efforts will be directed toward fans like you, ensuring that we build a strong, fan-friendly series for the future."[50]

As the season opener approached, the Indy Racing League changed its tag line from "I am Indy" to "I am Indy. One series. All the stars."[51] IndyCars had twenty-six teams for the opening race of the season at Homestead-Miami Speedway. This race was unique, as for the first time in motorsports history all races would be broadcast in high definition. George had spent $10 million for the system that would allow on-board cameras with the ability of a 360-degree view to be in six cars per race. The lipstick-sized cameras were installed inside a protective shell mounted on the car's air intake. IndyCar also teamed with MediaZone to provide the capability for subscribers to watch the race on their computers.[52]

Looking to the future, George commented, "2009 represents the opportunity for us to really look at where the series' best opportunities for growth are. I think it's likely we'll see more of a balance between ovals and road circuits than we have today." As planning for the series' future began, the looming question was how many additional races would be added to the existing IndyCar schedule and whether or not any historic venues on the Indy Racing League calendar would be dropped to make way for venues transitioning from the Champ Car schedule.[53] IndyCar believed two geographical areas had the type of demographics to grow the fan base—Portland, Oregon, and the Northeastern United States. Other markets of interest included Mexico, whose Tourism Board was sponsoring driver Mario Dominguez on the Pacific Coast Motorsports team.[54]

Putting Open-Wheel Racing Together

Reunification had been achieved at a great cost. Over the thirty years of the Indy car war, open-wheel racing had lost the support of many of its long-term fans, its sponsors and the media. NASCAR had soared to become the leading motorsports racing series in the nation.

What is known is that in an effort to crush the Indy Racing League and because of the escalating costs to support a racing team far in excess of the sponsorships the teams were able to secure, CART had blown through its $100 million war chest in less than two years. Much of this money was spent directly on trying to keep the racing teams alive so that there could be a series. Since both Champ Car and IndyCar are privately held, it is not known how much money the Hulman-George family had spent also supporting Indy-Car's racing teams to keep their series alive. Undoubtedly, it is in the millions of dollars.

For IndyCar to regain or hope to regain its stature, several long-term initiatives were necessary. First, the series needed a signature sponsor. Over the years, IndyCar had been successful in gaining two series sponsors, Pep Boys and Northern Light Technology, but neither sponsor lasted long. The first sponsor, Pep Boys, was sued by Indy Racing League for reneging on its sponsorship agreement. The second sponsor, Northern Light Technology, ended the relationship after the second year of a five-year agreement after the economy went south. Since 2003, the Indy Racing League had been without a title sponsor.

A second big issue for the Indy Racing League was developing well-known drivers who could power the sport. During the years when open-wheel racing ran under the USAC banner and during the early years of CART, there were many familiar drivers. Names such as A. J. Foyt, Roger Ward and Bill Vukovich dominated the landscape. That is one advantage that NASCAR had. Many of their top drivers were household names such as Danica Patrick,

Jeff Gordon and Dale Earnhart. The sad reality is many of the up-and-coming drivers abandoned open-wheel racing for NASCAR. Drivers such as Danica Patrick, who was listed as the "most popular" driver in IndyCar for six consecutive years (2005–2010), jumped to NASCAR. The bottom line for the drivers was that they had a much higher earning potential with NASCAR than with the Indy Racing League. Why? First, because NASCAR ran more races, but second, and more important, with more name recognition, there was more opportunity for sponsorships and endorsement deals. IndyCar had made some progress in increasing the driver's star power. Dario Franchitti, who began racing in CART in 1997 and switched to the Indy Racing League in 2002, was the series champion for four years (2007, 2009–2011)[1] and won the Indianapolis 500 three times (2007, 2010 and 2012). Another three-time Indianapolis 500 winner (2001, 2002 and 2009), Helio Castroneves appeared on *Dancing with the Stars,* winning the mirrored ball trophy in 2007.[2]

Just before the 2008 Indianapolis 500, IndyCar announced that Honda would continue to supply engines for the series for an additional five years. With a new engine configuration anticipated in the next couple of years and wanting to attract other engine manufacturers, the league formed the Manufacturers' Roundtable to openly discuss the engine and chassis rules.[3] League officials were very pleased with the turnout for the first meeting, which included representatives from Audi, BMW, Chevrolet, Fiat, Mazda and Volkswagen as well as engine builders Ilmor and Cosworth. What the representatives learned from Brian Barnhart at the meeting was that the next engine to power IndyCar was going to be turbocharged. They also learned that IndyCar hoped to increase the number of engine manufacturers participating in the series. IndyCar believed this would result in increased promotional dollars to the series. The benefit to the engine manufacturers was technical advances and being able to showcase their engines' capabilities.[4]

As the first half of the 2008 IndyCar series drew to a conclusion, Terry Angstadt, IndyCar's commercial division president, enthused, "We cannot be happier with what we have seen over the first half of the unified IndyCar series season. Key areas like attendance, ratings and sponsorship are all pointing in the right direction and we anticipate further growth and momentum heading into the second half of the season."[5] They had good reasons to be optimistic. After the difficulties of fielding a full complement of cars in the previous season, there were twenty-six cars participating in the series. And there was a strong increase in attendance at the gate. Even better, the ever-important television viewership was up for six of the nine races and had increased overall by 17 percent.[6] More viewers would translate to more value to the sponsors and more income to the series from promoters and sponsors.

Adding to the buzz around IndyCar was the announcement that Paul Tracy, one of Champ Car's top drivers and winner of the 2003 championship, was returning to the series. He would join George's Vision Racing, with Derrick Walker of Walker Racing as crew chief for the Rexall Indy Edmonton Grand.[7] Tracy joined Ed Carpenter, George's stepson, and A. J. Foyt IV as part of the team[8] and would finished fourth in the race.

Just when things were looking up for IndyCar after reunification, dark clouds appeared on the horizon. This time it wasn't the internal squabbling among open-wheel racing. It was the economy. General Motors, responding to the weakest motor sales in a decade, announced it was cutting its spending by $10 billion, suspending its dividend and selling $4 billion in assets. Although General Motors wasn't specific about how much spending it was going to trim from its support of motor sports, everyone involved in the sport knew significant cuts were coming.

Humpy Wheeler, president of Lowe's Motor Speedway, said, "GM's cutback is no surprise. They are going through their toughest time in history and are cutting back everywhere, so why not racing? I think everybody in big-time racing needs to brace themselves for more of the same from many other companies." He also cautioned, "We have been through these challenges before. What everyone needs to focus on is cutting costs—whether it be the top Cup teams or those who race every Saturday night at the short track level. Racing is going to change drastically—and has needed to do so for a long time—as a result of this economy. Five years from now, it will be much more efficient because this is survival for many."[9]

For the 2009 racing season, IndyCar announced it would run more street races and hoped to achieve a balance of 50 percent ovals and 50 percent street and road races. Initially, it added two well-received street races from the traditional CART/Champ Car line-up, the Toyota Grand Prix of Long Beach and the Streets of Toronto race. In order to make room for the additional road races on the IndyCar schedule, officials decided to drop two existing oval races, New Hampshire and Las Vegas. This decision did not sit well with some of the promoters and fans of IndyCar who either had a vested interest in the tracks or preferred oval racing.

Jerry Gappens, president and general manager of the New Hampshire Motor Speedway, couldn't believe these venues had been dropped. Recalling a meeting between IndyCar and Bruton Smith, the president of Speedway Motorsports (which owned the New Hampshire Motor Speedway and the Las Vegas Motor Speedway), Gappens said, "I sat in a meeting and watched Bruton ask them for a race here, which they seemed extremely interested in doing, pending scheduling conflicts with Japan. In addition, in that same meeting, they asked him to host the series finale in Las Vegas, which Mr. Smith agreed to and even offered the speedway and financial support for it to happen this year. Having attended that meeting in early June, it's hard to believe that neither facility is on the new schedule." Gappens also recounted some of the history behind the relationship with the Indy Racing League: "I think it is a slap in the face to Bruton Smith, our chairman, and to our company which have both been very supportive of the Indy Racing League since its inception. From a historical perspective, Bob Bahre, the former owner of New Hampshire Motor Speedway, was one of the first to agree to go with the Indy Racing League when they split from Championship Auto Racing Teams in 1995."[10]

Terry Angstadt, president of the commercial division for the Indy Racing League, explained that neither the New Hampshire Motor Speedway nor the Las Vegas Motor Speedway was on the schedule because of the size of the venues. New Hampshire seated 92,000, while Las Vegas could hold 125,000. Angstadt said of the decision not to race in either of these venues, "We said that putting 30, 40, 50,000 people in a big beautiful oval like they own didn't make sense for either one of us, in our opinion, so that's really what it came down to."[11]

Angstadt was positive about the new schedule. "We think it is a good move towards balance. Because Champ Car brought a lot of opportunities and a few challenges as exclusively road racing, we think that working towards that 50–50 balance is good. So by incorporating three and possibly four [street and road course races] for the future for now, with continuing interest in some of the other premier markets, we think that a 10–8 for '09, 10 ovals, eight street and road, is a good balance. And there is real interest in a couple more historic Champ Car venues for the future."[12]

With IndyCar adding street races and road courses to its schedule, it decided the new engine configuration available for the 2011 racing season: the horsepower would be increased from 500 to 750. This would enable the cars to have greater acceleration, speed and torque. It also hoped it would have three or four engine manufacturers participate in the series. To counteract the increased horsepower, the next generation of chassis would have less ground effects, thereby lessening the speeds on the ovals.[13]

When the broadcast agreement with ABC was extended for an additional four years, there was a new wrinkle. Having invested in the capabilities for the cars to have on-board cameras and production equipment for high definition broadcasts, the agreement stipulated that all IndyCar races would be broadcast in high definition. ABC would carry five of the 2009 IndyCar races. Thirteen races would be carried on cable channel Versus. The ten-year agreement with Versus includes a one-hour show the day before a race focusing on qualifying and other race-relevant stories.[14]

In October, Paul Tracy filed suit against Forsythe Racing, claiming a breach of contract. His complaint alleged he was owed $2.25 million plus any bonuses for the 2008 season and that his contract with Forsythe Racing included a $1-million buyout clause. Tracy indicated he had not received any funds from Forsythe Racing in 2008.[15]

In November, IndyCar made history when it signed a multi-year agreement with Apex-Brazil as the supplier of ethanol to fuel its race cars. Terry Angstadt, IndyCar's commercial division president, explained, "We continue to strive to be on the leading edge of the 'greening' of racing. The IndyCar Series was the first motorsports series to mandate the use of renewable fuel, and now we will work with the ethanol industry both in the United States and Brazil to promote the use of all types of ethanol by consumers."[16]

As the economic crisis brought on by subprime loans deepened, auto racing felt the sting of reduced budgets. When Honda announced it was putting its Formula One team up for sale and exiting the Formula One series, concern spread through both IndyCar and the American Le Mans series that Honda might also end its relationship with these two series. Honda was quick to reassure racing fans that they were committed to the racing industry. A statement issued by Honda said, "Racing has played an essential role in Honda's history as a company, and the competition that racing provides has always been a cornerstone of Honda's corporate values. We race to learn, we race to win. We plan to continue both of those traditions in 2009 and beyond."[17] On the heels of Honda's announcement, Audi disclosed that it would only run the season opener of the American Le Mans Series, a series that they had dominated in the LMP1 class.[18]

Stepping up to the plate to help relieve some of the financial pressure was chassis manufacturer Dallara, which announced a reduction in its prices in 2009 with an average projected team savings of 11 percent. Speaking on behalf of Dallara, IndyCar's project manager Andrea Toso said, "Everybody knows that this is a difficult time, and we have to do our best now to help the teams. If we can help the teams go through this difficult time, it is in the best interest of the manufacturers, the series and the teams. If we don't do anything now, maybe one year from now it's too late. We hope that all suppliers and partners will understand this initiative and follow through."[19] Joining Dallara was IndyCar's exclusive gearbox supplier, Xtrac, which cut prices on its pneumatic paddleshift system as well as on the service charges for 2009.[20]

Auto racing is an expensive sport. As the economy continued to spiral downward, teams were growing more concerned about their ability to retain or attract sponsors and about the cost of equipment. All the IndyCar teams needed to do was to look at how the economy had impacted NASCAR, which saw its television viewership for the first ten races of the 2009 season down by 10.8 percent. Additionally concerning to NASCAR's management was the sudden decline of 12 percent in the earnings of its primary sponsor, Sprint Nextel.[21] Although attendance at IndyCar races was up as was the viewership of television broadcasts, the looming question was how the economy would impact IndyCar.

Turmoil at the Brickyard

The thirty-year Indy car war was expensive, especially during the final decade when George formed the Indy Racing League and ultimately won the battle for control of open-wheel racing. George's sisters woke up to the reality of the expenses incurred and the continuing expenses to maintain the series. A report by SpeedTV.com claimed, "Between paying persons, supplying cars, engines and parts for other teams, firing high-powered public relations firms and starting his own IRL team—plus remaking the Indianapolis Motor Speedway to accommodate Formula One—George has spent more than $600M during the past 13 years."[1]

Barely a year after reuniting open-wheel racing and days after the conclusion of the 2009 Indianapolis 500, George was summoned to a board meeting of the Indianapolis Motor Speedway Corporation. Primarily a family affair, the board consisted of George; his mother, Mari Hulman George; his sisters, Josie George Krisiloff, Nancy George and Kathi Conforti-George; and attorney Jacky Snyder.

Rumors swirled around the racing community and Indianapolis about the board meeting. Some sources reported that George had been stripped of his roles at the Indianapolis Motor Speedway as well as the Indy Racing League. The Hulman-George family tried to put a positive spin on the meeting. George, while denying the rumors that he had been removed from his position, told the press the focus of the meeting was to develop strategies to improve the Indy Racing League. Mari Hulman George, the matriarch of the family and chair of the board, issued a press release stating, "There was a general discussion about the challenges and opportunities facing all of our companies and where most of our energies need to be spent. All of our properties are doing well, given the challenges of the current economy, [but] the Indy Racing League represents our greatest growth opportunity and therefore deserves the most attention at this point."[2]

Not surprisingly, there was great concern among various racing teams about the goings-on at IndyCar headquarters. The ability for the series to continue largely depended upon the continued willingness of the Indianapolis Motor Speedway and the Hulman-George family to support the league during economic rough spots. Without this economic support, the series could fold. In response, various IndyCar teams voiced strong support for George, issuing a statement which read, "During the past week, there have been many rumors and innuendos about our CEO Tony George. We, the IndyCar team owners, want to express our full support to Tony. As an innovator and leader of our sport, he continually strives to help and improve IndyCar racing, and for that we are exceptionally grateful."[3]

Despite the efforts to tamp down the chatter of George's dismissal, the rumors continued unabated. With another board meeting set for July 1 where George would unveil his plan for IndyCar, all eyes in the open-wheel racing world were focused on Indianapolis. The future became clearer when George quit his role as CEO not only of the Indianapolis Motor Speedway but also of its parent, Hulman and Company.[4] This would enable George to focus his attention on Vision Racing and other business interests. While not involved in the day-to-day business, George would continue to serve on the board of directors for both companies.

The board turned to Jeffrey Belskus to assume the mantle as the president and CEO of the Indianapolis Motor Speedway Corporation. W. Curtis Brighton became the president and CEO of Hulman and Company. IndyCar would continue with Terry Angstadt as the president of the commercial division and Brian Barnhart as president of the competition division.[5]

About a week after his separation from the Indianapolis Motor Speedway Corporation and the Indy Racing League, George spoke publicly about his decision:

> At a board meeting last week, I was asked to continue as CEO of the Indy Racing League, reporting to a new president and CEO of IMS. In my view, this would have created an unnecessary bureaucratic layer between the people in the operations of the IRL and the CEO of IMS that had not previously existed. From my perspective of my experience as president and CEO of the Indianapolis Motor Speedway, I am acutely aware that the interests of Indy-car racing as a sport, the IRL as a league and the most important motorsports race in the world, are mutually dependent and interconnected, both now and in the future, I did not feel that a subordinate position as CEO of the IRL was a management vehicle which would allow me to accomplish the objectives that the family and the board requested me to pursue, I declined the position.[6]

Toward the end of July, George, obviously hurt by the decision of the family, wrote on the Vision Racing Web site, "I continue to be perplexed by the board's recent decision to relieve me from my responsibility as CEO of the enterprise. To date, I have not received a reasonable explanation as to why, the statement they released to the press notwithstanding, I feel as though, after 20 years, I am entitled to one. I understand that maybe they don't feel they owe me an explanation."[7]

Despite the distractions of the family dispute, business at the Indy Racing League continued without disruption. The management team was concerned about the lack of competitive racing on the tracks. With a new chassis and engine combination expected in 2012, they focused on other possible remedies to improve racing while being cost effective. With assistance from Honda Performance Development, the Indy Racing League instituted a push-to-pass button to permit a driver to increase the speed of the car for a short time. The system, first implemented at the Meijer Indy 300, provided a driver with the ability to use the push-to-pass system 20 times for 12 seconds each.[8] The push-to-pass system did not originate with the Indy Racing League, as it had previously been used by Champ Cars.[9] Les MacTaggart, IndyCar's senior technical advisor, explained the benefits to the driver and race teams. "It's to provide the driver, if they're already making a passing maneuver, an additional tool to complete the pass. It provides teams with options which they have to choose how they're going to run, so it brings more strategy from a team aspect."[10]

Rumors are hard to tamp down. During late July, rumors began circulating throughout IndyCar that George and billionaire John Menard, the owner of a chain of home improvement stores throughout the Midwest, were engaged in conversation to buy out the Indy Racing League from George's family. There was also speculation that George and Menard were engaged in conversation about purchasing the troubled Milwaukee Mile track.[11] At the Indy Meijer 300 race in late July, George acknowledged a relationship with John Menard as a sponsor of Ed Carpenter, a driver for George's Vision Racing team and George's stepson. George also addressed the rumors that he and Menard were forming a group to purchase the Indy Racing League. "I haven't had any conversations with him regarding that or taking over Milwaukee [Mile]. I don't know that either one of us wants to do that. We've been building our relationship with the IndyCar program now for two years and he has been sponsoring Ed [Carpenter]. The indications are he wants to continue that."[12]

Management of the Indy Racing League took two steps forward in solidifying the series. The first was the "Road to Indy" developmental series. Brian Barnhart explained the goals of the program: "In creating the Road to Indy, we are trying to bridge the gap between the premier open-wheel racing divisions and the entry level open-wheel series by creating a clear career path for aspiring drivers. With the Road to Indy, a driver has the opportunity to hone his professional racing skills at an early stage of his or her career and has a chance to build upon those skills in a professional environment while driving similar-style open-wheel racing vehicles on similar tracks at every step."[13]

The first step in creating the "Road to Indy" was the earlier announcement of the Indy Racing League sanctioning races for the U.S. F2000 series being revived by Andersen Productions, Ltd., which was owned by brothers Dan and John Andersen. This series was important to the Indy Racing League because it was the entry step of drivers hoping to participate in open-wheel racing.[14] The other steps on the "Road to Indy" were the Star Mazda Championship series and the Indy Firestone Lights series. All three series joined IndyCar during the festivities for the Indianapolis 500. Both the U.S. F2000 series and the Star Mazda Championship race have a race at the O'Reilly Raceway Park in Clermont, Indiana, the night before the Indianapolis 500, while the Firestone Lights series holds its Firestone Freedom 100 race at the Indianapolis Motor Speedway on Carb Day, the Friday before the Indianapolis 500.[15]

The second announcement, heralded on a billboard on Times Square in New York City, was that Izod would be the series sponsor of the Indy Racing League, which had gone ten years without this critical part of the puzzle. In the six-year agreement, Izod agreed to provide funding of $100,000 for up to 25 cars to the team owners. Additional monies would be spent on marketing of the series. Brian Barnhart exclaimed, "The fact it's somebody outside the motorsports realm takes us into people's living rooms that may not be race fans. I think it will be a great match for both organizations. They bring a marketing expertise that we've never had before."[16]

In November, employees were rocked by the elimination of 25 jobs at the Indy Racing League and its sister company, IMS Productions. The action was part of an effort to improve the operational efficiency of both units.[17]

In response to the continuing economic malaise, the Indianapolis 500 announced it would have only 12 days of racing activity from opening day through qualification. Qualifying would be limited to one weekend.[18] This would save the teams and the Indianapolis Motor Speedway money. Also significant to the teams was a reduction in the cost of the engine for the 2010 season. Honda reduced the cost of their engine lease for teams participating in the full 17-race series by $27,000 to $935,000. For a team participating only Indianapolis 500, the cost was reduced by $75,000.[19]

In January 2010, George abruptly stepped down from the board of

Hulman and Company. His life had been spent in auto racing, and now he wasn't involved with the family company, the Indianapolis Motor Speedway or the Indy Racing League. The only involvement he had was his Vision Racing team. It was a blow when John Menard decided not to continue funding of this racing team. George made the difficult decision to close the Firestone Lights team down. The announcement was made on the Vision Racing team Web site, which said, "Efforts to find a solid sponsor partnership have been difficult, but will continue so that we may take to the track once again. We hope to see you all at the track in the near future."[20]

The rumor mill was now ripe with the speculation that the Hulman-George family would sell the Indianapolis Motor Speedway. The leading contender was the International Speedway Corporation, owner of multiple racetracks including the Daytona International Speedway. Jeff Belskus, CEO for the Speedway, said, "I chuckle whenever I hear ISC is going to buy IMS because it's not for sale. It's an asset of this business and to the extent any asset can be sold, it can be sold. But that is really an esoteric conversation because the Indianapolis Motor Speedway is not for sale. The Indianapolis Motor Speedway is a long-standing part of history, so I chuckle to myself because it's not for sale. It's like the Vanderbilts selling the railroad or the Rockefeller Family selling Standard Oil in previous centuries."[21]

A New Start

In February, the Indy Racing League announced its new CEO. In doing so, they left the world of motorsports, hiring Randy Bernard, who had taken the Professional Bull Riders, Inc., from virtual anonymity. His hiring was promoted by Josie George Krisiloff, who had been impressed by his work ethic and his leadership of the Professional Bull Riders. Under Bernard's leadership, which began in 1995, the Professional Bull Riders prize money grew from $330,000 in 1994 to over $11 million in 2008.[1] In a difficult economic period, when auto racing and IndyCar were experiencing a decline in attendance, the Professional Bull Riders saw a 10.7 percent increase in attendance at their events in 2009.[2]

Although he had no experience in auto racing, Bernard was perceived as being very astute in marketing sporting events. Belskus commented on his skill set: "Randy is the right person at the right time to head the Indy Racing League. He brings a superb sports marketing and promotion background, excellent CEO skills, energy and enthusiasm at a time when the IZOD IndyCar Series is positioned for growth."[3]

Some of the titans of auto racing were clearly impressed by Bernard in their early meetings and openly supported him. Chip Ganassi said, "I like the guy because he's a workaholic. You ask the guy a question; he gives you an answer. I like that. I'm sure his inflow of information is coming at him like water from a fire hose and he's trying to swallow it all. I could tell in my first meeting with him it wasn't his first rodeo." Roger Penske was also impressed: "I met him before he took the job and I think he's a business guy. He built PBR from scratch. When you talk to him he is talking about the right things. He is talking about purses. He is talking about people in the stands. He is growing the brand and trying to do things differently." Penske also commented about Bernard's work ethic: "I told him 'Hey, let's get together' and he said 'how about tomorrow?' I had to tell my wife I had to go into the office bright and early on a Sunday morning, and he was there waiting on me. He was like a sponge."[4]

Randy Bernard.

Bernard clearly understood that the challenge at IndyCar was to increase revenues. "I never tried to be an expert on bull riding and I will never try to be an expert on racing. That's not my job. My job is to see how many more people I can get to come to that event and how many people can watch that event on TV. I have to be a devil's advocate to figure out what is in the best interest of the fans."[5]

Bernard understood he had a huge learning curve. Underlying his five-point plan for resurrection of the league was the need to understand the history and culture of open-wheel racing. Bernard said, "I will spend hours in the Hall of Fame Museum. I will want to spend hours with past champions who will give me insight, and I will also want to spend a lot of time with fans. I want to hear their input. I want to see what they think of the sport." Bernard's five-point plan included developing relationships with the team owners, fans and sponsors, creating a consistent marketing platform and becoming profitable. He acknowledged that long-term profitability could not be through cost-cutting but rather was dependent upon the growth of interest in the sport, which would grow revenues.[6]

Although Bernard had not grown up in the auto racing world, he clearly understood the importance of race drivers to the success of the league. He also understood that NASCAR and Formula One were siphoning off the best drivers America had. Open-wheel racing, be it CART, Champ Car, the IRL or IndyCar, had been unable to keep pace with the sponsorship money flowing into the NASCAR or Formula One teams or the drivers' compensation. In an attempt to retain the current drivers, Bernard wanted to increase the prize money. To do that, Bernard clearly had to increase the visibility of the sport and garner more sponsors both for the league as well as for the teams.[7]

For the long-term benefit of open-wheel racing, Bernard would emphasize developing drivers from the ground level. Bernard explained, "Within six months you will see us develop more grassroots. Karting is going to be a very big issue with me. If there are 25,000 to 50,000 kids out there karting, why aren't we capitalizing on that? I want them looking up to Graham Rahal and Danica Patrick and Helio Castroneves and say 'Hey, that's what I want to do when I grow up.'"[8]

At IndyCar headquarters, Barnhart was outlining the goals and challenges for the new chassis to be implemented in 2012: "Our chassis is the most complex challenge in world motorsports because of the variety of race courses where we compete. It must be designed to run at 235 mph at the Indianapolis Motor Speedway, and protect drivers and spectators in high-speed crashes. It must be able to perform on superspeedways, speedways and short ovals as well as natural terrain road courses and temporary circuits."[9]

Barnhart had been in discussions with chassis suppliers including Dallara, Swift, DeltaWing and Lola. The requirements included that the chassis should be lighter weight, it should have more space for sponsor logos and be easily identifiable, it must be safe for the drivers and spectators, and it must be cost-effective for the teams. IndyCar also had a preference for the chassis to be manufactured in the United States, preferably in Indiana, and for adherence to IndyCar's green technology.[10]

The call for a new chassis brought out several interested parties, including the then-current IndyCar manufacturer, Dallara, as well as start-ups DeltaWing and BAT Engineering. DeltaWing introduced its new chassis, designed by Ben Bowlby of Ganassi Racing,[11] at the Chicago Auto Show. Its radical design focused on reducing the weight of the automobile as well as reducing drag. It claimed to achieve record-breaking track performance while reducing the power requirements by one half over the more recent car designs.[12] Three highly regarded engineers, Bruce Ashmore, Alan Mertens and Tim Wardrop, joined forces to form BAT Engineering to produce a competitive design for the chassis. Bruce Ashmore was Lola's chief designer, Alan Mertens was a designer for March and Galmer, while Tim Wardrop was a G-Force designer.[13]

After a brief two months on the job, Bernard believed IndyCar racing needed to have more major events than just the Indianapolis 500. NASCAR has three major events—the Daytona 500, Talladega and the Coca-Cola 600. Horse racing has three major events—the Kentucky Derby, the Belmont and the Preakness. Going back over the past 100 years of open-wheel racing, the racing had always been dominated by one race, the Indianapolis 500. Acknowledging this fact, Bernard said while attending the Long Beach Grand Prix, "You have the Indianapolis 500, and then you have a bunch of vanilla events. Not to take away from this great event here [at Long Beach], but it's not a national event, which we need to have two or three majors that stand apart and make them big, big events. I think what we're working on might help with that."[14] Bernard did not unveil his plans.

In order to garner more excitement, the Indianapolis 500's Pole Day was changed. Rather than have the pole position decided by the fastest qualifying speed, Speedway officials decided to have a shootout of the top nine fastest cars on the first day of qualifying. On Pole Day, twenty-four slots were available out of the thirty-three total slots in the race. Each car could make up to three qualifying runs. The initial qualifying period would be between 11 a.m. and 4 p.m. At 4:30 p.m., the nine fastest cars would line up for a "shootout." Each car would run four laps to determine the starting position for the top nine slots in the field. Belskus said, "This new format for Indianapolis 500 qualifying will deliver even more action and intensity for fans. Drivers will go all out during the first session on Pole Day to get a chance to make a run for the pole. Then they'll need to dig even deeper to find the speed for the pole in the last 90 minutes. Plus there still will be plenty of spots up for grabs on Bump Day with all of the dramatic, last-minute bumping that generations of fans have loved about Indy."[15] Winner of the pole in the new qualifying format was Helio Castroneves with a four-lap qualifying speed in the shootout of 227.970 mph.[16]

Without a background in auto racing, Bernard formed a committee to help him in the selection of the new chassis. The seven-member committee was led by General William Looney, a four-star general in the United States Air Force. Included on the committee were representatives of the IRL, racing teams, engine experts and chassis experts.[17] In July, IndyCar announced that the new chassis for the 2012 season would be built by Dallara in Indiana. The Dallara chassis included the tub, the safety cells and other components to IndyCar specs.[18] The rules allowed other manufacturers to provide changeable bodyworks, known as aero kits, such as wings and sidepods. The aero kits would give the teams a chance to customize their cars not only in terms of visual appeal but also in terms of aerodynamics.[19] Despite the fact that the new chassis was predicted to cost 45 percent less than the current model,[20] some team owners believed the cost of changing the chassis was too much during the economic downturn. And understandably, team owners would have liked the old parts they had in stock to be interchangeable with the new design.[21]

In November 2010, Chevrolet announced it would return to Indy car racing by providing aero kits and becoming an engine supplier. The engine, to be built by Ilmor, a company owned by Penske, was a twin, turbocharged, direct-injected V-6. The engine would be used by Team Penske, the most winning team in open-wheel racing.[22] The decision by IndyCar to return to a turbocharged engine was the driving factor behind Chevrolet's decision to return as an engine manufacturer.[23] The announcement by Chevrolet was the answer to one of IndyCar fans' dreams: competition. Bernard exclaimed, "What I've heard from day one is fans and everyone in IndyCar wanted competition. The second thing they wanted was an American manufacturer. This is the first step. Chevy coming back and competing with such a rich heritage is fantastic."[24] Bernard continued, "Chevrolet brings a strong passion for racing, technology, relevance and innovation, which is a great fit for us with our new car platform."[25] Chevrolet did bring a passion for racing back to IndyCar. They had participated as an engine manufacturer from 1986 through 1993 before taking a nine-year hiatus. They returned to open-wheel racing from 2002 through 2005. Utilizing the V-8 engine, Chevrolet scored victories in 104 races, won the Indianapolis 500 7 times and had 6 champion racers.[26]

Within a week of the announcement by Chevrolet, Lotus announced at the Los Angeles Auto Show that it was returning to open-wheel racing as an engine supplier as well as providing aero kits. They started by sponsoring KV Racing Technology, with driver Takuma Sato in 2010. Danny Behar, Lotus Group CEO, said, "We really want to fight and compete with the big guys. But we have a Lotus way to do things. We always try to understand what we are getting into. That's why we started this year with a very small activity with Takuma Sato with one car to understand IndyCar racing and to see whether there was an opportunity for us to become a real contender."[27]

The positive news of three engine suppliers was dampened when Firestone announced in March 2011 that they were withdrawing from IndyCar racing. This followed the pullout of their parent, Bridgestone, from F-1 racing the previous December.[28] This news was concerning to the teams who had been lobbying to keep Firestone as the tire supplier. The sentiment of the teams was expressed by Conquest Racing boss Eric Bachelart, who told Sport.com, "We all want to keep running with Firestone. We know those people, we trust their product and we have to save the deal. [Firestone is] the best partner ever and we can't afford to lose them so we're hoping they'll review their decision."[29] The racing teams indeed felt very safe running on Firestone tires—in twenty-one years of racing, there had not been a single incident caused by a tire failure.[30]

What must have been very concerning to IndyCar management was that Firestone had been the only tire supplier to IndyCar since 2000.[31] Tires are obviously a crucial component of a race car, and IndyCar would need to find a new supplier pronto. Within a week, Firestone and the Indy Racing League had reached a new agreement keeping Firestone as a tire supplier through the 2012 racing season.[32] But there was a significant cost to both the league as well as to the teams for the new agreement. Historically, Firestone had provided the teams tires gratis, with an average value of about $750,000 per team per year. Now, the teams would have to pay for the tires.[33] Although Firestone agreed to continue as the tire supplier for the IndyCar series, they did not plan to continue as the sponsor of the Indy Lights Series.[34]

With the racing teams continuing to be concerned about the cost of the new chassis, IndyCar decided to postpone the implementation of the aero kits until the 2013 racing season. Each aero kit cost only $75,000, but to outfit a multiple-car team including spare parts, and different aero kits for the different types of racing, the cost would increase to approximately $500,000 per team. The new chassis would use the default aero kit provided by Dallara.[35]

Riding the Bucking Bull

As the 2011 racing season got underway, IndyCar announced the use of double-file restarts for the oval races. The idea was proposed by Chip Ganassi and Roger Penske, who had seen the success of double file restarts for NASCAR. But the drivers, concerned about the fragility of the Indy racing cars, were opposed to this plan.[1] The difficulties with the double file restarts began with the opening race at St. Petersburg, where there were multiple car crashes and injuries as the drivers tried to navigate a sharp corner in turn one that effectively took the track from two lanes to one. The difficulty was that unlike NASCAR, Indy cars are not made to be involved in bumping. The cars have fragile front wings, which if touched could destroy the downforce and braking ability of the car or could slice through the tires.[2]

Officiating errors would become the storyline for the year. At the Milwaukee 225 in mid–June, Dario Franchitti was going into his pit when he clipped a tire laid out at the edge of Will Power's pit. Most people expected Franchitti to receive a penalty for this occurrence similar to the penalty incurred by Takuma Sato for hitting pit equipment earlier in the race. But a penalty was not forthcoming for the apparent infraction by Franchitti. A review by IndyCar officials after the race indicated that there was enough "reasonable doubt" not to assess a penalty. The officials felt Power's crew had laid out the equipment prematurely and had put it on the edge of the pitbox in an apparent attempt to make Franchitti's entrance into his pit difficult.

The difficulties for race director Brian Barnhart escalated at the Toronto race in mid–July. Will Power spun after being clipped by Franchitti. Both IndyCar and broadcast personnel tweeted that Franchitti had been handed a stop-go penalty for causing Power to spin, but a penalty was not assessed. Racing officials ruled this was a "racing incident." Power, upset by Franchitti's actions and the lack of a penalty, ranted, "He's the guy that mouths off about everyone and whines about everyone, and he's the guy racing dirty who never gets penalized by IndyCar. It's just not right." He continued, "I'm not surprised he didn't get a penalty, he never gets a penalty. IndyCar won't penalize them because Chip Ganassi goes up there and gives it to them. It's just wrong."[3]

The difficulties escalated at the New Hampshire race. Barnhart halted the race with 10 laps remaining because of rain. When the race was red-flagged, Ryan Hunter-Reay was in the lead. Despite light rain continuing to fall on the track, Barnhart decided to restart the race. On the restart, Hunter-Reay slipped two positions, handing the lead to Oriol Servia and second place to Scott Dixon. When Danica Patrick spun in turn four, causing a multiple-car crash, the entire field was sent back to racing under a yellow flag. Most race observers believed Servia had won the race, having been in first position when the race was called. However, Barnhart decided to have the race results reflect those at the restart, handing the win to Hunter-Reay. This obviously brought protests from Servia and second-place finisher Scott Dixon. Servia said, "I think it was really wet out there and we shouldn't have gone out, but they threw the green and I was ahead when the yellow went out. Any racing, even here, when you call the leader that is the way it stands. They called me the leader and then they decide to reverse it. I'm very upset." Also negatively impacted by the decision on the restart was Will Power, who was locked in the points race with Dario Franchitti. Power was one of the racers involved in the multiple-car crash at the end of the race. Frustrated, Power in a post-race television interview said of Barnhart, "He makes such bad calls all the time. This has got to be it. They cannot have this guy running the show. That was a decision to put a lot of drivers in danger … it was no condition to race in. Shame on him." His middle finger salute was caught on camera and broad-cast live to the television audience.[4] In response to the outburst, IndyCar fined Power $30,000 and placed him on probation for the remainder of the racing season. Power was given the option of working off the fine through media appearances on behalf of IndyCar.[5]

Barnhart later admitted the decision to restart the race was an error. He maintained that he did not have information from the drivers or team owners indicating the track was too slippery to race, as there was no direct link to them. Barnhart explained the decision to restart the race: "We could have just tooled around behind the pace car and thrown the checkered flag and the yellow at the same time at 225 and we would have made a lot of fans angry in the race grandstands. Based on the information we had, we were going to try and put on a show for them. Unfortunately, it turned out to be the wrong way to do that."[6]

The race results were appealed by the Newman/Haas racing team (Oriol Servia) and the Target/Chip Ganassi team (Scott Dixon). Barnhart recused himself from the hearing and appointed an independent committee consisting of Jerry Gappens (manager of the New Hampshire Motor Speedway), Rollie Helmling (former president and CEO of USAC) and Jeff Stoops (USAC's chairman of the board). The review focused on whether or not Barnhart as race director had the authority to make the ruling and to roll back the race results. Upon listening to the presentations made by the various participants, the committee issued a statement reaffirming Barnhart's authority and upheld the race results.[7]

The season of controversy continued at the Twin Ring race at Motegi, Japan, when Helio Castroneves passed J. R. Hildebrand under yellow flags on the last lap of the race. At the time of the infraction, Castroneves was running 7th. While he later acknowledged he was wrong in passing, Castroneves believed the infraction would result in his placing 8th in the race. Instead, Barnhart dropped him to the back of the lead lap, resulting in his final ranking of 22nd. Upset by the severe drop in ranking, Castroneves tweeted, "Very disappointing finishing 7th and being put to 22nd. This is just ABSURD !!! It is sad to see just one person being responsible for bringing down the entire series. Brian is inconsistent and even changes the rule book when it is convenient for him, and his own personal interests." He concluded his rant by saying that Brian Barnhart was "a circus clown."[8] IndyCar officials responded by assessing Castroneves a $30,000 fine "for use of improper, profane or disparaging language" in reference to officials for comments made toward the race director via Twitter. As with the fine for Will Power, Castroneves could work off the fine through media appearances on behalf of IndyCar.[9]

Despite the turmoil in the driver ranks, the television ratings for IndyCar continued to show improvement under Bernard's leadership. Average viewership on Versus, now NBC Sports, increased 10 percent to 400,000 for each race. Celebrating the Indianapolis 500's 100th anniversary, ABC reported a 16 percent increase in viewership up to 6.7 million.[10]

After several months on the job, Bernard was fine-tuning his strategy to raise the visibility of IndyCar. He had been very unhappy with the results of the Milwaukee 225 race held at the historic Milwaukee Mile. This race, which was broadcasted on ABC, had a mere 13,000 spectators in the stands, which was not the image Bernard wanted to portray. In an effort to increase the attendance at the races and television viewership, Bernard was thinking about asserting more control over the poorly performing races by taking on responsibilities such as ticketing, promotion and marketing—responsibilities normally handled by the race promoter, not the sanctioning body.

This strategy wasn't without risks. It was the same strategy CART had used in its final months when it was suffering from poor attendance at races and low television ratings. Tim Frost, a Chicago-based motorsports business consultant, explained the risks of this high risk/high reward strategy: "It can cost $3 million to $5 million to do a street or road race. It's a bit less to do an oval race, but it's still a major financial commitment. He better make sure he has the expertise to handle things like ticket sales, corporate hospitality, sponsorship sales, and food and beverage. There are a million of details to deal with beyond just advertising an event, and if you don't execute those things right, and you're operating a number of races, you can lose a lot of money in a hurry."[11]

In an effort to energize the series, Bernard planned a season finale for the Las Vegas Motor Speedway. Departing from the standard format, he was interested in having race car drivers from any series participating, subject to approval by IndyCar. The carrot for the drivers? A $5-million prize to be split with a fan if a non-regular IndyCar driver could start from the back of the pack and win the race. Bernard explained the rationale: "The whole point is to bring in some of the best drivers from around the world to show them and [the viewing audience] how good our [IndyCar] drivers are. This isn't a circus. We're not taking all comers. We want the best drivers to come and challenge our drivers. We think our series drivers are that good."[12]

Bernard had negotiated this race being televised on ABC, and he set a goal of a 1.2 viewership rating for the race. If achieved, it would be a significant improvement over the 2010 season-finale Miami-Homestead viewership rating of a mere 0.3 (or 330,000 households). This race would have stiff competition for television viewership. Also scheduled that day was a NASCAR race and the possibility of a National Football League game if the football lockout was resolved.[13]

Not everyone was thrilled with the proposed Las Vegas race. There were teams and drivers who believed the $5-million prize should be divided among the regular participants in IndyCar. Bernard dismissed that idea, saying, "It's time to shake things up."[14] The $5 million in prize money would be split between the driver and a yet-to-be-named fan. Like the Mega Million or the Powerball lotteries, the winner would have the choice of either taking cash up front or having an annuity with a forty-year payout. The annuity option would result in a pre-tax payment of $62,500 annually to the fan while if the lump sum option were chosen, the pre-tax payment was estimated at $1.3 million.[15] The cost to IndyCar regardless of the method chosen for receipt of the payment would be less than the $5 million advertised value to the winners.

Through this promotional effort, Bernard succeeded in achieving increased interest in this race. The driver chosen for the IndyCar challenge was Dan Wheldon, who just months earlier had won the Indianapolis 500.

Unfortunately, Wheldon was killed in a multiple-car crash on the beginning of lap 12 when his car ran up over the back of another racer and became airborne. Many fans and pundits of IndyCar believed the cause of the wreck was having too many cars in the field—34 for a 1.5-mile oval—and the $5-million prize to Dan Wheldon if he was able to come from the back of the pack to win the race.[16] The drivers' reaction to the race did not reflect the fans' perception of the race venue or the $5-million challenge being the cause behind the wreck; they defended IndyCar. Dario Franchitti said, "It's very unfair to criticize Randy, completely wrong. And finger pointing is not going to do any good here at all."[17]

In December, after an analysis of the crash by IndyCar, both the prize money and the number of cars on the track were dismissed in the official report. Rather, IndyCar attributed the crash to the interplay between the Dallara chassis and the recently repaved track. The track's grooves had not been established, which enabled the cars to race all over the track rather than in the one or two grooves normal at oval tracks. The report also indicated that there was no way to determine prior to the race that the track was not safe. The standard two-day compatibility tests done in November 2010 did not reflect any safety issues with the track.[18]

The crash at Las Vegas not only tarnished IndyCar's image, it also proved expensive. The promotion of the event had resulted in nearly 70,000 spectators at the event. Unlike most races, where IndyCar's role is limited to that of being the sanctioning body, at the Las Vegas race, IndyCar also took on the role of promoter. In the end, IndyCar refunded the majority of the tickets to the event.[19]

After a long racing season with unforced errors leading to controversy, Bernard had little option but to remove Barnhart as the race director. Barnhart would remain with IndyCar as the director of operations. His responsibilities would include the behind-the-scenes logistics and event operations.[20] Hired to fill in the role of race director, Beaux Barfield brought experience to the position, most recently as the race director of the American LeMans Series. In his younger days, he had been an open-wheel racer. He was known to many people in open-wheel racing, having spent four years as a race steward for Champ Car.[21]

At the conclusion of the controversial 2011 racing season, Dario Franchitti was the IndyCar champion. For many years IndyCar had wanted to present a trophy to their champion. Upon the purchase of Champ Car, they wanted the Vanderbilt Cup trophy, which had been tied up in the Champ Car bankruptcy proceedings. Not able to secure the Vanderbilt Cup, they chose another historic trophy, the Astor Cup, to be presented to Franchitti.

The Astor Cup was commissioned by Vincent Astor, the millionaire son of John Jacob Astor IV. The cup was first presented to the winner of the Astor Cup Race at Sheepshead Bay Speedway in 1915 (to Gil Anderson of the Stutz team) and 1916 (to Johnny Aitken of the Speedway Team). Like the Borg-Warner Trophy, awarded to the winner of the Indianapolis 500, the Astor Cup Trophy resides at the Indianapolis Motor Speedway Hall of Fame Museum with replica trophies for the championship driver and team owner.[22]

One of the teams negatively impacted by the new chassis and engine requirements was Newman/Haas Racing. After having been a part of open-wheel racing for 29 years and joining IndyCar in 2008, they announced in December 2011 they were not going to be participating in open-wheel racing. Carl Haas, the founder and co-owner, explained the decision: "The economic climate no longer enables Newman/Haas Racing to participate in open wheel racing at this time."[23]

As 2011 came to a close, Bernard negotiated a race at Quindao, China, to replace the Twin Ring race at Motegi, Japan. The 3.87-mile circuit race would be run on the same weekend as Quindao's International Beer Festival. Bernard explained the rationale for going to Quindao for a race: "Last year, at our sponsorship summit, China was the number 1 place our sponsors wanted to go outside of the United States. As the world's global economy continues to grow and evolve, China, the world's second largest economy, has become a top priority with most American businesses and the sponsors that are committed to IndyCar."[24]

IndyCar also announced changes to its TEAM program, which provided financial support to teams participating in the series. Prior to 2011, any team participating full time in the series was eligible for participation in the TEAM program. For 2011, this support was limited to the top 22 teams. In February, IndyCar announced the TEAM program for 2012 would be limited to 20 teams. Of the 20 teams to be provided support, 18 finished in the top 22 teams during the IndyCar 2011 season. The other two teams, Carpenter Racing and Lotus Dragon Racing, were selected after making presentations to IndyCar of their marketing and organizational plans. To qualify for a guaranteed $1.1 million in financial support, participants in the TEAM program had to participate in qualifications for the Indianapolis 500 and the road trip to Quindao. Total prize money for the IndyCar season including the Indianapolis 500 was estimated at $39 million.[25]

More good news was received at IndyCar headquarters when Firestone agreed to extend its contract to provide tires through 2012. Additionally, they also agreed to continue as the title sponsor for the Firestone Indy Lights Series.[26]

After Tony George quit the Hulman and Company board in July 2009, the board was expanded for the first time with people outside of the Hulman-George inner circle. First additions included Andre B. Lacy, chairman of Indianapolis-based logistics and distribution firm LDI, and Michael L. Smith, the former chairman of medical insurance company Anthem, Inc. Having benefitted from the expertise and views of these outsiders, Mari Hulman George announced an additional expansion of the board to eleven members in March 2012. The new members included Jeffrey Belskus, a longtime Indianapolis Motor Speedway employee; John F. Ackerman, the chairman of private equity fund Cardinal Capital Partners; Mark D. Miles, the CEO of Central Indiana Cooperative Partnership, Inc.; and James T. Morris, the president of Pacers Sports Entertainment.[27]

Following through on his promise to strengthen the IndyCar feeder series, Bernard announced that the Skip Barber Racing School would join forces with IndyCar to create the Skip Barber Racing Academy for those interested in becoming professional race car drivers but lacking either professional racing or karting experience. As a prerequisite to the academy, a candidate needed to complete a three-day Formula Car Racing School. The top thirty-three participants in the racing school would be chosen for the academy and, after completion, would be able to participate in the Skip Barber Shootout with the possibility of sponsored participation in the Mazda Road to Indy.[28]

The 2012 racing season opened with the new Dallara chassis and three engine providers—Honda, Chevrolet and Lotus. IndyCar officials hoped the new chassis would generate increased interest in the races and that having three engine manufacturers would increase the competitiveness of the races. In various racing team's headquarters, there continued to be a lot of complaints about the cost of the new equipment, and particularly the cost of the aero kits, which had been mandated but not yet implemented.

With the adoption of new equipment, unanticipated issues frequently arise. That was certainly true for the new turbocharged engines. While preparing for the third race of the season, the Toyota Grand Prix of Long Beach, James Hinchcliffe, a driver for the GoDaddy.com team, went to the Infineon Raceway (now Sonoma Raceway) for testing. During the tests, the car experienced the unanticipated failure of its Chevrolet engine. Chevrolet engineers tore down the engine and discovered a problem they believed would impact all eleven cars running in the IndyCar series with Chevrolet engines. As a result, they issued an order to immediately change the engine on all eleven teams. Among the IndyCar mandates is that when an engine is changed prior to its expected life of 1,850 miles, the car would incur a ten-spot penalty. This penalty applied to all eleven teams, which replaced their Chevrolet engines.[29] Better to take a penalty at the beginning of the race than to have an increased probability of an engine failure during the middle of the race.

Some IndyCar teams felt the mandated ten-spot penalty was unjust, given that it was a manufacturer's problem for all of the teams running with Chevrolet engines. IndyCar technical director Will Phillips defended the league's position on the penalty. "The teams and the manufactures came together as a team. If there are no teams, the manufacturer can't run their product. And if there are no manufactures, the teams have nothing to run on."[30] With concern for the impact upon the fans of the Indianapolis 500, IndyCar announced that the ten-spot penalty for changing engines would not apply to the Indianapolis race but would rather be implemented on the next race on the schedule, to be held at Belle Island in Detroit.[31]

Meanwhile, Honda was having its own problems with its engines. The engines had not performed well during the first four races of the season. In order to achieve parity with the Chevrolet teams, Honda wanted to make changes to the engine configuration for the ten cars running with Honda engines. Honda had the support of Borg-Warner, the suppler of turbochargers for both Honda and Chevrolet, for a slightly altered compressor cover whose function was to equalize the performance of the two types of turbochargers. Chevrolet threatened a protest before the Grand Prix of Long Beach, causing IndyCar officials to order the removal of the replacement parts.[32] After the race, IndyCar officials declared the proposed modification was legal, resulting in Chevrolet's immediately filing a protest. To hear the protest, a three-member panel was named including Hans Peter Kollmeier, the former head of Mercedes-Benz Motorsport's engine and powertrain, selected by General Motors/Chevrolet; Jim Voyles, an attorney and partner in the law firm of Voyles, Zahn and Paul, selected by Honda; and Jack Snyder, an attorney and member of the Indianapolis Motor Speedway board, selected by IndyCar.[33] After a ten-hour hearing of technical and legal arguments, the three-member panel ruled that the modification to the turbocharger wanted by Honda was permitted under IndyCar rules. With the ruling having gone against Chevrolet, they filed an appeal.[34] Brian Barnhart solicited retired Indiana Supreme Court judge Theodore Boehm to mediate the dispute between the two parties. Like the three-member panel, Judge Boehm ruled in favor of Honda.[35] John Barnes of Panther Racing was one of the people critical of the handling of this issue by IndyCar. He posted on his Twitter account, "Today is the day to resolve TURBOGATE! I hope @indycar gets their act together. It has been embarrassing." IndyCar officials took offense to this tweet, fined him $25,000, and placed him on probation for the remainder of the year.[36]

The engine difficulties also extended to newcomer Lotus, which had signed up four teams—HVM Racing, Dragon Racing, Bryan Herta Autosports and Dreyer Reinbold Racing. After a change in ownership resulted in unanticipated delays, Lotus was unable to fulfill all of its commitments. In late April 2012, they were dropped by Bryan Herta Autosports and Dreyer Reinbold Racing as their engine supplier. Randy Bernard of the Indy Racing League promised to help the two teams secure new engines.[37]

After the inability of Lotus to supply engines to two of the teams, it seemed unfair for these teams to be penalized ten spots on the starting grid for changing their engine supplier. As a result, the Indy Racing League issued a rule for "Supplemental Guidelines for Engine Manufacturers" prohibiting teams from seeking other engines unless there were extraordinary circumstances. Trevor Knowles, the IRL's director of engine development, explained the rationale for the rule: "The intent of the rule is to try to help to build a partnership between a team and its engine manufacturer. Having a long-term commitment helps ease concerns about confidentiality of any information a manufacturer might share with a team. It also limits a manufacturer's ability to drop a team from its line-up if they are going through a bad patch. Without it, one would see a drift of all the teams with the best results to the manufacturers with the best results creating a big imbalance across the field."[38]

Also experiencing problems with the Lotus engine was Dragon Racing. In a dispute that began before the season opened, Lotus and Dragon Racing could not agree about what contracts were signed. Adding additional stress to the relationship, Lotus delivered the chassis and engine to Dragon Racing the day before preliminary activities began for the season opener in St. Petersburg. Unable to get satisfactory resolution from Lotus, Dragon Racing returned the engines and all the spare parts. The Associated Press reported that Dragon Racing's principal, Jay Penske, had filed legal action in California saying, "Dragon has had enough of Lotus' deceit and wrongdoing. Dragon has put an end to its ill-fated relationship with Lotus and now seeks recompense for the damages inflicted upon it."[39]

Although not formally announced, it was apparent Dragon Racing would adopt the Chevrolet engine. A dead giveaway of this action was the wearing of Chevrolet shirts by the Dragon Racing crew rather than the previously issued Lotus shirts. And Chevrolet engineers were seen going in and out of the Dragon Racing garage. Behind the scenes Roger Penske was helping his son to change engine manufacturers. The elder Penske's company, Ilmor Engineering, manufactured the Chevrolet racing engine.[40] The announcement of

Dragon Racing's change in engine manufacturers came on May 16. Dragon Racing's two drivers, Sebastien Bourdais and Katherine Legge, had just eleven days to test the new engine-and-chassis combination and qualify before the running of the Indianapolis 500.[41]

As the teams got ready for the Indianapolis 500, eleven teams were fined $15,000 each for infractions during the pre-qualifying technical inspection. Including other fines assessed, the Indianapolis 500 garnered $275,000 from thirteen teams.[42] The teams that were fined were unhappy that they had not been told in advance that the league was going to strictly enforce the rules. With money being tight for the teams, the penalties were another thorn in the racing teams' sides. In an effort to try to explain why the penalties were assessed, Beaux Barfield, race director, said, "I know a lot of the teams are upset at the fines, and it might sting a bit right now. But we want to make sure that the big prize—$7 million in total prize money on Sunday and $3 million to win—is earned fairly."[43]

At the Pole Day shoot out, Chevrolet had eight of the top nine spots. But on race day, driving cars powered by Honda engines, Dario Franchitti won the race and his teammate, Scott Dixon, placed second. This led to griping by some Chevrolet teams that Honda had been "sandbagging" during the qualifications and they had been put at a competitive disadvantage by the decision to allow Honda to use its carburetor cover. There were also charges by some in the Chevrolet camp who believed the Chip Ganassi Team had used an upgraded Honda engines for the race. Will Phillips, IndyCar's vice president of technology, acknowledged that the Honda's engines could have upgraded calibration and mapping; however, the same could be said for Chevrolet and Lotus engines. Phillips strongly denied that the Ganassi team had an advantage with the engines: "The manufacturer does not pick who gets which engine, IndyCar does that. The Honda engines for the race were already allocated prior to qualifying."[44]

The multiple officiating errors, the fines assessed, the equipment requirements and the "turbogate" brouhaha led to discontent among various IndyCar teams. Throughout the month of May, rumors were floating throughout open-wheel racing and Indianapolis of a brewing rebellion. Despite efforts to tamp down the level of discontent, it continued to fester, and by the time of the running of the Indianapolis 500 it was a full boil. It had started with the driver discontent the previous racing season that had resulted in the removal of Brian Barnhart as the series race official. And there continued to be many who believed that Bernard's decision to have the $5-million Las Vegas Challenge was a primary contributor to the death of popular driver Dan Wheldon.

In an interview with Indianapolis radio station The Fan, Robin Miller of Speed TV talked about the discontent: "There's always this under bed of unhappiness in auto racing, and it usually starts with the car owner, then permeates to the fans and drivers. Everything is never good enough, it's always bad news. Is it perfect? No, but it's a helluva lot better than it was three or four or five years ago. If the car owners are unhappy because they are not getting their way or because they don't have their yes-man little puppet in there, then I suggest they go and find something else to do."[45]

Seven days after the running of the Indianapolis 500, Bernard finally acknowledged that there was an effort to get him ousted as head of IndyCar. He posted to his Twitter account, "It is true that an owner is calling others trying to get me fired. I have had several owners confirm this. Disappointing." Many fans believed the source of the discontent was Ed Carpenter, Tony George's stepson. Carpenter denied his involvement, tweeting, "For those accusing me of being a conspirator, I'm not the one talking and creating this story." Carpenter wasn't the only suspect in the palace revolt. Some believed it might be Roger Penske, who had been upset over the Honda turbocharger decision. But Penske was publicly supporting Bernard. Michael Andretti had been named as the leader of the insurrection by Robin Miller, which Andretti denied in a tweet: "Very disappointed in Robin Miller reporting things before knowing the truth! The truth is I'm not leading any lynching."[46] Bernard later tweeted that the team owner behind the rumor was not Ed Carpenter, Roger Penske, Jay Penske, or Bobby Rahal. Andretti admitted to having been in a dust-up with Bernard, but he continued to deny he was behind the palace revolt: "Yeah, I unloaded on Randy the other day, but it wasn't about his job; it was about trying to fix some things. There's no lynch mob. It's not about getting his job. It's about helping [the series]."[47]

Bernard's strategy of exposing the discontent and seeking a show of support from the Indianapolis Motor Speedway management appears to have worked, at least on a short-term basis. Various car owners were showing support for Bernard, and the rumors were diminishing.[48] But this was the calm in the middle of the storm. It was about to come raging back.

As in 2011, the racing teams wanted IndyCar to back off on the requirement for the aero kits. The underlying reason was cost. Each kit cost $75,000. But if a team participated in a full season, they would need at least two different aero kits for each car—one for high-speed oval racing and a different one for street races and road races. For one of the large racing teams, such as Ganassi, Penske or Andretti, the cost for the aero kits could approach $500,000.

The teams were being squeezed financially. With the loss of Lotus as an engine supplier, the cost of the engine leases increased. The Dallara chassis, initially with an estimated cost of $385,000, was actually costing the teams closer to $600,000. Another burr under the team owners' saddles was the cost of replacement parts, which were more expensive than the old chassis parts and couldn't be used in the new chassis.

Some of the team owners hoped that by not adapting the aero kits, the engine manufacturers would reduce the cost of the engine lease. Team owner A. J. Foyt told Speed.com, "I'd like to see the engine manufacturers take the money they were going to spend on those kits and take a little more off the engine lease." Unfortunately, the reality was that the engine manufacturers had been spending money on research and development costs for the aero kits and were unlikely to reduce the costs even if the implementation was postponed.[49]

The on-track action resumed with the Detroit Grand Prix. The track selected was the 2.08-mile Belle Isle course, which hadn't been used for an IndyCar race since 2008. The race was to be 90 laps. Just as in the initial races at the Indianapolis Motor Speedway in 1909, the Belle Isle course didn't hold up well to the punishment of the race cars. The track began to deteriorate, with asphalt crumbling. On lap 44, James Hinchcliffe hit the wall going into a turn. Recognizing the danger caused by the condition of the track, race officials red-flagged the race at lap 45. The organizers of the Detroit Grand Prix spent the next two hours patching the track with quick-drying concrete filler and epoxy resin. Meanwhile, spectators abandoned the race and ABC switched the race telecast over to its sister station, ESPN. After the delay, the race was restarted, but only an additional 15 laps were run.[50]

Controversy surfaced again the next weekend following the Firestone 500 at the Texas Motor Speedway. Justin Wilson won the race after Graham Rahal bumped the wall with two laps remaining.[51] In the post-race technical review, Wilson's car was discovered to have an unapproved sidepod. But not only was he allowed to keep the win, the penalty was a mere five points and $7,500.[52] With thirteen teams having been fined in aggregate $275,000 during pre-inspection technical issues for the Indianapolis 500, you can imagine the uproar caused by IndyCar's actions. Upon reflection, Bernard acknowledged that the officiating call wasn't right. "In hindsight, we should have been more stringent and harsh. If someone wins and gets caught cheating, they shouldn't get points or any dollars, and I think you'll see that change."[53]

The following weekend, IndyCar ventured to the historic Milwaukee Mile track for a 225-lap race. Once again, IndyCar had an unforced error with its officiating. This time, on the 103rd lap, Scott Dixon was penalized for jumping the restart of the race. The only problem was that he didn't.

When the IndyCar officials reviewed the tape of the start, they were looking at the wrong restart. To add insult to injury, the restart used by the officials had been waved off. Needless to say, team owner Chip Ganassi was exasperated. He fumed, "That was a call on a restart that never happened." Race director Beaux Barfield acknowledged the error: "We thought we were looking at the correct [replay]. If we would have played it four or five seconds more, we would have realized [the field] got to the start/finish line and then got the yellow flag. That was my mistake."[54] But the damage had been done. There was nothing Barfield could do to reverse the error. As a result, Dixon finished eleventh in the race and his series ranking dropped from second to third.[55]

Then another shoe dropped for Bernard. This time not from the team owners or the drivers but rather from China. Quindoa's government was under the leadership of a new mayor, and he wasn't happy with the agreement reached by his predecessor with IndyCar. The major issue was the race's being scheduled for the same day as Quindao's International Beer Festival. Notification was given by Quindoa barely two months before the mid–August running of the race, which did not give IndyCar officials enough time to schedule a replacement.[56] Having fallen below the required sixteen-race schedule, the cancellation jeopardized many of the contracts with sponsors and television.[57] Worse yet, China did not fulfill the monetary agreement for a $4-million sanctioning fee that was crucial for the finances of the league.[58]

Adding to Bernard's woes, television ratings had a double-digit decline for the series during the 2012 year. This would directly impact the value to various sponsors not only for the series but also for the teams. As had been seen in earlier episodes of declining television ratings, track owners frequently renegotiated the sanction fees for the races as the value of the race had declined for them also. Additionally, it became known that the series sponsor, Izod, was planning on leaving.[59]

After a year of turmoil, the *Indianapolis Business Journal* reported Bernard's firing and subsequent negotiation of his severance package in late October. This report was refuted by Indianapolis Motor Speedway officials.[60] With the drama was being played out in the newspapers for all to see, Graham Rahal tweeted, "Come on people. Either keep Randy or fire him but this is foolish and embarrassing for the sport."[61] The chaos at the Indianapolis Motor Speedway's headquarters on West 16th Street generated by this report resulted in a hastily called teleconference board meeting. The result was an official announcement of Bernard's leaving by "mutual separation."[62]

The response by the team owners was split. There were those who were happy Bernard had departed from the IRL, but there were others who were disappointed in the decision. Issuing a statement of support for the Indianapolis Motor Speedway was Michael Andretti; the statement read, "We believe that the board of directors of the Indianapolis Motor Speedway Corporation, IMS President and CEO Jeff Belskus and the Hulman-George family will make the right decisions that leverage the many strengths of IndyCar for the benefit of the fans, teams, drivers, promoters, and sponsors."[63] Roger Penske was critical of Bernard's apparent firing. He told the Associated Press, "It's a big disappointment; the board continues to show poor judgment. There is no future plan. The series had momentum. New cars, new engines, new race formats, all brought about by Randy. No business can run with a senior management change every two years."[64] Likewise, Bobby Rahal of Rahal Letterman Lanigan Racing was disappointed in Bernard's departure: "I've never seen a series with so many good things going for it consistently shooting itself in the foot. We've got great races. Randy put some great people in place there and got rid of a lot of the dead wood and I would just love to know the reasoning [for Sunday's board decision]. It's just embarrassing."[65]

More intrigue was added to the IndyCar drama when Tony George, once again, resigned from Hulman and Company's board of directors. His comments to the press about his decision fueled speculation that he was again trying to regain control of IndyCar. He said, "I realize that my recent efforts to explore the possibility of acquiring IndyCar represent the appearance of a conflict, and it is in everybody's best interest that I resign from the Hulman & Company board. It goes without saying that I want to do what is in the best interest for this organization."[66]

Sports Business Journal reported that George led a group of investors to buy IndyCar. The investors included Roger Penske, Chip Ganassi, Michael Andretti, Kevin Kalkhoven and Zak Brown, the principal of the Indianapolis-based sports marketing firm Just Marketing International.[67] Later the details of the deal came out. George's group was willing to buy the series for $5 million, subject to a satisfactory agreement being reached on participation in the Indianapolis 500. Additionally, the group indicated they had $25 million in working capital to support the series. Proposed leadership included Zak Brown as the CEO and commissioner of the series; Mike O'Driscoll, the chairman of Jaguar Heritage, the COO and president of the series; Terry Angstadt, the former president of the IndyCar commercial division; Claire Roberts, the CEO of ArbiterSports, an NCAA subsidiary technology group; and George.[68]

The offer was attractive from the standpoint that it would stop IndyCar's dependence upon the Indianapolis Motor Speedway and Hulman and Company for financial support. But the $5 million was a lowball offer in comparison to other sports leagues. It was 10 percent of the cost of a Major League Soccer franchise and less than 25 percent of the value of the Indianapolis Indians,[69] the hometown AAA minor-league team affiliated with the Pittsburg Pirates.

Selling IndyCar would have some serious negative impacts upon the Indianapolis Motor Speedway. The Speedway's influence would be limited. No longer would they make the decisions regarding the suppliers, the chassis and engine makers, or the rules for the league. They would be reduced to another track where the series ran. On a longer-term basis, they also ran the risk that if the group purchasing the series were to fail, they would have to pick up the pieces to ensure the Indianapolis 500 would have a sanctioning body.[70] Given the risk of selling IndyCar, the familiar refrain by the Indianapolis Motor Speedway of the business's not being for sale is not surprising. Jeff Belskus went on to say they had not received nor reviewed an offer from the George group.[71]

Epilogue

Open-wheel racing was again in crisis. Some pundits believed there were strong parallels to the collapse of CART/Champ Car and predicted the Indy-Car series couldn't be saved.[1] Certainly, whomever Hulman and Company selected to lead the resurgence of the league had his work cut out for him. The biggest issues to be addressed continued to be the ones plaguing Indy-Car/CART/Champ Car for years—low attendance at races outside of the Indianapolis 500, tepid television viewership leading to a frequent turnover of sponsors, and the lack of recognizable stars among the race car drivers. There was also the challenge of regaining the interest of thousands of fans who had abandoned Indy car racing, having grown tired of the turmoil and internal feuding for the past three decades. Larry DeGaris, the director of academic sports marketing programs at the University of Indianapolis, identified another problem underlying the television viewership and race attendance: "They have a very serious problem with an aging demographic. They have to appeal to a younger audience."[2]

On an interim basis, assuming the mantle of the IndyCar CEO role was Jeff Belskus, president of the Indianapolis Motor Speedway and Bernard's former boss. As the Speedway began a search, Belskus indicated that the board was looking for a candidate with "experience as a CEO, [who is] a good businessperson and [who] has experience in sports and entertainment. Experience in motorsports would be a bonus but not a requirement."

The Speedway reportedly received eight to ten unsolicited resumes from people interested in the position. The Speedway also had three strong internal candidates—Jeff Belskus, Doug Boles and Mark Miles. Belskus, a long-term Hulman and Company and Indianapolis Motor Speedway employee, had a strong accounting background. He had served as the CFO for both the Indianapolis Motor Speedway and Hulman and Company and was also the CEO after Tony George's departure in 2009. Douglas Boles joined the Indianapolis Motor Speedway in a public relations role in 2011. An attorney, he was one of the founders of Panther Racing. Immediately preceding his joining the Speedway, he was employed by Atlanta-based Ignition, a marketing firm with high-powered clients such as Coca-Cola, Delta, Arby's Foundation, John Deere and Honda. The third internal candidate was Mark Miles, who had recently joined the board of directors. He was the president and CEO of the Central Indiana Corporate Partnership, a coalition of leading central-Indiana-based businesses and university presidents focused on the betterment of central Indiana. His background included fifteen years as the CEO of the ATP Tour (the men's pro tennis tour). He also was at the forefront of Indianapolis's successful hosting of the Pan American Games in 1987 and Super Bowl XLVI in 2012.[3]

It did not take long for the Hulman and Company board to make a decision about leadership. But the decision wasn't about the leadership of Indy-Car; rather it was about the leadership of the holding company, Hulman and Company. On November 20, Mari Hulman George announced Mark D. Miles as new CEO for Hulman and Company. Miles was a savvy power player in the Indianapolis community. After graduating from Wabash College, he went to work for three powerhouse Indiana politicians: former Indianapolis mayor William H. Hudnut III, former senator Richard Lugar and former Indiana senator and vice presidential candidate Dan Quayle. Using his skills navigating the political spectrum, he then joined one of Indianapolis' leading companies, Eli Lilly & Company, in their local, state and national governmental affairs efforts. Miles was also the chair of the Indianapolis campaign to lure the 1987 Pan American games to the city. He gained additional experience in the sports world when he led the men's tennis circuit, the ATP, to new heights. Under his direction, prize money grew from $42 million in 1992 to $85 million in 2005. He was also chair of the 2012 Super Bowl committee, which brought Super Bowl XVLI to Indianapolis.[4]

One person singing Miles' praises was Frank Supovitz, senior vice president of events for the National Football League, who had worked with Miles on Super Bowl XLVI. Supovitz said, "Mark is one part big thinker, one part consensus builder and 100 percent passionate about Indianapolis and its place on the national sports landscape. I have no doubt he will take IndyCar and its associated businesses to an entirely new level."[5]

Having led the Central Indiana Corporate Partnership, Miles understood the economic impact upon Indianapolis of the events at the Indianapolis Motor Speedway and associated race-related businesses. A study by the Indiana University Public Policy Institute reflected a $510-million economic impact generated annually by the Indianapolis Motor Speedway, the IndyCar teams, the Dallara facility and visitors attending the Indianapolis 500, the

Brickyard 400 and the Moto GP. Included in the economic impact was approximately $235 million in wages to a workforce estimated at 6,200 jobs.[6]

From his years with the ATP, Miles understood the global reach of the Indianapolis 500. In an interview with John Oreovitz, Miles commented, "During those years living and traveling outside of the United States more than 50% of the time, I can tell you it's absolutely true: You can't go anywhere in the world and have a conversation with any people who have any kind of worldview and not have them know about Indy, IndyCar and the Indianapolis Motor Speedway. So I come to this challenge with the perspective that we have a remarkable opportunity with a remarkable, potent, global brand."[7]

Miles also understood the need to get the various constituencies—team owners, drivers, promoters, sponsors and suppliers—to begin working together instead of being at odds with each other. Politically astute, Miles said, "I realize there are personalities and history [with IndyCar], but I'll work very hard to bring a fresh perspective and build some trust." He had been through a similar situation when he took over the ATP. Miles reminisced, "There were really hard feelings, worse than hard feelings. There were competitive events being organized to run against each other. It was a mess."

Mark Miles.

Things were so bad at the ATP he had been told by some insiders the group would fold before he got his bags unpacked at the London office. Miles issued a call to action to the various constituencies who had been squabbling since before the split of USAC and CART. "But the sport, I hope to find, will recognize that [success] is predicated on our ability to work together."[8]

As he rolled up his sleeves at the helm of Hulman and Company, Miles had his work cut out for him in association with IndyCar. One of the items on his agenda was the continual surfacing of rumors that IndyCar and/or the Indianapolis Motor Speedway would be sold. This speculation, which first surfaced shortly after the death of Tony Hulman, continued to be in play despite consistent efforts by Mari Hulman George and the Indianapolis Motor Speedway to quell the chatter. And for the past three years, the speculation had reached a crescendo point with the various efforts of Tony George to buy the IndyCar series. Upon his appointment as CEO of Hulman and Company, Miles attempted, once again, to quell the rumors: "I think that the destinies of IMS and the Indianapolis 500-Mile Race and IndyCar Series are inextricably welded, woven together. So we are determined to grow the Indy-Car Series as a sport, and that will help the Indianapolis 500-Mile Race in the process."[9]

Chief among the concerns was the diminishing number of spectators at the various IndyCar races as well as the Indianapolis 500 and lower television viewership, which drives the value of the series. Other issues needing to be resolved were finding a new IndyCar series sponsor; resolution of the issues surrounding tire suppliers, engine suppliers, and the aero kits; and finding both a sponsor and tire supplier for the Indy Lights series.[10] Another issue lurking in the background was the possibility of Formula One establishing a new regional championship for the Americas. Formula One already ran the Grand Prix of Austin (Texas), the Grand Prix of Montreal (Canada) and the Grand Prix of San Paolo (Brazil) and was exploring a fourth Grand Prix race, possibly in New Jersey. Under discussion was the establishment of establishing a GP 2 and GP 3 series that would use the same four tracks and would increase the exposure of Formula One from four to eight races. Formula One already ran successful GP 2 and GP 3 races in Asia, Europe and the Middle East. This could be a long-term threat to IndyCar if Formula One established a grass-roots interest in their brand of open-wheel racing.[11]

Miles would not have the day-to-day responsibilities of running IndyCar. The task of stabilizing the series initially fell to Belskus, who had taken over the responsibilities after the departure of Bernard. Understanding the necessity to turn the series around, Belskus immediately reached out to various IndyCar constituencies. Belskus commented, "I spent a lot of time in the last three weeks working and engaging with team owners, promoters and sponsors, engaging fans and understanding what opportunities we have and what the barriers are to those opportunities."[12] By the end of November 2012, the *Indianapolis Business Journal* reported that Miles was looking for a candidate to run IndyCar with experience in auto racing and with solid sponsor contacts. Miles also indicated that the job of running IndyCar as well as the Indianapolis Motor Speedway was too big for any one person.

An interesting list of potential candidates for the IndyCar czar starting circulating throughout the open-wheel racing world. They included Zak Brown, the CEO of Just Marketing International, who had been tagged as the person who would run the series if Tony George had been successful in his bid to buy the series; Scott Atherton, the head of the American LeMans Series; George Pyne, the former NASCAR chief operations officer; Mike O'Driscoll, the former Jaguar managing director; and Andrew Craig, who led CART when it became a public company.[13]

While pondering the management structure for IndyCar, there were other nuts-and-bolts issues needing to be addressed. Lotus, which had struggled to provide engines for the IndyCar series, was released from its supplier contract in mid–December. This meant the remaining engine suppliers, Chevrolet and Honda, would each be required to fill the engine requirements for up to 60 percent of the field.[14] IndyCar management was able to renew the tire supply contract with Firestone through 2018. Prior to his departure, Bernard had been talking with Hoosier Racing Tire Company, reportedly the biggest supplier of racing tires in North America, about becoming the tire supplier for IndyCar. It would have been a boost to Hoosier Racing Tire to add IndyCar to the stable of series running on its tread, and it was reportedly willing to spend as much marketing money as Firestone if it was selected.[15]

Much of the continuing unhappiness of the IndyCar teams was the cost of the Dallara DW12 chassis, which was well in excess of the anticipated cost. In January 2013, Belskus negotiated a deal with Dallara to reduce the cost of spare parts by 14 percent for the 2013 racing season—not exactly the 20 percent reduction desired by the teams, but certainly an improvement. The savings to the teams was estimated at approximately $50,000 per car.[16]

Another challenge was that the Indianapolis Motor Speedway, once the crown jewel of auto racing, was showing its age. It badly needed a facelift, particularly in comparison to the new Circuit of the Americas facility in Austin, Texas, and the planned $400 million in upgrades to the Daytona International Speedway. Derek Daly, a former Indy car driver and a sports commentator for WISH-TV in Indianapolis, said of the facility, "The luster is gone from the Indianapolis Motor Speedway. It creates an unattractive sports platform for commercial sponsors to get involved. The problems will take years to fix. The sooner they get started the better." Miles acknowledged the need: "If you think of any major professional event or high-level collegiate event, the facility has a lot to do with the vitality of the event aesthetically and for the fan experience and economically."[17]

Understanding that the Indianapolis Motor Speedway facilities were not keeping pace with other race tracks, Miles instituted a full review of the needs of the Speedway. The master plan reflected needs of $120 million, which included lighting ($20 million), grandstand upgrades ($15 million), video boards around the track ($15 million) and measures to address Americans with Disabilities Act needs ($10 million). Other industry experts pegged the costs at nearer $200 million.[18] The question was how to fund these needs.

Referring to the Indiana University Public Policy Institute study reflecting the $510-million economic impact of the Indianapolis Motor Speedway on the state of Indiana, Miles commented, "This study shows how the Indianapolis Motor Speedway and its associated industries form a powerful engine that helps drive the Indiana economy. The Super Bowl brought a tremendous economic impact to Indianapolis and Indiana in 2012, and this state is very fortunate that IMS, its events and associated industries deliver an even greater economic contribution every single year."[19] With his experience in the political affairs area for Eli Lilly & Company, behind the scenes, Miles worked with the Indiana General Assembly to provide monies for some much-needed upgrades to the Speedway. The legislation crafted would have the Indianapolis Motor Speedway receiving up to $5 million per year for the next 20 years, for upgrades for a total of $100 million. The funding would be through the Indiana Motorsports Funding District. The loan, guaranteed by Hulman and Company, would be repaid through an increase in sales and income taxes paid by the Indianapolis Motor Speedway. Recognizing the importance of motorsports to Indiana's economy, which employs an estimated 23,000 Hoosiers at an average salary of $63,000, the state also created a fund of up to $5 million per year for use by other motorsports-related companies. This fund would be administered by the Indiana Economic Development Corporation.[20]

To understand the full scope of the needs of the Indianapolis Motor Speedway and IndyCar and also to help determine the long-term viability of IndyCar, the Indianapolis Motor Speedway engaged the Boston Consulting Group to review their operations. Their 115-page report was issued after conversations both with folks at the Indianapolis Motor Speedway and IndyCar and also with some focus groups. After having fought for the past seventeen years to position IndyCar as the open-wheel racing league, the report confirmed the linkage between IndyCar and the Indianapolis Motor Speedway. Additionally, and possibly more importantly, the report recommended the Hulman-George family not sell the Indianapolis Motor Speedway or Indy-Car.

The focus groups also helped to define what separates IndyCar from its rival NASCAR in the minds of fans. Top among the list was that spectators placed more emphasis on increasing speeds than the engineering of the race car.[21] For Indy car fans, who had thrived during the 1950s, 1960s and 1970s when speeds were increasing on a rapid pace, it had been a long twenty-three years since Arie Luykendyk's speed record established in 1990 was broken.[22] As a roadmap to the future, the Boston Consulting Group's report suggested implementing marketing strategies to position "IndyCar as having the most skilled, daredevil drivers and not theatrical, off-track personalities." It also offered some concrete suggestions for implementation including condensing the season, adding a second international season, and having a three-race play-off with the finale to be in Indianapolis.[23]

Since his arrival at Hulman and Company, Miles had been reevaluating the management structure of IndyCar and the Indianapolis Motor Speedway. From his comments, there is no doubt that he was thinking of streamlining the two organizations. "Folks have sort of thought that we are just looking for a person to replace Randy and I don't know if that's where we'll end up. First thing is, our organization has kind of built two organizations and you've got a structure of the Indianapolis Motor Speedway organization that has sales and marketing and licensing and communications and then you've got the exact same functions staff differently at the IndyCar organization, across the street from each other. So I think anybody coming to it would say, 'Could we be a higher-performing, more effective organization with more money to invest in human resources if we put those together?'"[24]

Prior to the running of the 2013 Indianapolis 500, Miles selected Derrick Walker to be the president of Operations and Competition. Walker had a unique blend of qualifications. He worked for many years for the Penske organization before becoming a team owner. When hired by IndyCar, he was the general manager of the Ed Carpenter Racing Team. In announcing his selection, Miles said of Walker, "Derrick stood out because his decades of experience in North American open-wheel racing blend ownership and management of his own race teams and other teams. He understands how to balance the technical and financial operations of our sport, and his confident leadership will provide a firm, clear direction for long-term IndyCar operations and competition."[25]

Prior to Miles' selection of Walker, Penske had told the Associated Press, "We've never had a strong enough leader as they do in NASCAR to say, 'Hey guys, here's the rules, here's how we race, and guess what, if you don't like it, park your car outside and sit in the stands. That's what we need. We need some leadership.'"[26] Walker appeared to be the type of leader the participants in IndyCar would respect. Of his appointment, Walker acknowledged the need for strong leadership: "I think when you look at the quality of the field of IndyCar, it demands a strong governing body that has a vision and the leadership that is required to match the quality of our teams. We have a responsibility and obligation to be as good as we can as a governing body."

Walker's appointment was cheered by race car drivers and team managers. Penske team member Will Power, who drove for Team Australia (which Walker headed between 2005 and 2007 on the Champ Car circuit), said, "I think Derrick Walker is the perfect choice. He is a brilliant man who understands all facets of racing and I think his time as a team owner will be very important in his new role with IndyCar because he knows what the teams are faced with." Mike Hull, the managing director for Target/Chip Ganassi Racing, said, "I think it's a great selection because of the wealth of experience that he has is hard to match and he provides relevance to the direction that IndyCar wants to go and Mark Miles is creating positive change by hiring people like Derrick."[27]

One of the things IndyCar fans had been missing was the historical innovation of open-wheel racing, which led to new automotive breakthroughs and higher speeds. Mike Hull acknowledged this: "Innovation comes from the generation that Derrick and I represent. I understand that innovation and technology has been reigned in a bit by cost containment but I think there still has to be a positive way for us to tell the positive story of technology in IndyCar racing because it is well advanced of other forms of motorsports but it takes it on the chin because it is referred to as a spec series."[28] Miles and Walker both understood the need to return to open-wheel racing's historical roots. Miles pledged that IndyCar would seek to have more technical innovation while still trying to make the sport safer. Walker put some meat on the bones, saying, "In the short term, we'll look for incremental changes to our cars through components such as aerodynamic, horsepower and tires. In a way, we're going back to the future. Indy cars have always been about innovation and speed, and our goal is to open the door for that again."[29]

By July, Miles had formulated his strategy for his team going forward. Rather than have two silos, one at the Indianapolis Motor Speedway and a second at IndyCar, with duplicate functions, the team would be function-based across Hulman and Company. With the exception of the hiring of Walker to run race operations, Miles utilized people who already had ties to the organizations to fill the roles. Belskus would be the president of Hulman and Company as well as their CFO. Doug Boles, who had been the chief public relations officer, would become the Speedway's president responsible for its day-to-day operations. Robby Greene, the interim COO of IndyCar, was chosen as the head of IMS Productions, a multimedia production company that provides live production services for national sporting and entertainment events for multiple television networks including ABC, CBS, NBC,

Fox, ESPN, NBC Sports and CBC. The only job remaining to be filled was the president of Hulman Motorsport Properties, which was responsible for all IMS and IndyCar sales, marketing, public relations, television and broadcast licensing, and licensing of intellectual property.[30]

IndyCar also addressed the continuing residual of "turbogate" by mandating that all cars beginning with the 2014 series would run with a twin turbocharged engine. Derek Walker commented on the change: "In an effort for parity throughout the turbocharger range, mandating a twin turbocharger system simplifies our efforts to ensure even closer competition. Both manufacturers displayed a willingness to use a common turbo spec for 2014, so it made sense to mandate a twin turbocharger that maintains the performance we've come to expect while keeping the technology relevant to the automobile industry."[31]

Even though Honda and Chevrolet agreed with the twin turbocharged engines, they were limited to charging $695,000 per engine lease to the teams. The all-in cost of the design, development and manufacture of the engine was higher than could be recouped by the engine lease. Simply put, the engine manufacturers were supporting the teams much in the same fashion that the tire companies had historically supported racing teams. Additionally, the engine supply contract required both companies to supply up to 60 percent of the field. While indicating a willingness to provide engines for an additional two or three years, Honda requested that IndyCar pursue additional engine manufacturers to participate in the series. Roger Griffiths, Honda Performance Development technical director, explained: "When you've got seven or eight cars and you're subsidizing them, that's one thing. But when you've got 12 or 13 or 14 and you're subsidizing them, that's completely different, and it's hard for us to maintain that level of subsidy."[32]

With an eye to Formula One's success in running events in Asia, the Middle East and Europe and with experience during his tenure as the chief of the ATP in foreign events, Miles was evaluating having a "mini-series" outside of the United States during the off-season. Just as CART turned toward foreign markets, which have an appeal to multi-national companies, some sports marketers believed IndyCar racing would be a viable marketing option for companies outside of the United States. With experience having run a team, Derrick Walker explained the benefit to racing outside of the United States for the IndyCar teams: "Right now we've got a lot of downtime and there's only so much testing you can do. Our teams need income and an international component could help provide some additional income helps strengthen their financial position."[33]

As the IndyCar team began developing the race schedule for the 2014 season, Miles started thinking about trying to reenergize the happenings around the Indianapolis 500. Over the years, the format had changed, with reduced time in Indianapolis. Opening day, which had been a big event back in the 1950s and 1960s, had lost its importance. How could Miles and his team bring the activities at the Speedway back to a fever pitch? Miles' solution was creating a Month of May event—a month-long celebration of racing at the Indianapolis Motor Speedway. His solution was to have an IndyCar race at the Speedway prior to the Indianapolis 500. Miles explained to Racer.com, "We only had a few thousand people on [Indianapolis 500] opening day this year and we keep doing the same things and it's not working. I want to protect the Indianapolis 500 but we need to look at what we can do to help the race and IndyCar. We need to make more out of the month and I don't see how starting off with a road race could hurt it."[34] A road race would utilize the course built during Tony George's tenure as part of the Formula One strategy. Since the end of Formula One races at the Indianapolis Motor Speedway, the use of the road course had been limited to motorcycle racing. Many spectators found the Formula One races to be boring, and the track needed upgrades to support a return of this type of racing. Funding from the Indiana Economic Development Commission would help in making the improvements.

Miles made the announcement of the Grand Prix of Indianapolis: "The Grand Prix of Indianapolis is all about elevating the Indianapolis 500 and the IndyCar series with more thrilling content for our loyal supporters and fans. This will be a very different event than the '500' and will be one of three major weeks of excitement at IMS in May, all leading to the 98th Indianapolis 500 on May 25." The Speedway planned to spend $5 million to upgrade the course with harder turns and to increase speeds.[35]

As Miles approached his first anniversary at Hulman and Company, his imprint upon the Indianapolis Motor Speedway and IndyCar was being felt. He had streamlined the operations of both facilities. He had addressed the residual issues of "turbogate," and IndyCar was now in search of additional engine manufacturers to relieve the pressure placed upon Toyota and Honda. Miles had begun to address the physical upgrades needed at the Indianapolis Motor Speedway and had crafted a plan for the financing of the improvements. He had also implemented the Boston Consulting Group's suggestion of compressing the racing schedule. In 2014, IndyCar planned to run 15 races over a 19-week period. Miles believed the compressed schedule would help IndyCar increase its television viewership. He explained how the previous racing schedule with wide gaps between races had a negative impact upon IndyCar: "To be quite candid, we raced in Baltimore and then took a month off, then we waited a couple of weeks and then we were in Fontana. I don't think that's a recipe for presenting yourself in the optimal way to the public."[36]

Possibly most importantly, the 2013 racing season was without the controversy and internal family dissentions that had caused so much turmoil over the past thirty years.

There was much work remaining to be done. The damage done by the Indy car war would not be undone in a year. If the various stakeholders—teams, drivers, sponsors, equipment manufacturers and promoters—pulled together, open-wheel racing could have a shot at regaining its lost stature.

Chapter Notes

Prologue

1. Economaki, "Survey Says NFL Is Leading American Sport," *National Speed Sport News*, Jan. 16, 2008, 27.

2. Kirby, "The Way It Is: Debating the Great Spec Car Plague," http://www.gordonkirby.com/categories/columns/theway/2006/the_way_it_is_no7.html, May 15, 2006.

3. Rudeen, "British Bullet at Indy," http://sportsillustrated.cnn.com/vault/article/magazine/MAG1072607/index.htm, May 29, 1961.

4. Ibid.

5. Ibid.

6. Ibid.

7. Ibid.

8. Kirby, "The Way It Is: Looking at the Challenges Facing America's Open-Wheel Racing," http://www.gordonkirby.com/categories/columns/theway/2006/the_way_it_is_no1.html, Apr. 6, 2006.

9. Ludvigsen, *Dan Gurney: The Ultimate Racer*, 72.

10. Kirby, "The Way It Is: Looking at the Challenges Facing America's Open-Wheel Racing," http://www.gordonkirby.com/categories/columns/theway/2006/the_way_it_is_no1.html, Apr. 6, 2006.

11. Ibid.

12. Kirby, "The Way It Is: Why Dan Gurney Is America's Greatest Racing Man," http://www.gordonkirby.com/categories/columns/theway/2006/the_way_it_is_no38.html, Dec. 18, 2006.

13. Ludvigsen, *Dan Gurney: The Ultimate Racer*, 73.

14. Case, "Revolution at Indianapolis," http://allamericanracers.com/revolution-at-indiana polis/.

15. Ibid.

16. Cadou, "Now It Comes Out—the Money (and Secrets)," *National Speed Sport News*, May 23, 1984, 3.

17. Waltz, "Andy Granatelli Unveils Turbine Powered Indy Car," http://www.nationalspeedsportnews.com/racing-history/torn-from-the-headlines/andy-granatelli-unveils-turbine-powered-indy-car/, accessed Dec. 21, 2013.

18. Cadou, "Now It Comes Out—the Money (and Secrets)," *National Speed Sport News*, May 23, 1984, 3.

19. Ibid.

20. Ibid.

21. "Tobacco Money Makes Its Move into Auto Racing," *National Speed Sport News*, Jan. 20, 2010, 17.

Chapter 1

1. Shaffer, *CART: The First 20 Years*, 19.

2. Collins, "Rising Costs Making Owners Restless," *Indianapolis Star*, May 28, 1978.

3. Kirby, "The Way It Is: The Tragedy of History Repeating Itself," http://www.gordonkirby.com/categories/columns/theway/2012/the_way_it_is_no350.html, Aug. 27, 2012.

4. Shaffer, *CART: The First 20 Years*, 20.

5. Ibid.

6. Cadou, "USAC Loses Eight Officials in Air Crash," *National Speed Sport News*, Apr. 26, 1978, 3.

7. Wallen, Fleisher and Harker, *United States Auto Club*, 234.

8. Hollingsworth, "IRL and CART," www.automedia.com/IRL_and_CART/pht20030901.

9. Mylenski, "Risk-Taking Rogue Pat Patrick Strikes It Big in Oil—and Racing," http://articles.chicagotribune.com/1998–08–14/sports/9808140060_1_championship-auto-racing-teams-american-racing-series-united-states-auto-club, Aug. 14, 1998.

10. Ibid.

11. Shaffer, *CART: The First 20 Years*, 20.

12. "Key Meeting Friday on USAC's Troubles," *National Speed Sport News*, Aug. 16, 1978, 3.

13. "USAC Panel Oks Fuel, Power Plan," *Indianapolis Star*, Aug. 19, 1978, 26.

14. Miller, "500 Miles of an Unfunny Folly," *Indianapolis Star*, Sept. 7, 1978, 40.

15. "USAC Directors Make 3 Changes," *Indianapolis Star*, Sept. 8, 1978, 33.

16. Cadou, "Goodyear Indicates USAC Pullout May Be Near," *National Speed Sport News*, Sept. 20, 1978, 3.

17. Ibid.

18. "USAC Board Sets Emergency Meeting," *National Speed Sport News*, Nov. 8, 1978, 3.

19. Ibid.

20. Economaki and Oursler, "Champ Racing in Turmoil, CART Quits USAC," *National Speed Sport News*, Nov. 22, 1978, 3.

21. Miller, "USAC's Life Threatened by CART," *Indianapolis Star*, Nov. 19, 1978.

22. "Are Car Owners Bidding for Control of USAC?" *National Speed Sport News*, Oct. 25, 1978, 3.

23. Shaffer, *CART: The First 20 Years*, 23.

24. Miller, "USAC's Life Threatened by CART," *Indianapolis Star*, Nov. 19, 1978.

Chapter 2

1. Miller, "USAC's Life Threatened by CART," *Indianapolis Star*, Nov. 19, 1978.

2. Economaki and Oursler, "CART Schedule Announced; Rift with USAC Widens," *National Speed Sport News*, Nov. 29, 1978, 3.

3. Carraccio, "A Look at IndyCar's Revolving Door of CEOs," http://www.autoracing1.com/article.asp?id=3873, Nov. 19, 2012.

4. Economaki and Oursler, "CART Schedule Announced; Rift with USAC Widens," *National Speed Sport News*, Nov. 29, 1978, 3.

5. "Newly Formed CART Is Sanctioned by SCCA," *Indianapolis Star*, Dec. 11, 1978, 30.

6. Economaki and Oursler, "CART-SCCA Deal Triggers Indy Stock-Block Thinking," *National Speed Sport News*, Dec. 13, 1978, 3.

7. Clymer, *Indianapolis 500 Mile Race History*, 200.

8. Economaki and Oursler, "Six Tracks Remain USAC; Indy Goes Stock Block!" *National Speed Sport News*, Jan. 3, 1979, 3.

9. Ibid.

10. Cadou, "USAC's New Rules, What Do They Mean?" *National Speed Sport News*, Jan. 3, 1979, 3.

11. Economaki and Oursler, "CART Big Guns Shell USAC, Key Defensive Move Seen," *National Speed Sport News*, Jan. 10, 1979, 3.

12. Ibid.

13. "Indy Is Open to All: TV Pact Is Key Issue," *National Speed Sport News*, Jan. 17, 1979, 3.

14. Moore, "USAC Makes Rulings for Equivalency," *Indianapolis Star*, Jan. 21, 1979.

15. Economaki and Oursler, "USAC Sets Stock-Block Formula at 600 Horses," *National Speed Sport News*, Jan. 24, 1979, 3.

16. "Three CART Races for TV; Indy Stick w/USAC Regs," *National Speed Sport News*, Jan. 31, 1979, 3.

17. Economaki and Oursler, "USAC Sets Stock-Block Formula at 600 Horses," *National Speed Sport News*, Jan. 24, 1979, 3.

18. "Three CART Races for TV; Indy Stick w/USAC Regs," *National Speed Sport News*, Jan. 31, 1979, 3.

19. "Indy Is Open to All: TV Pact Is Key Issue," *National Speed Sport News*, Jan. 17, 1979, 3.

20. Carraccio, "A Look at IndyCar's Revolving Door of CEOs," http://www.autoracing1.com/article.asp?id=3873, Nov. 19, 2012.

21. Miller, "Foyt Quits CART: Rejoins USAC," *Indianapolis Star*, Feb. 1, 1979, 33.

22. Economaki and Oursler, "Major Obstacle to CART-USAC Peace Removed," *National Speed Sport News*, Feb. 28, 3.

23. "Administration's Energy Saving Plan Could Halt US Auto Racing," *National Speed Sport News*, Mar. 7, 1979, 3.

24. "CART Wins over USAC in Apr. 22 TV Battle," *National Speed Sport News*, Mar. 28, 1979, 3.

25. Miller, "Judge Gives CART Go Sign," *Indianapolis Star*, May 6, 1979, 1.

26. Allyn, "Foyt Easy Ontario Victor as USAC Fields 21 Cars," *National Speed Sport News*, Mar. 28, 1979, 3.

27. "CART Enters 44 Cars in Record Indy 500 Field," *National Speed Sport News*, Apr. 18, 1979, 3.

28. Ibid.

29. Cadou, "Ban a Shock to CART," *National Speed Sport News*, Apr. 25, 1979, 3.

30. Miller, "First Court Victory Goes to CART," *Indianapolis Star*, May 4, 1979, 33.

31. Miller, "CART Mired in Legal Lumbering," *Indianapolis Star*, May 5, 1979, 19.

32. Miller, "CART Still Waiting on IMS Reply," *Indianapolis Star*, Apr. 24, 1979, 23.

33. Miller, "The Rejected 6 Ask Cloutier 'What For?'" *Indianapolis Star*, Apr. 22, 1979.

34. Miller, "CART Still Waiting on IMS Reply," *Indianapolis Star*, Apr. 24, 1979, 23.

35. Miller, "CART Mired in Legal Lumbering," *Indianapolis Star*, May 5, 1979, 19.

36. Miller, "First Court Victory Goes to CART," *Indianapolis Star*, May 4, 1979, 33.

37. Miller, "6 Top '500' Entries Rejected," *Indianapolis Star*, Apr. 21, 1979, 1.

38. Cadou, "Ban a Shock to CART," *National Speed Sport News*, Apr. 25, 1979, 3.

39. Miller, "6 Top '500' Entries Rejected," *Indianapolis Star*, Apr. 21, 1979, 1.

40. Miller, "The Rejected 6 Ask Cloutier 'What For?'" *Indianapolis Star*, Apr. 22, 1979.

41. "SCCA Seeking ACCUS' Intervention," *Indianapolis Star*, Apr. 23, 1979, 22.

42. Moore, "It's USAC's Responsibility: Cloutier," *Indianapolis Star*, Apr. 25, 1979, 53.

43. Cadou, "Ban a Shock to CART," *National Speed Sport News*, Apr. 25, 1979, 3, 16.

44. Economaki and Ousler, "Penske Offers 'Performance Bond,'" *National Speed Sport News*, Apr. 25, 1979, 3.

45. Miller, "Race Talks Fail; Hearing Today," *Indianapolis Star*, May 3, 1979, 35.

46. Ibid.

47. Moore, "CART Files Suit vs. USAC, IMS," *Indianapolis Star*, Apr. 27, 1979, 31.

48. Ibid.

49. Miller, "Judge Gives CART Go Sign," *Indianapolis Star*, May 6, 1979, 1.

50. "'Make Cloutier Talk,' Court Asked," *Indianapolis Star*, May 2, 1979, 31.

51. Cadou, "CART Petitions Federal Court to Upset USAC's Indy Turndown," *National Speed Sport News*, May 2, 1979, 3.

52. Miller, "Judge Gives CART Go Sign," *Indianapolis Star*, May 6, 1979, 1.

53. "Trials Sham of Speed," *Indianapolis Star*, May 21, 1979, 22.

54. Ibid.

55. "7 '500' Trials Protests Denied," *Indianapolis Star*, May 22, 1979, 1.

56. Ibid.

57. Ibid.

58. Ibid.

59. "CART Backs Extra Qualifying," *Indianapolis Star*, May 24, 1979, 1.

60. "USAC OKs New Try for Bumped Racers," *Indianapolis Star*, May 23, 1979, 1.

61. "Pit Pass," *Indianapolis Star*, May 25, 1979, 33.

62. Overpeck, "Extra Qualifications Voted Out," *Indianapolis Star*, May 25, 1979, 1.

63. "11 'Bumped' Cars Can Requalify Today," *Indianapolis Star*, May 26, 1979, 1.

64. Overpeck, "35 Cars Await Starting Flag," *Indianapolis Star*, May 27, 1979, 1.

65. "Pit Pass," *Indianapolis Star*, May 27, 1979.

Chapter 3

1. Moore, "Racing Factions Seek Settlement," *Indianapolis Star*, May 24, 1979, 39.

2. "Pocono Talks Are On," *National Speed Sport News*, May 30, 1979, 3.

3. Overpeck, "1980 '500' by Invitation Only," *Indianapolis Star*, June 2, 1979, 1.

4. Miller, "CART Calls Truce to Talk Peace," *Indianapolis Star*, June 12, 1979, 23.

5. Overpeck, "1980 '500' by Invitation Only," *Indianapolis Star*, June 2, 1979, 1.

6. "USAC Claims CART Violated Antitrust Act," *Indianapolis Star*, June 12, 1979, 23.

7. Economaki and Oursler, "New CART-USAC Reconciliation Plan Being Presented in Indy by Smartis," *National Speed Sport News*, June 13, 1979, 3.

8. Moore, "USAC, CART Bomb Out," *Indianapolis Star*, June 16, 1979, 27.

9. Miller, "Ontario Hitches Ride on CART," *Indianapolis Star*, July 3, 1979, 24.

10. Ibid.

11. Oursler, "$6.3 Million Conspiracy Suit Is Filed by Pocono," *National Speed Sport News*, Sept. 5, 1979, 3.

12. "Cooper Quits as Speedway President," *Indianapolis Star*, May 8, 1982, 1.

13. Moore, "Cooper's Plan for Speedway: Evolution, Not Revolution," *Indianapolis Star*, Oct. 19, 1979, 39.

14. "Cooper New Indianapolis Head, Reaction Favorable," *National Speed Sport News*, Oct. 24, 1979, 3.

15. "CART Gets PPG as Sponsor, 4 NBC TV Races," *National Speed Sport News*, Oct. 31, 1979, 3.

16. "Indy Inks 'Lend-Lease' Deal with Pocono," *National Speed Sport News*, Nov. 7, 1979, 3.

17. "1979 Poor Year at Gate: Goodyear," *National Speed Sport News*, Jan. 9, 1980, 2.

18. "Impasse in Indy-Car Talks; Goodyear Sharply Critical," *National Speed Sport News*, Jan. 23, 1980, 3.

19. "Indy Car 'Peace Conference' Falls Apart After Walkout," *National Speed Sport News*, Jan. 16, 1980, 2.

20. Miller, "Goodyear Enters Indy-Car Battle," *Indianapolis Star*, Jan. 24, 1980, 37.

21. "Impasse in Indy-Car Talks; Goodyear Sharply Critical," *National Speed Sport News*, Jan. 23, 1980, 3.

22. Miller, "Goodyear Enters Indy-Car Battle," *Indianapolis Star*, Jan. 24, 1980, 37.

23. Miller, "CART Teams to Get Indy Invites," *Indianapolis Star*, Jan. 25, 1980, 37.

24. Miller, "USAC-CART Talks Flag," *Indianapolis Star*, Feb. 1, 1980, 32.

25. Miller, "Angry Foyt Turns In USAC Card," *Indianapolis Star*, Feb. 5, 1980, 21.

Chapter 4

1. Miller, "Speedway President Offers CART, USAC Peace Plan," *Indianapolis Star*, Feb. 16, 1980, 31.

2. "USAC OK's Modified Cooper Peace Plan," *Indianapolis Star*, Feb. 21, 1980, 32.

3. "CART's Reply: Definite 'Maybe,'" *Indianapolis Star*, Feb. 23, 1980, 29.

4. "Peace Proposal Pleases Most, Not CART Head," *National Speed Sport News*, Feb. 20, 1980, 3, 12.

5. Ibid.

6. "USAC, CART Like Looks of Cooper Proposal," *National Speed Sport News*, Feb. 27, 1980, 3.

7. Ibid.

8. Miller, "CART Says 'Let's Go,' USAC Shows E-Z Board," *Indianapolis Star*, Mar. 2, 1980.

9. "Penske Says Solution Close in CART-USAC Wrangling," *Indianapolis Star*, Mar. 28, 1980, 23.

10. Overpeck, "USAC, CART Form New Racing League," *Indianapolis Star*, Apr. 4, 1980, 28.

11. "CART Is Back in Business," *Indianapolis Star*, July 2, 1980, 15.

12. Miller, "USAC Nixes CRL; Reopens War?" *Indianapolis Star*, July 1, 1980, 26.

13. Cadou, "USAC's Declaration of Independence May Mean War," *National Speed Sport News*, July 2, 1980, 3.

14. Ibid.

15. "Cooper Quits as Speedway President," *Indianapolis Star*, May 8, 1982, 1.

16. Cadou, "USAC Rules Out Participants on Board," *National Sport Speed News*, Aug. 20, 1980, 3.

17. Cadou, "Cooper Decides: USAC to Stay On at Indy," *National Sport Speed News*, Sept. 3, 1980, 2.

18. Miller, "Cooper Declares Independence," *Indianapolis Star*, June 24, 1980, 24.

19. "Does USAC Vote Signal the End?" *National Speed Sport News*, July 9, 1980, 3.

20. "Milwaukee Vote Goes to CART," *Indianapolis Star*, July 9, 1980, 19.

21. Miller, "USAC Focus on Sprint, Dirt Cars," *Indianapolis Star*, Sept. 25, 1980, 35.

22. Miller, "Bank Denies Lease to Save Pocono," *Indianapolis Star*, Mar. 1, 1981.

23. "Pocono Rejoins '81 USAC Sked," *Indianapolis Star*, Mar. 4, 1981, 19.

24. "USAC Schedule Claims Two '500s,'" *Indianapolis Star*, Dec. 13, 1980, 38.

25. "13 CART Shows for '81 Season," *National Sport Speed News*, Oct. 8, 1980, 3.

26. "CART and PPG Set $1 Million Point Fund," *National Sport Speed News*, Nov. 12, 1980, 3.

27. Guehler, "CART Spells Out Its $1 Million' 500-Mile Michigan Race July 19," *National Speed Sport News*, Mar. 4, 1981, 3.

28. Miller, "82 USAC Rules Eliminate Cosworth," *Indianapolis Star*, Jan. 7, 1981, 35.

29. "Speedway's Cooper Lauds Move to Stock Engines," *Indianapolis Star*, Jan. 8, 1981, 34.

30. "Pocono Entries Out, CART Cars Absent," *National Speed Sport News*, May 20, 1981, 3.

31. "Record Set for Indy 500 Entries," *National Speed Sport News*, Apr. 15, 1981, 2.

32. Miller, "More Animosity than Honesty at Speedway," *Indianapolis Star*, May 21, 1981, 41.

33. "Board Hears Sneva Case," *Indianapolis Star*, May 22, 1981, 37.

34. Freudenthal, "Vollstedt Appeal Denied; Drivers Meet at 11 a.m," *Indianapolis Star*, May 23, 1981, 31.

35. Cadou, "Much Bitterness in First 2 Days of Indy Hearing," *National Speed Sport News*, June 10, 1981, 3.

36. "Andretti Indy Appeal to ACCUS," *National Speed Sport News*, Nov. 11, 1981, 3.

37. "USAC Says No to Andretti," *National Speed Sport News*, Nov. 18, 1981, 3.

38. Ibid.

39. "ACCUS Refusal to Hear Andretti Gives Unser 500," *National Speed Sport News*, Feb. 3, 1982, 2.

40. Cadou, CART Puts Pocono 500 Off Limits," *National Speed Sport News*, June 10, 1981, 3.

41. "CART Ban Set Aside," *National Speed Sport News*, July 1, 1981, 3.

42. "No CART Appeal on Pocono 7 Suspensions," *National Speed Sport News*, July 8, 1981, 3.

43. "Pocono-CART Lawsuit Now at $9.9 Million," *National Speed Sport News*, July 15, 1981, 3.

44. Cadou, "Exotic Engines OK for Indy '82—USAC," *National Speed Sport News*, Aug. 5, 1981, 2.

45. "Cooper Quits as Speedway President," *Indianapolis Star*, May 8, 1982, 1.

46. "CART, Pocono Make Peace; Set Aug. 15 500," *National Speed Sport News*, May 5, 1982, 2.

47. "CART Sponsor PPG Backs 500," *Indianapolis Star*, May 30, 1982, 2D.

48. Ibid.

49. Ibid.

50. "Drivers Seek CART Sanction for Indy 500," *National Speed Sport News*, Nov. 10, 1982, 3.

51. "USAC Retains Indy 500 Sanction," *National Speed Sport News*, Jan. 12, 1983, 3.

52. "Attendance Upswing Noted at U.S. Events," *National Speed Sport News*, Dec. 15, 1982, 2.

Chapter 5

1. Allyn, "CART Eliminates Skirts in Move to Slow Cars," *National Speed Sport News*, Sept. 1, 1982, 3.

2. Ibid.; "USAC's New Rules Parallel to CART's," *National Speed Sport News*, Oct. 6, 1982, 2.

3. Miller, "Don Is a Dandy at 205.198," *Indianapolis Star*, May 12, 1983, 37.

4. "CART Reveals Engine Specs," *Indianapolis Star*, Sept. 8, 1983, 35.

5. Oursler, "As CART's Rules Expire, What to Do Is Question," *National Speed Sport News*, July 20, 1983, 3.

6. "'84 CART Year at $10 Million!" *National Speed Sport News*, Feb. 29, 1984, 3.

7. Cadou, "Oversupply of Race Cars Is Talk of Indy Town," *National Speed Sport News*, Apr. 25, 1984, 3.

8. Ibid.

9. Ibid.

10. Economaki and Oursler, "CART Chief, Indy 500 Boss in Hush-Hush Rules Parley," *National Speed Sport News*, July 18, 1984, 3.

11. Stilley, "Return Indy Car Racing to the Ovals—CART's Patrick," *National Speed Sport News*, Aug. 1, 1984, 3.

12. Ibid.

13. Mylenski, "Risk-Taking Rogue Pat Patrick Strikes It Big in Oil—and Racing," http://articles.chicagotribune.com/1998–08–14/sports/9808140060_1_championship-auto-racing-teams-american-racing-series-united-states-auto-club, Aug. 14, 1998.

14. "U.S. Race Fans Jammed Speedways During 1984," *National Speed Sport News*, Jan. 9, 1985, 5.

15. CART Prize $ Jumps 15% to Record $11.5 Million," *National Sport Speed News*, Jan. 16, 1985, 3.

16. Stilley, "Only 15 'Old' Cars Among Indy Entries," *National Sport Speed News*, Apr. 17, 1985, 3.

17. Stilley, "Indy Entries Jump to 77 as April 5 Deadline Passes," *National Sport Speed News*, Apr. 10, 1985, 2.

18. Stilley, "Only 15 'Old' Cars Among Indy Entries," *National Sport Speed News*, Apr. 17, 1985, 3.

19. "Fastest Indy 500 Field Set, Average Speed up 4 MPH," *National Sport Speed News*, May 15, 1985, 3.

20. Turner, "GM Believes It Has a Better Idea for Indy," *National Sport Speed News*, May 15, 1985, 3.

21. Turner, "CART's New Rules 'a Kick in the Face' Says Buick," *National Sport Speed News*, July 3, 1985, 3.

22. Cadou, "A Slowdown at Indy Goal of USAC and CART," *National Sport Speed News*, June 5, 1985, 3.

23. Turner, "New CART Indy Car Rules Cut Downforce, Not Power," *National Sport Speed News*, July 3, 1985, 3.

24. Ibid.

25. Turner, "CART's New Rules 'a Kick in the Face' Says Buick," *National Sport Speed News*, July 3, 1985, 3.

26. "CART Network to Broadcast Sixteen Races," *National Sport Speed News*, Dec. 18, 1985, 3.

27. "ABC-TV Wins Rights to Show Indy 500 Live," *National Sport Speed News*, Aug. 21, 1985, 3.

28. "USAC & CART Meet to Discuss Ways of Slowing Indy Cars," *National Sport Speed News*, Sept. 3, 1986, 3.

29. "IMS' Tony George Joins USAC's Board," *National Speed Sport News*, Jan. 28, 1987, 3.

30. "Another $15.5 Million Year for CART Series," *National Speed Sport News*, Feb. 25, 1987, 3.

31. Stilley, "Crash Tests Coming for Future Indy Cars," *National Speed Sport News*, Aug. 26, 1987, 3.

32. "Stock Blocks Are Cornerstone of New All-U.S. Indy Car Series," National Speed Sport News, Nov. 18, 1987, 3.

33. "Attendance at Major U.S. Race Events Jumps 11%," *National Sport Speed News*, Jan. 6, 1988, 3.

34. "Dissent over CART Regs, Some Look to Detroit," *National Sport Speed News*, July 13, 1988, 3.

35. "ACCUS Accepts CART," *National Sport Speed News*, Sept. 14, 1988, 3.

36. "CART Studying FISA Ban on out-of-Country Races," *National Sport Speed News*, Nov. 2, 1988, 2.

37. Oursler, "CART Replaces F-1 in Detroit, Sets Japan Bow," *National Sport Speed News*, Nov. 9, 1988, 3.

38. Economaki, "Battle Lines Forming in CART-FISA Feud," *National Sport Speed News*, Nov. 16, 1988, 3.

39. "CART's Japanese Race Scrubbed," *National Sport Speed News*, Dec. 14, 1988, 3.

40. Waters, "CART Plans for 1990 Include Canada, Europe, Japan," *National Sport Speed News*, Feb. 15, 1989, 2.

41. Franck, "CART-FISA Negotiations On but TV Rights Pose Problem," *National Sport Speed News*, July 5, 1989, 3.

42. Waltz, "CART Rules Dispute Hot Topic at Pocono," *National Sport Speed News*, Aug. 21, 1989, 3.

43. Franck, "Penske Takes Issue with USAC," *National Sport Speed News*, Sept. 6, 1989, 3.

44. "Indy Car Owners Meet, Seek Restructuring of CART," *National Sport Speed News*, Oct. 11, 1989, 3.

45. "CART Expands Board, Retains Pres. Caponigro," *National Sport Speed News*, Nov. 1, 1989, 3.

46. "Controversy Surfaces in CART as Sponsor Unhappy with Head," *National Sport Speed News*, Nov. 29, 1989, 3.

Chapter 6

1. "Indy Head Cloutier Heart Victim at 81," *National Sport Speed News*, Dec. 13, 1989, 3.
2. "CART Issues Pink Slip to Caponigro, Picks Capels to Lead Club through '90," *National Sport Speed News*, Dec. 20, 1989, 3.
3. "IMS Picks Tony George," *National Sport Speed News*, Jan. 10, 1990, 5.
4. "Auto Racing Attendance Continues to Climb," *National Sport Speed News*, Jan. 10, 1990, 2.
5. Ibid.
6. "'90 CART/PPG Series Worth $20 Million; Car Specs Continue as Major Problem," *National Sport Speed News*, Jan. 17, 1990, 2.
7. "Safer and Slower Cars for Indy's 1990 500: See USAC-CART Peace," *National Sport Speed News*, Jan. 31, 1990, 2.
8. LeMasters, "Rules Issue at Indy Won't Die," *National Sport Speed News*, May 16, 1990, 3.
9. "CART Names Bill Stokkan Chairman," *National Sport Speed News*, Apr. 11, 1990, 3.
10. "CART Chairman: Entertainment Thrust Needed," *National Sport Speed News*, Jan. 11, 1991, 2.
11. LeMasters, "Indy Speaks Out on Rule Changes," *National Sport Speed News*, Aug. 1, 1990, 3.
12. "CART's Rules Rhubarbs Resurface at Detroit GP," *National Sport Speed News*, June 20, 1990, 3.
13. "CART Drops Detroit, Adds Australian Run," *National Sport Speed News*, Aug. 22, 1990, 3.
14. Ibid.
15. Franck, "Detroit Indy Car Race May Not Be Dead," *National Sport Speed News*, Sept. 5, 1990, 3.
16. LeMasters, "Round-Trip Detroit GP Ride for Stokkan," *National Sport Speed News*, Sept. 19, 1990, 3.
17. "Renew Detroit GP, Denver Site Issue," *National Sport Speed News*, Oct. 3, 1990, 3.
18. Oursler, "Tensions Are Rising in CART-FISA Feud," *National Sport Speed News*, Oct. 10, 1990, 3.
19. Ibid.
20. LeMasters, "CART Gains Indy's George as Ally in FISA Tiff," *National Sport Speed News*, Dec. 12, 1990, 3.
21. Ibid.
22. Miller, "Major '500' Rules Changes Coming," *Indianapolis Star*, May 26, 1991, B-1.

23. Lemasters, "Turbos May Go Says Indy Boss," *National Sport Speed News*, May 29, 1991, 3.
24. Miller, "Major '500' Rules Changes Coming," *Indianapolis Star*, May 26, 1991, B-1.
25. Lemasters, "Turbos May Go Says Indy Boss," *National Sport Speed News*, May 29, 1991, 3.
26. Miller, "CART May Ask George to Revamp Racing," *Indianapolis Star*, Sept. 6, 1991, A-1.
27. Lemasters, "Turbos May Go Says Indy Boss," *National Sport Speed News*, May 29, 1991, 3.
28. Ibid.
29. Miller, "CART Has Much to Gain in Deal with Indy," *Indianapolis Star*, Sept. 6, 1991, B-3.
30. Miller, "CART May Ask George to Revamp Racing," *Indianapolis Star*, Sept. 6, 1991, A-1.
31. Miller, "CART Chairman Favors Democratic Indy-Car Board," *Indianapolis Star*, Oct. 28, 1991, D1.
32. Ibid.
33. Miller, "George Has a Take-It-or-Leave-It Deal for CART," *Indianapolis Star*, Oct. 31, 1991, D1.
34. "Membership of New Indy-Car Board Under Debate," *Indianapolis Star*, Oct. 13, 1991, D-2.
35. Miller, "CART Not Ready to Relinquish Sovereignty to George," *Indianapolis Star*, Nov. 10, 1991, D-3.
36. Lemasters, "Indy-CART Marriage Off," *National Sport Speed News*, Dec. 4, 1991, 3.
37. Miller, "George Has a Take-It-or-Leave-It Deal for CART," *Indianapolis Star*, Oct. 31, 1991, D-1.
38. Lemasters, "Indy-CART Marriage Off," *National Sport Speed News*, Dec. 4, 1991, 3.
39. "Racing Attendance Jumps Despite Sluggish Economy," *National Sport Speed News*, Jan. 8, 1992, 5.
40. Lemasters, "All Sweetness & Life at CART; Bonus in Change to For-Profit," *National Sport Speed News*, Jan. 29, 1992, 3.
41. Lemasters, "Indy's George Moves Ahead with Plan to Solve Indy Car Woes," *National Sport Speed News*, Feb. 19, 1992, 2.
42. Lemasters, "TV, Sponsor and Date Problems Face IndyCar," *National Sport Speed News*, Mar. 11, 1992, 3.
43. Ibid.
44. Ibid.
45. Miller, "George Plan Sent Back Once Again," *Indianapolis Star*, June 7, 1992, E-1.
46. Ibid.
47. Lemasters, "New Indy Proposal Leaves CART Cold," *National Sport Speed News*, June 10, 1992, 2.

48. Lemaster, "Indy Walls to Come Tumbling Down," *National Sport Speed News*, June 3, 1992, 2.

49. Lemasters, "IMS' George Pleased with NASCAR Test," *National Sport Speed News*, July 1, 1992, 3.

50. Miller, "George Takes Huge Risk to Unify Racing," *Indianapolis Star*, July 26, 1992, E-1.

51. Ibid.

52. Ibid.

53. "IndyCar Plans Huge '93 Fines for Rules Sins," *National Speed Sport News*, Nov. 18, 1992, 2.

54. Lemasters, "CART Rule Forces Honda to Re-evalute Indy Car Program," *National Speed Sport News*, Feb. 10, 1993, 3.

55. Ibid.

56. "No Nissan Indy Effort, Massive Cuts in NPTI Staff," *National Speed Sport News*, Mar. 3, 1993, 3.

57. "New USAC Regs Allow Single-Example Indy Engines," *National Speed Sport News*, Mar. 10, 1993, 2.

58. LeMasters, "Firestone Picks '95 for Indy Car Return," *National Speed Sport News*, May 19, 1993, 3.

59. "Honda Indy Car Project Gets Green Light for '94," *National Speed Sport News*, Sept. 15, 1993, 3; "Honda's Indy Decision Imminent," *National Speed Sport News*, Sept. 8, 1993, 2.

60. Lemasters, "CART Returns to 'Big Board' Status; Still Hunting New CEO," *National Speed Sport News*, Nov. 17, 1993, 2.

61. Lemasters, "IMS-USAC Plans Rock Indy Car Set," *National Speed Sport News*, Mar. 16, 1994, 3.

Chapter 7

1. Mittman, "George Ignites Car Wars," *Indianapolis Star*, Mar. 12, 1994, D-1.

2. Lemasters, "IMS-USAC Plans Rock Indy Car Set," *National Speed Sport News*, Mar. 16, 1994, 3.

3. Mittman, "George Ignites Car Wars," *Indianapolis Star*, Mar. 12, 1994, D-1.

4. "IndyCar Girds for IMS Fight," *National Speed Sport News*, June 15, 1994, 3.

5. Martin, "Tony G. at PIR?" *National Speed Sport News*, June 29, 1994, 3.

6. Ibid.

7. Martin, "Tony G. at PIR?" *National Speed Sport News*, June 29, 1994, 3.

8. Martin, "New IRL Engine Rules Rile Penske," *National Speed Sport News*, Aug. 17, 1994, 3.

9. Miller, "George Unveils Name, Leaders for New Circuit," *Star*, July 9, 1994, E-1.

10. Mittman, "George Ignites Car Wars," *Indianapolis Star*, Mar. 12, 1994, D-1.

11. Mittman, "Circuit Leaving Some Confused," *Indianapolis Star*, July 9, 1994, D-1.

12. Martin, "New IRL Engine Rules Rile Penske," *National Speed Sport News*, Aug. 17, 1994, 3.

13. Koenig, "Course of Change," *Indianapolis Star*, July 31, 1994, A-1.

14. Ibid.

15. "No IRL Sked as Yet, But '96 TV Is All Set," *National Speed Sport News*, Jan. 18, 1995, 2.

16. Lemasters, "$1 Million IRL Bow for DisneyWorld," *National Speed Sport News*, Jan. 25, 1995, 3.

17. Lemasters, Indy Car's Craig Speaks of Conciliation, IRL, TV," *National Speed Sport News*, Feb. 8, 1995, 3.

18. IRL Engine Delay," *National Speed Sport News*, Mar. 15, 1995, 3.

19. Lemasters, "$1 Million IRL Bow for Disney World" *National Speed Sport News*, Jan. 25, 1995, 3.

20. "IndyCar-IRL War of Words Hits New High" *National Speed Sport News*, June 21, 1995, 2.

21. Mittman, "Indy-Car War On for Real," *Indianapolis Star*, Dec. 20, 1995, G-1.

22. Miller, "George's IRL Plans Will Damage Indy's Respectability," *Indianapolis Star*, July 5, 1995, B-1.

23. "An Unanimous 'Nay'" Vote on IRL Edict," *National Speed Sport News*, July 12, 1995, 3.

24. "IndyCar-IRL War of Words Hits New High," *National Speed Sport News*, June 21, 1995, 2.

25. "An Unanimous 'Nay'" Vote on IRL Edict," *National Speed Sport News*, July 12, 1995, 3.

26. Martin, "Open Indy Quals to All or We Strike!" *National Speed Sport News*, Sept. 27, 1995, 3.

27. Martin, "Penske says 'No' to Rival 500 at Michigan," *National Speed Sport News*, Oct. 11, 1995, 3.

28. Miller, "CART Officials Say They May Not Be Making May Pit Stop in Indy," *Indianapolis Star*, Oct. 11, 1995, B-1.

29. Mittman, "Indy-Car War On for Real," *Indianapolis Star*, Dec. 20, 1995, G-1.

30. "Principals Speak as IRL-IndyCar Battle Heats Up," *National Speed Sport News*, Oct. 25, 1995, 3.

31. Lemasters, "U.S. 500 Race Shocks Fans and Sponsors," *National Speed Sport News*, Jan. 10, 1996, 3.

32. Ibid.

33. Koenig, "Indy-Car Racing Split Also

Brings Division of Sponsor's Spending," *Indianapolis Star*, May 19, 1996, E-1.

34. "Details of Failed IRL-IndyCar Discussions Now Made Public," *National Speed Sport News*, July 19, 1995, 2.

35. "IRL's Long: Indy Control Key Issue," *National Speed Sport News*, July 26, 1995, 2.

36. Koenig, "CART/IRL Split Has Stalled Sport's Economic Growth," *Indianapolis Star*, Sept. 22, 1996 E-1.

37. Martin, "Strong Words as CART-IRL Tiff Heats Up," *National Speed Sport News*, Jan. 10, 1996, 14.

38. Lemasters, "Valvoline Out at IMS; Pennzoil Takes Over," *National Speed Sport News*, Mar. 13, 1996, 3.

39. Lemasters, "The Big Day Is Finally Here for New Tony George Series," *National Speed Sport News*, Jan. 24, 1996, 3.

40. Miller, "IRL Is Competitive, but It's Certainly Not Major-League Racing," *Indianapolis Star*, Jan. 29, 1996, D-2.

41. Miller, "New CART Season Strong on Competition," *Indianapolis Star*, Feb. 25, 1996, C-2.

42. Miller, "IRL, CART Sit, but No Fire in Peace Pipe," *Indianapolis Star*, Feb. 25, 1996, C-2.

43. Koening, "Indy-Car Racing Split Makes Engine Firms Shift Allegiances," *Indianapolis Star*, Feb. 25, 1996, E-1.

44. "CART-IRL Talks Continue, May Resolution Unlikely," *National Speed Sport News*, Feb. 28, 1996, 3.

45. Ibid.

46. "CART-IRL Talks Continue, May Resolution Unlikely," *National Speed Sport News*, Feb. 28, 1996, 3.

47. Martin, "IndyCar Board Rebuffs Roger on Peace Plan," *National Speed Sport News*, Feb. 28, 1996, 3.

48. Koenig, "CART Ordered to Drop Indy-Car Name," *Indianapolis Star*, Mar. 20, 1996, F-1.

49. Martin, "IMS Tells CART 'Nix the Name,'" *National Speed Sport News*, Mar. 27, 1996, 2.

50. "CART Fires Back," *National Speed Sport News*, Apr. 3, 1996, 3.

51. Martin, "IMS Fires Back with New Suit," *National Speed Sport News*, May 8, 1996, 3.

52. "Details Made Known of Indy's CART Suit," *National Speed Sport News*, May 15, 1996, 3.

53. "Chassis Regs Complete IRL's 1997 Car Plans," *National Speed Sport News*, Apr. 3, 1996, 3.

54. Martin, "IRL Car Specs Preclude Running in IndyCar Events," *National Speed Sport News*, Apr. 10, 1996, 2.

55. "IRL's 'Look to Europe,'" *National Speed Sport News*, Apr. 10, 1996, 2.

56. "Letterman, Newman Side with CART in Indy War," *Indianapolis Star*, May 10, 1996, Q-6.

57. Koenig, "The Race Is On for Indy-Car Sponsors," *Indianapolis Star*, Mar. 1, 1996, C-1.

58. "Arie, Roberto Head 77-Car Indy Entry List," *National Speed Sport News*, Apr. 17, 1996, 3.

59. Cavin, "Strong Words at 'Other 500,'" *Indianapolis Star*, May 11, 1996 D-1.

60. Miller, "The Battle Lines Have Been Drawn. With CART Teams Racing at Michigan in Protest, the Indianapolis 500 Is ... A RACE DIVIDED," *Indianapolis Star*, May 24, 1996, S-1.

61. Koenig, "Both Races Suffer from Racing Civil War," *Indianapolis Star*, May 27, 1996, S-9.

62. Martin, "After Volatile Month of May, Time to Move On for CART?" *National Speed Sport News*, June 12, 1996, 2.

63. Koenig, "Indy-Car Racing Split Also Brings Division of Sponsor's Spending," *Indianapolis Star*, May 19, 1996, E-1.

64. Koenig, "NASCAR Takes Lead in Race for Sponsors," *Indianapolis Star*, Mar. 8, 1996, F-1.

65. Koenig and Francis, "Indy-Car Feud's Fallout Still Being Felt," *Indianapolis Star*, June 1, 1996, D-1.

66. "Indy's 500 Winner of TV Battle," *National Speed Sport News*, June 12, 1996, 2.

Chapter 8

1. Miller, "CART Vows to Continue War with Indy," *Indianapolis Star*, June 2, 1996, B-1.

2. "Penske: 'Indy Return Not a Closed Book,'" *National Speed Sport News*, June 26, 1996, 2.

3. Miller, "CART-IRL Boiler Is Cooling," *Indianapolis Star*, Aug. 11, 1996, B-9.

4. Miller, "Speedway Message to CART Regulars Is 'Suite Dreams,'" *Indianapolis Star*, July 14, 1996, B-9.

5. Koenig, "CART/IRL Split Has Stalled Sport's Economic Growth," *Indianapolis Star*, Sept. 22, 1996, E-1.

6. Koenig, "CART, IRL TV Ratings Continue to Slide," *Indianapolis Star*, May 9, 1997, C-4.

7. Martin, "Gossage: No Texas CART Race," *National Speed Sport News*, Sept. 18, 1996, 3.

8. Miller, "CART to Steer Around Showdown," *Indianapolis Star*, Oct. 4, 1996, F-1.

9. Miller, "IndyCar, CART Spell Out, Settle Differences for Racing Acronym," *Indianapolis Star*, Dec. 22, 1996, C-10.

10. "Absolutely, Positively, FedEx Signs to be CART's Sponsor," *National Speed Sport News*, Dec. 10, 1997, 2.

11. Martin, "Penske Ponders IRL Indy Run," *National Speed Sport News*, Feb. 19, 1997, 3.

12. Martin, "Penske Indy Posture Divides CART Teams," *National Speed Sport News*, Mar. 5, 1997, 3.

13. Mittman, "Indy-Only Format for 500 May Open Door for CART," *Indianapolis Star*, May 9, 1997, C-4.

14. Koenig, "Fans Shouldn't Hold Breath Waiting for CART's Return to Indianapolis," *Indianapolis Star*, May 18, 1997, C-7.

15. Mittman, "No Real Winners in IRL, CART Feud; Tony George Says IRL Not at War with Anyone, Hopes in Time People Will View Series Differently," *Indianapolis Star*, May 24, 1997, D-1.

16. Miller, "IRL Retools the Rules, Opens Doors for CART," *Indianapolis Star*, May 17, 1997, A-1.

17. Mittman, "No Real Winners in IRL, CART Feud; Tony George Says IRL Not at War with Anyone, Hopes in Time People Will View Series Differently," *Indianapolis Star*, May 24, 1997, D-1.

18. *Associated Press*, "Indy 500 Field Expanded to 35; Johnny Unser, St. James Back In," http://articles.latimes.com/1997–05–19/sports/sp-60301_1_johnny-unser, May 19, 1997.

19. Cavin, "U.S. Auto Club Still Part of Speedway Despite Debacle," *Indianapolis Star*, May 22, 1998, J-9.

20. Martin, "Luyendyk Puts Hammer Down for 2nd Indy Score," *National Speed Sport News*, June 4, 1997, 2.

21. Cavin, "500, IRL Drop USAC as Sanctioning Body," *Indianapolis Star*, June 17, 1997, A-1.

22. Miller, "George's Change of Heart Bleeds Hypocrisy," *Indianapolis Star*, Sept. 12, 1997, C-1.

23. Miller, "Owners, Drivers Favor Changes," *Indianapolis Star*, Sept. 12, 1997, C-4.

24. Miller, "May Daze Prompts Numerous Questions," *Indianapolis Star*, Sept. 14, 1997, C-7.

25. Lemasters, "IMS Cuts Week of Practice, 2nd Time Trial Weekend Next Year," *National Speed Sport News*, Sept. 17, 1997, 3.

26. Mittman, "Road Course at Speedway Is 'Feasible,'" *Indianapolis Star*, Sept. 18, 1997, D-1.

27. "Absolutely, Positively, FedEx Signs to Be CART's Sponsor," *National Speed Sport News*, Dec. 10, 1997, 2.

28. Martin, "Reebok Will Not Sponsor IRL Tour," *National Speed Sport News*, Jan. 7, 1998, 3.

29. Martin, "Pep Boys Adds to IRL Season Opener," *National Speed Sport News*, Jan. 28, 1998, 3.

30. Koenig, "IRL May Earn $101 Million in Sponsorships," *Indianapolis Star*, Feb. 13, 1998, D-10.

31. Mylenski, "Risk-Taking Rogue Pat Patrick Strikes It Big in Oil—and Racing," http://articles.chicagotribune.com/1998–08–14/sports/9808140060_1_championship-auto-racing-teams-american-racing-series-united-states-auto-club, Aug. 14, 1998.

32. Koenig, "Auto Circuit Ready to Race on Wall Street," *Indianapolis Star*, Mar. 8, 1998, L-6.

33. Koenig, "CART Stock Has a Fast Start," *Indianapolis Star*, Mar. 11, 1998, C-1.

34. Mayer, "CART Seeks up to $84 Million in IPO," *National Speed Sport News*, Jan. 7, 1998, 3.

35. Ibid.

36. Lemasters, "CART Race a Reality," *National Speed Sport News*, Apr. 15, 1998, 3.

37. Miller, "NASCAR's TV Success Puts CART, IRL to Shame," *Indianapolis Star*, July 1, 1998, B-1.

38. Miller, "Lack of Drivers Familiar to Racing Fans Casts a Major Cloud over IRL, CART," *Indianapolis Star*, May 15, 1998, D-1.

39. Miller, "CART Owners Offer Plan for Return to the '500,'" *Indianapolis Star*, Nov. 8, 1998, A-1.

40. Ibid.

41. Miller, Cavin and Koenig, "New IRL Rules Likely to Dash Reunion Hope," *Indianapolis Star*, Nov. 18, 1998, A-1.

42. Miller, "New IRL Rules Likely to Dash Reunion Hope," *Indianapolis Star*, Nov. 18, 1998, A-1.

43. Ibid.

44. "New IRL Pact Has FOX with ABC for '99," *National Speed Sport News*, Jan. 6, 1999, 3.

45. Mayer, "CART-NASCAR Tie?—Not Likely: France," *National Sport Speed News*, Dec. 15, 1999, 3.

46. Ibid.

47. Ibid.

48. Lemasters, "Is CART-IRL Resolution Near?" *National Speed Sport News*, Apr. 7, 1999, 2.

49. Martin, "Three Killed by Debris; IRL Cancels Race," National Speed Sport News, May 5, 1999, 3.

50. Mayer, "Penske Sells Nearly All!" *National Speed Sport News*, Apr. 21, 1999, 3.

51. Mayer, "It All Boils Down to Numbers & Shareholders," *National Speed Sport News*, May 19, 1999, 3.

52. Martin, "George on CART: 'We Won't

Change,'" *National Speed Sport News*, Sept. 29, 1999, 3.

53. Oreovicz, "Despite 22 Events CART Targets 500," *National Speed Sport News*, Nov. 10, 1999, 2.

54. Martin, "IRL Signs Northern Light to $50 Million Sponsorship," *National Speed Sport News*, Feb. 2, 2000, 3.

55. Martin, "Ray Garners Championship; Brack Wins 500! As IRL Endure Season of Triumph and Tragedy," *National Sport Speed News*, Dec. 15, 1999, 8.

56. Martin, "'Little Al' Opens Up on CART-IRL Move," *National Speed Sport News*, Mar. 22, 2000, 3.

57. Martin, "Fans Cheer Unser upon Indy Return," *National Speed Sport News*, May 17, 2000, 2.

58. Martin, "CART and IRL Champs to Share 500 Front Row," *National Speed Sport News*, May 24, 2000, 2.

59. Indianapolis Motor Speedway, http://www.indianapolismotorspeedway.com/indy 500/history/stats/results/?year=2000.

60. Martin, "Fans Cheer Unser upon Indy Return," *National Speed Sport News*, May 17, 2000, 2.

61. Martin, "Penske Researching Indianapolis Return," *National Speed Sport News*, June 7, 2000, 2.

62. Oreovicz, "CART Board Ousts Craig," *National Speed Sport News*, June 21, 2000, 3.

63. Martin, "IMS Returns to Traditional Schedule," *National Speed Sport News*, July 12, 2000, 2.

64. Oreovicz, "Mercedes Orders End to CART Engine Supply," *National Speed Sport News*, Sept. 13, 2000, 3.

65. Oreovicz, "CART Engine Suppliers Resist Plans to Cut Power," *National Speed Sport News*, July 26, 2000, 3.

66. Oreovicz, "Top Jag F-1 Job Steals CART Boss," *National Speed Sport News*, Sept. 20, 2000, 3.

67. Mayer, "Major Changes Possible for 'New CART,'" *National Speed Sport News*, Dec. 12, 2001, 3.

Chapter 9

1. Oreovicz, "Finally, CART Has Its Man!" *National Speed Sport News*, Dec. 6, 2000, 2.

2. Cavin, "IRL Won't Push CART Merger," *Indianapolis Star*, Feb. 9, 2001, D-1.

3. Cavin, "500, IRL Drop USAC as Sanctioning Body," *Indianapolis Star*, June 17, 1997, A-1.

4. Mayer, "Buys by CEO Heitzler, Others Raise Questions," *National Speed Sport News*, June 20, 2001, 3.

5. Oreovicz, "CART Alters Engine Regs, Ford and Honda Cry 'Foul,'" *National Speed Sport News*, June 20, 2001, 3.

6. Oreovicz, "Appeals Panel Rebuffs CART on Disputed Popoff Valve, *National Speed Sport News*, July 11, 2001, 2.

7. Oreovicz, "CART's Popoff Problem Solved," *National Speed Sport News*, July 18, 2001, 2.

8. Oreovicz, "CART Alters Engine Regs, Ford and Honda Cry 'Foul,'" *National Speed Sport News*, June 20, 2001, 3.

9. Kaplan, "ISL Files Countersuit Against Ex-partner CART," http://www.sportsbusiness daily.com/Journal/Issues/2001/04/20010416/ No-Topic-Name/ISL-Files-Countersuit-Agai st-Ex-Partner-CART.aspx, Apr. 16, 2001.

10. Mayer, "CEO Heitzler Is No. 1 Target as CART Directors Sit Down," *National Speed Sport News*, Dec. 5, 2001, 2.

11. Hawkins, "Extreme G-Forces Prompt Race Cancellation," www.abcnews.com/US/sto ry?id93412&page, Apr. 30, 2001.

12. Oreovicz, "Russell's CART Tenure Ends," *National Speed Sport News*, Oct. 3, 2001, 3.

13. Mayer, "Major Changes Possible for 'New CART,'" *National Speed Sport News*, Dec. 12, 2001, 3.

14. Mayer, "Controversy Swirls Around CART; Leadership Quality Is Questioned," *National Speed Sport News*, July 18, 2001, 3.

15. Mayer, "CART TV? Not Yet, But Possible," *National Speed Sport News*, Aug. 1, 2001, 3.

16. Mayer, "Expensive New CART TV Pact Offers More Hours," *National Speed Sport News*, Aug. 22, 2001, 3.

17. Martin, "IRL and ABC/ESPN Extend Through '07," *National Speed Sport News*, Sept. 5, 2001.

18. Mayer, "The Heitzler File, Part 1," *National Speed Sport News*, July 25, 2001, 3.

19. Ballard, "Coming to Grips," *Indianapolis Star*, July 5, 2001, C-1.

20. Ibid.

21. Oreovicz and Martin, "No More Turbos for Toyota," *National Speed Sport News*, Oct. 3, 2001, 3.

22. Oreovicz, "Heitzler Goes, Pook Is Eyed as New CEO," *National Speed Sport News*, Dec. 12, 2001, 3.

23. Mayer, "Is CART Shareholder Planning Lawsuits?" *National Speed Sport News*, Nov. 20, 2002, 29.

24. Mayer, "CART Discloses $1.4 Million in Extra Expenses," *National Speed Sport News*, Oct. 31, 2001.

25. Mayer, "CEO Heitzler Is No. 1 Target as

CART Directors Sit Down," *National Speed Sport News*, Dec. 5, 2001, 2.

26. Oreovicz, "Heitzler Goes, Pook Is Eyed as New CEO," *National Speed Sport News*, Dec. 12, 2001, 3.

27. Mayer, "No 'Poison Pill' for CART's Forsythe," *National Speed Sport News*, Sept. 18, 2002, 3.

28. Mayer, "Major Changes Possible for 'New CART,'" *National Speed Sport News*, Dec. 12, 2001, 3.

29. Oreovicz, "Heitzler Goes, Pook Is Eyed as New CEO," *National Speed Sport News*, Dec. 12, 2001, 3.

30. Mayer, "Major Changes Possible for 'New CART,'" *National Speed Sport News*, Dec. 12, 2001, 3.

31. Oreovicz, "Pook Swings into Action as CART Strengthens Plan," *National Speed Sport News*, Jan. 30, 2002, 3.

32. Ibid.

33. Oreovicz, "CART Takes on Promoter's Role," *National Speed Sport News*, Mar. 6, 2002, 31.

34. Oreovicz, "Pook Swings into Action as CART Strengthens Plan," *National Speed Sport News*, Jan. 30, 2002, 3.

35. Mayer, "Despite Losing Forecast, Wall Street Backs CART CEO," *National Speed Sport News*, Mar. 13, 2002, 3.

36. Mayer, "If You Sue Me, I'll Sue You," *National Speed Sport News*, Apr. 3, 2002, 2.

37. Ballard, "Open-Wheel Series Entering New Eras, CART Moves Forward with Eyes on 2005," *Indianapolis Star*, Jan. 17, 2003, D-1.

38. Cavin, "The Changing Face of Open-Wheel Racing," *Indianapolis Star*, Dec. 14, 2001, D-3.

39. Oreovicz, "Honda Appears Ready to Join IRL," *National Speed Sport News*, May 1, 2002, 3.

40. Ibid.

41. Oreovicz, "Pook Claims CART Is Moving Forward," *National Speed Sport News*, June 5, 2002, 25.

42. Mayer, "Ecclestone on CART: 'No Interest,'" *National Speed Sport News*, June 12, 2002, 22.

43. Oreovicz, "CART Takes Strides to Help Competitors," *National Speed Sport News*, Aug. 21, 2002, 21.

44. Oreovicz, "CART Back to Turbos," *National Speed Sport News*, June 19, 2002, 3.

45. Ibid.

46. Martin, "Castroneves Keeps Point Lead," *National Speed Sport News*, July 3, 2002, 23.

47. Oreovicz, "CART Announces Assistance Program for Struggling Teams," *National Speed Sport News*, June 19, 2002, 27.

48. Oreovicz, "CART Takes Strides to Help Competitors," *National Speed Sport News*, Aug. 21, 2002, 21.

49. Ibid.

50. Oreovicz, "CART Back to Turbos," *National Speed Sport News*, June 19, 2002, 3.

51. Securities and Exchange Commission, CART 10-Q, http://www.sec.gov/Archives/edgar/data/1051825/000095015202006428/l9555 51ae10vq.txt.

52. Mayer, "Financial Trouble for CART?" *National Speed Sport News*, Aug. 21, 2002, 3.

53. Ibid.

54. Mayer, "Major Investor Seeks Break Up, or Sale of CART," *National Speed Sport News*, Sept. 11, 2002, 3.

55. Ibid.

56. Mayer, "No 'Poison Pill' for CART's Forsythe," *National Speed Sport News*, Sept. 18, 2002, 3.

57. Martin, "Andretti Takes Three Cars to IRL," *National Speed Sport News*, Sept. 25, 2002, 2.

58. Knutson, "Will CART Become an F-1 Feeder Series?" *National Speed Sport News*, Oct. 16, 2002, 2.

59. Oreovicz, "Chris Pook Clears Air on CART & Bernie," *National Speed Sport News*, Oct. 30, 2002, 2.

60. Mayer, "Words May Come Back to Haunt CART," *National Speed Sport News*, Oct. 23, 2002, 2.

61. Oreovicz, "Chris Pook Clears Air on CART & Bernie," *National Speed Sport News*, Oct. 30, 2002, 2.

62. Mayer, "Words May Come Back to Haunt CART," *National Speed Sport News*, Oct. 23, 2002, 2.

63. Oreovicz, "Bridgestone Sticking with CART," *National Speed Sport News*, Nov. 6, 2002, 22.

64. Oreovicz, "Ford Announces Support for CART," *National Speed Sport News*, Nov. 27, 2002, 6.

65. Mayer, "CART Loses $8.3 Million in Third Quarter," *National Speed Sport News*, Nov. 20, 2002, 2.

66. Mayer, "Is CART Shareholder Planning Lawsuits?" *National Speed Sport News*, Nov. 20, 2002, 29.

67. "CART Won't Return to England for Now," *National Speed Sport News*, Nov. 27, 2002, 6.

68. Mayer, "Racing in Europe Is Costly for CART," *National Speed Sport News*, Jan. 15, 2003, 14.

69. Ibid.

70. Mayer, "New Era Begins for CART Shareholders," *National Speed Sport News*, Dec. 11, 2002, 2.

71. Oreovicz, "CART Begins Rebuilding

Process," *National Speed Sport News*, Jan. 22, 2003, 27.

72. Oreovicz, "CART Turns On the Lights," *National Speed Sport News*, Jan. 22, 2003, 23.

73. Oreovicz, "CART Begins Rebuilding Process," *National Speed Sport News*, Jan. 22, 2003, 27.

74. Mayer, "CART Attendance Questioned," *National Speed Sport News*, Jan. 29, 2003, 3.

75. Securities and Exchange Commission, CART 10-K for 12/31/2003, http://www.sec.gov/Archives/edgar/data/1051825/000095015204006473/l09292ae10vk.txt.

76. Martin, "IRL Ready to Use IndyCar Again!" *National Speed Sport News*, Jan. 8, 2003, 3.

77. "IRL Becomes Indy Racing League IndyCar Series," http://www.crash.net/indycar/news/16966/1/irl_becomes_indy_racing_league_indycar_series.html, Jan. 8, 2003.

78. Oreovicz, "Several New Teams Commit," *National Speed Sport News*, Jan. 8, 2003, 11.

79. Mayer, "CART Sues Road America," *National Speed Sport News*, Feb. 19, 2003, 2.

80. Oreovicz, "CART Axes Road America," *National Speed Sport News*, Mar. 12, 2003, 2.

81. Mayer, "CART Stock Hits New Low," *National Speed Sport News*, Mar. 12, 2003, 2.

82. Mayer, "CART Losing Numbers Game," *National Speed Sport News*, Mar. 19, 2003, 2.

83. Mayer, "Analyst Questions CART's Survival," *National Speed Sport News*, Mar. 19, 2003, 21.

84. Mayer, "CART's 10-K Poses Questions," *National Speed Sport News*, Apr. 2, 2003, 2.

85. Ibid.

86. "CART Loses $9 Million," *National Speed Sport News*, May 14, 2003, 2.

87. Oreovicz, "CEO Pook Defends CART's Position," *National Speed Sport News*, May 21, 2003, 3.

88. Mayer, "CART's Future Addressed," *National Speed Sport News*, June 11, 2003, 3.

89. Oreovicz, "CEO Pook Defends CART's Position," *National Speed Sport News*, May 21, 2003, 3.

90. Oreovicz, "CART Looks for Private Investors," *National Speed Sport News*, June 18, 2003, 3.

91. Martin, "Team-Owner Penske Says CART's Days Are Numbered," *National Speed Sport News*, July 2, 2003, 24.

Chapter 10

1. Oreovicz, "CART's Future Still Remains Uncertain," *National Speed Sport News*, July 16, 2003, 3.

2. Ibid.

3. Securities and Exchange Commission, CART 10-Q for 6/30/2003, http://www.sec.gov/Archives/edgar/data/1051825/000095015203007658/l02333ae10vq.txt.

4. Ballard, "CART Needs Deal to Continue," *Indianapolis Star*, Aug. 15, 2003, D-6.

5. Securities and Exchange Commission, CART 10-Q for 6/30/2003, http://www.sec.gov/Archives/edgar/data/1051825/000095015203007658/l02333ae10vq.txt.

6. Oreovicz, "CART Stays Silent About Critical Board Meeting," *National Speed Sport News*, July 23, 2003, 4.

7. Oreovicz, "Future of CART Being Decided Behind Closed Doors," *National Speed Sport News*, Aug. 6, 2003, 7.

8. Oreovicz, "CART Gets Offer for Shares," *National Speed Sport News*, Aug. 20, 2003, 3.

9. Oreovicz, "OWRS Deal Under Review," *National Speed Sport News*, Oct. 1, 2003, 2.

10. Oreovicz, "Is CART Saved by New Deal, or Not?" *National Speed Sport News*, Sept. 17, 2003, 6.

11. Oreovicz, "CART Stock Falls Below NYSE Criteria," *National Speed Sport News*, Oct. 8, 2003, 33.

12. Oreovicz, "CART Announces Sked, SEC Filings," *National Speed Sport News*, Nov. 19, 2003, 29.

13. CART Plans Acquisition Meeting," *National Speed Sport News*, Nov. 26, 2003, 2.

14. Oreovicz, "CART Merge Vote Called Off," *National Speed Sport News*, Dec. 10, 2003, 2.

15. Ibid.

16. Ballard, "Philosophies to Clash as Judge Hears CART Case," *Indianapolis Star*, Jan. 28, 2004, D-1.

17. Ballard, "IRL Won't Get Chance to Pull Plug on CART," *Indianapolis Star*, Jan. 29, 2004, A-1.

18. Ballard, "With Judge's Ruling, Race Begins for Circuit," *Indianapolis Star*, Jan. 30, 2004, D-1.

19. "Champ Car to Pay Molson for TV Production," *National Speed Sport News*, Jan. 26, 2005, 10.

20. Ballard, "Philosophies to Clash as Judge Hears CART Case," *Indianapolis Star*, Jan. 28, 2004 D-1.

21. Ballard, "Open-Wheel Unity: Desirable, Difficult," *Indianapolis Star*, May 24, 2005, D-1.

22. Oreovicz, "Champ Car Finalizes TV with Networks," *National Speed Sport News*, Jan. 19, 2005, 18.

23. "Champ Car to Pay Molson for TV Production."*National Speed Sport News*, Jan. 26, 2005, 10.

24. "George Tackles Role of Team Owner," *National Speed Sport News*, Febraury 16, 2005, 2.

25. Wikipedia, "Kelley Racing," http://en. Wikipedia.org/wiki/Kelley_racing.

26. "George Tackles Role of Team Owner," *National Speed Sport News*, Feb. 16, 2005, 2.

27. Martin, "Briscoe at Ganassi; Is Texas in Trouble?" *National Speed Sport News*, Jan. 19, 2005, 5.

28. Martin, "Race Date Leaves IRL, PIR at Crossroads," *National Speed Sport News*, Apr. 27, 2005, 2.

29. Oreovicz, "Champ Car to Talk with Honda," *National Speed Sport News*, May 25, 2005, 44.

30. Ballard, "Open-Wheel Unity: Desireable, Difficult," *Indianapolis Star*, May 24, 2005, D-1.

31. Ibid.

32. Oreovicz, "Champ Car Locks Up Long Beach Grand Prix," *National Speed Sport News*, June 1, 2005, 3.

33. Martin, "Indy 500 Fanfare Boosting IRL's Image," *National Speed Sport News*, June 8, 2005, 6.

34. Martin, "Chevy Will Leave the IRL," *National Speed Sport News*, Aug. 24, 2005, 25.

35. Martin, "Honda Says It's Ready to Power All of IRL in '07," *National Speed Sport News*, Oct. 19, 2005, 4.

36. Oreovicz, "Conspiracy? Attendance Dips to New Low," *National Speed Sport News*, Aug. 31, 2005, 2.

37. Oreovicz, "Champ Car Can't Clear Obstacles, Axes Ansan," *National Speed Sport News*, Oct. 5, 2005, 3.

38. Oreovicz, "New Champ Car Chassis Lightens Financial Strain," *National Speed Sport News*, Oct. 12, 2005, 3.

39. Ibid.

40. Oreovicz, "Strategic Series," *National Speed Sport News*, Nov. 9, 2005, 20.

41. Oreovicz, "Champ Car's First 'Turbo Tour' Takes Drivers to Media Masses," *National Speed Sport News*, Mar. 15, 2006, 37.

42. Oreovicz, "Strategic Series," *National Speed Sport News*, Nov. 9, 2005, 20.

43. Kirby, "The Way It Is: Tony George's dystopian vision Is Upon Us," http://www.gordonkirby.com/categories/columns/theway/2006/the_way_it_is_no9.html, May 29, 2006.

44. "George Scoffs at Merger Rumors," *National Speed Sport News*, Mar. 1, 2006, 2.

45. Martin, "IRL's George Warms Up to Unification," *National Speed Sport News*, Mar. 29, 2006, 5.

46. Martin, "Penske Not Buying Unification," *National Speed Sport News*, Mar. 29, 2006, 23.

47. Martin, "Merger Not Coming Any Time Soon," *National Speed Sport News*, May 17, 2006, 20.

48. Ibid.

49. Martin, "Merger Talks Crawling Along," *National Speed Sport News*, May 31, 2006, 3.

50. Kirby, "The Way It Is: Tony George's Dystopian Vision Is Upon Us," http://www.gordonkirby.com/categories/columns/theway/2006/the_way_it_is_no9.html, May 29, 2006.

51. "Champ Car, IRL Nearing Merger," *Indianapolis Star*, June 25, 2006, A-1.

52. Ibid.

53. Kravitz, "Racing Merger Must Not Stall," *Indianapolis Star*, July 7, 2006, D-1.

54. Oreovicz, "George, Kalkhoven Merger Comes to a Standstill," *National Speed Sport News*, July 5, 2006, 25.

55. Oreovicz, "Champ Car Lands Television Deal with ABC/ESPN," *National Speed Sport News*, Nov. 22, 2006, 10.

56. Oreovicz, "Big Business: Ford Pulls Out of Champ Car," *National Speed Sport News*, Jan. 31, 2007, 2.

Chapter 11

1. Oreovitz, "Series VP Resigns; Matos Chooses IPS," *National Speed Sport News*, Jan. 23, 2008, 3.

2. Ibid.

3. "Cotman Confirmed at IRL," Crash.net, http://www.crash.net/indycar/news/25730/1/cotman_switch_confirmed.html, Feb. 6, 2008.

4. "Another Missed Opportunity for Open-Wheel Merger," *National Speed Sport News*, Feb. 6, 2008, 3.

5. Oreovicz, "Around the Bend," *National Speed Sport News*, May 7, 2008, 2.

6. "US Open Wheel Merger Close for 2008?" Crash.net, http://www.crash.net/indycar/news/25744/1/merger_talks_stall.html, Feb. 8, 2008.

7. "Walker to Move Regardless?" http://www.crash.net/indycar/news/25746/1/walker_to_go_regardless.html, Feb. 11, 2008.

8. Cavin, "Champ Car's Walker Considers Switch to IRL," *Indianapolis Star*, Feb. 13, 2008, D-3.

9. "Series to File for Bankruptcy?" http://www.crash.net/indycar/news/25749/1/confusion_amid_bankruptcy_rumours.html, Feb. 13, 2008.

10. "US Open Wheel Merger Close for 2008?" http://www.crash.net/indycar/news/25744/1/merger_talks_stall.html, Feb. 8, 2008.

11. Martin, "Champ Car, IRL Merging Closer," *National Speed Sport News*, Feb. 13, 2008, 2.

12. "US Open Wheel Merger Close for 2008?" http://www.crash.net/indycar/news/25744/1/merger_talks_stall.html, Feb. 8, 2008.

13. "Merger Plans Hit Standstill?" http://www.crash.net/indycar/news/25744/1/merger_talks_stall.html, Feb. 10, 2008.

14. Cavin, "No Merger News but Many Questions," *Indianapolis Star*, Feb. 15, 2008, D-6.

15. "Series to File for Bankruptcy?" http://www.crash.net/indycar/news/25749/1/confusion_amid_bankruptcy_rumours.html, Feb. 13, 2008.

16. Ibid.

17. "US Open-Wheel Merger Agreed?" http://www.crash.net/indycar/news/25756/1/us_poised_for_unity_at_last.html, Feb. 19, 2008.

18. Cavin, "IRL Closer to Deal with Champ Car," *Indianapolis Star*, Feb. 20, 2008, D-1.

19. Oreovicz, "Kalkhoven: 'Leave It Alone,'" *National Speed Sport News*, Feb. 13, 2008, 2.

20. Oreovicz, "Groups Take Wait-and-See Approach," *National Speed Sport News*, Feb. 20, 2008, 2.

21. Cavin and Ballard, "IRL, CCWS Execs Plan to Meet," *Indianapolis Star*, Feb. 21, 2008, D-3.

22. Cavin, "No Deal Yet, but It's Closer," *Indianapolis Star*, Feb. 22, 2008, D-1.

23. "No Resolution to Merger Talks," http://www.crash.net/indycar/news/25765/1/still_ground_to_cover_before_unity.html, Feb. 22, 2008.

24. Martin, "War Over, 'Now the Work Starts,'" *National Speed Sport News*, Feb. 27, 2008, 3.

25. "IRL, Champ Car Make Up," *Indianapolis Star*, Feb. 23, 2008, 1.

26. Ballard, "5 Things Needed to Boost Success of IRL's IndyCar," *Indianapolis Star*, May 4, 2008, C-1.

27. Cavin, "Unification," *Indianapolis Star*, Feb. 23, 2008, D-1.

28. "AGR Backs Merger," http://www.crash.net/indycar/news/25767/1/andretti_its_a_huge_day.html, Feb. 23, 2008.

29. "Walker: It's What People Wanted," http://www.crash.net/indycar/news/25768/1/walker_its_back_to_the_future.html, Feb. 28, 2008.

30. Martin, "Reunited," *National Speed Sport News*, May 21, 2008, MD-2.

31. Martin, "Handshake Seals Open-Wheel Deal," *National Speed Sport News*, Mar. 5, 2008, 2.

32. Cavin, "IRL Meeting Draws Full Lineup of Champ Car Teams," *Indianapolis Star*, Feb. 26, 2008, D-1.

33. Martin, "Champ Car, IRL Merging Closer," *National Speed Sport News*, Feb. 13, 2008, 2.

34. Oreovicz, John, "Champ Car Firm Files for Bankruptcy," *National Speed Sport News*, Mar. 12, 2008, 2.

35. Cavin, "Unifying Series Isn't Cheap," *Indianapolis Star*, Feb. 28, 2008, D-1.

36. Ballard, "5 Things Needed to Boost Success of IRL's IndyCar," *Indianapolis Star*, May 4, 2008, C-1.

37. Martin, "War Over, 'Now the Work Starts,'" *National Speed Sport News*, Feb. 27, 2008, 3.

38. Martin, "George: Engine Availability Not an Issue," *National Speed Sport News*, Feb. 27, 2008, 25.

39. Cavin, "Era of Unity: Start the Excitement," *Indianapolis Star*, May 4, 2008, A-1.

40. Martin, "George: Engine Availability Not an Issue," *National Speed Sport News*, Feb. 27, 2008, 25.

41. Martin, "Transition of Equipment a 'Challenge,'" *National Speed Sport News*, Feb. 27, 2008, 3.

42. Martin, "George Outlines Future IRL Plans," *National Speed Sport News*, Apr. 9, 2008, 30.

43. "Forsythe Scales Back to Atlantic Effort," http://www.crash.net/indycar/news/25792/1/forsythe_bows_out_but_stays_in_atlantics.html, Feb. 29, 2008.

44. Cavin and Ballard, "Champ Car's Tracy Looks for a Ride," *Indianapolis Star*, Feb. 29, 2008, D-5.

45. "Tracy to Test for Germain Racing," *National Speed Sport News*, May 28, 2008, 12.

46. Martin, "Paul Tracy Wants to Race," *National Speed Sport News*, Apr. 9, 2008, 25.

47. "Andretti Green Promotions Secures 2009 IndyCar Series Date for GP of Toronto," *National Speed Sport News*, May 21, 2008, 42.

48. Martin, "Gossage, IRL at Odds over Future Texas Events," *National Speed Sport News*, June 11, 2008, 29.

49. Oreovicz, "Champ Car Firm Files for Bankruptcy," *National Speed Sport News*, Mar. 12, 2008, 2.

50. "Fans to Join Paul Newman in His Return to Indy 500?" *Indianapolis Star*, Mar. 25, 2008, D-2.

51. Martin, "DirecTV to Come on Board as IndyCar Series Title Sponsor," *National Speed Sport News*, Apr. 2, 2008, 3.

52. Ballard, "Fans Will Get HD Views from Cars," *Indianapolis Star*, Mar. 28, 2008, D-8.

53. Oreovicz, "Around the Bend," *National Speed Sport News*, May 7, 2008, 2.

54. Ibid.

Chapter 12

1. Wikipedia, "Dario Franchitti," http://en.wikipedia.org/wiki/Dario_Franchitti.

2. Kravitz, "Open-Wheeling Racing Begins Rebuilding After Unification," *Indianapolis Star*, May 4, 2008, C-1.

3. "Honda Gets Five More Years in the IRL, http://www.crash.net/indycar/news/26021/1/honda_extends_engine_deal.html/ May 24, 2008.

4. Martin, "Will It Be Turbos in 2011 for Indy Cars?" *National Speed Sport News*, July 2, 2008, 3.

5. "IRL Happy with Momentum," http://www.crash.net/indycar/news/26108/1/irl_happy_with_unification_upswing.html, July 4, 2008.

6. Ibid.

7. "Paul Tracy Confirms IndyCar Comeback with Walker," http://www.crash.net/indycar/news/26132/1/tracy_confirms_indycar_return.html, July 14, 2008.

8. Martin, "Forsythe to Enter Indy Lights," *National Speed Sport News*, July 23, 2008, 27.

9. Clayton, "GM Cutting Spending," *National Speed Sport News*, July 23, 2008, 2.

10. Martin, "More Road Courses for Indy-Car," *National Speed Sport News*, Aug. 6, 2008, 6.

11. Ibid.

12. Ibid.

13. Martin, "Engines Going Turbo in 2011," *National Speed Sport News*, Aug. 27, 2008, 2.

14. "ABC, Versus to Screen IndyCar," http://www.crash.net/indycar/news/26187/1/series_celebrates_new_tv_deals.html, Aug. 8, 2008.

15. "Tracy Takes Forsythe to Court," http://www.crash.net/indycar/news/26303/1/tracy_sues_for_breach_of_contract.html, Oct. 7, 2008.

16. "Apex-Brazil Signs On as New IRL Fuel Partner," http://www.crash.net/indycar/news/26358/1/series_hits_apex_with_new_fuel_partner.html, Nov. 19, 2008.

17. "Honda's US Programme to Continue," http://www.crash.net/indycar/news/26376/1/honda_to_continue_us_programme.html, Dec. 7, 2008.

18. Economaki, "Racing Suffers Body Blow," *National Speed Sport News*, Jan. 7, 2009, 4.

19. "Dallara to Cut Prices in '09," http://www.crash.net/indycar/news/26379/1/dallara_to_cut_costs_for_teams.html, Dec. 13, 2008.

20. "Xtrac to Offer Cheaper Support," http://www.crash.net/indycar/news/142832/1/xtrac_cuts_cost_for_teams.html, Feb. 10, 2009.

21. Economaki, "Business Pages, Not Sports Pages," *National Speed Sport News*, May 13, 2009, 4.

Chapter 13

1. "George Denies IMS 'Oust' Claims," http://www.crash.net/indycar/news/147501/1/george_still_at_ims_focused_on_irl.html, May 27, 2009.

2. Ibid.

3. Martin, "IndyCar Teams Unified in Show of Support for George," *National Speed Sport News*, June 3, 2009, 5, 33.

4. Martin, "In the End, Only Family Could Bring Down George," *National Speed Sport News*, July 8, 2009, 29.

5. Martin, "George Ousted from Speedway, IndyCar Roles," *National Speed Sport News*, July 8, 2009, 3.

6. Martin, "George: Role a Life-Long Position," *National Speed Sport News*, July 15, 2009, 22.

7. "George Continues to Seek Reason for Exit," http://www.crash.net/indycar/news/150400/1/george_wants_reason_for_push.html, July 26, 2009.

8. "Indy Introduces 'Push to Pass,'" http://www.crash.net/indycar/news/150529/1/indycar_series_introduces_push_to_pass.html, July 29, 2009.

9. Kallman, "Push to Pass Gets First Use at Indy," http://www.jsonline.com/sports/autoracing/95164034.html, May 28, 2010.

10. "Indy Introduces 'Push to Pass,'" http://www.crash.net/indycar/news/150529/1/indycar_series_introduces_push_to_pass.html, July 29, 2009.

11. Martin, "Taking a Hard Look at the Indy-Car Rumor Mill," *National Speed Sport News*, July 29, 2009, 23.

12. Martin, "Dispute Not Straining Family," *National Speed Sport News*, Aug. 5, 2009, 29.

13. Fenech, "Road to Indy Bridges Open-Wheel Gap," *National Speed Sport News*, Dec. 16, 2009, 2.

14. "IRL, Dan Andersen Reviving U.S. F2000 Series," *National Speed Sport News*, Oct. 28, 2009, 9.

15. Fenwick, "Road to Indy Bridges Open-Wheel Gap," *National Speed Sport News*, Dec. 16, 2009, 2.

16. Martin, "IndyCar Series Signs 6-Year Pact with IZOD," *National Speed Sport News*, Nov. 11, 2009, 3.

17. "Indianapolis, IRL Announces Job Cuts," http://www.crash.net/indycar/news/154689/1/ims_irl_announces_job_cuts.html, Nov. 16, 2009.

18. "Indy Qualifying Format Reduced to One Weekend," *National Speed Sport News*, Jan. 6, 2010, 9.

19. "Several Technical Changes Coming to

IndyCar in 2010," *National Speed Sport News*, Jan. 20, 2010, 2.

20. Martin, "George's 'Vision' Now Over," *National Speed Sport News*, Feb. 3, 2010, 8.

21. Martin, "George Resigns from Speedway Board; Belskus: IMS Not for Sale," *National Speed Sport News*, Jan. 17, 2010, 3.

Chapter 14

1. Wikipedia, "Professional Bull Riders," http://en.wikipedia.org/wiki/Professional_Bull_Riders.

2. Professional Bull Riders, http://www.pbr.com/en/news/press-releases/2009/2/pbrs-live-attendance-up-in-2009-season.aspx.

3. "Indy Racing League Appoints New CEO," http://www.crash.net/indycar/news/156523/1/league_reveals_new_ceo.html, Feb. 3, 2010.

4. Martin, "New CEO Bernard Could Deliver Much Needed Boost to the IndyCar," http://sportsillustrated.cnn.com/2010/writers/bruce_martin/04/05/Randy.Bernard.IndyCar/, Apr. 5, 2010.

5. Ibid.

6. Martin, "New IndyCar CEO Faces Steep Learning Curve," *National Speed Sport News*, Feb. 10, 2010, 11.

7. Martin, "New CEO Bernard Could Deliver Much Needed Boost to the IndyCar," http://sportsillustrated.cnn.com/2010/writers/bruce_martin/04/05/Randy.Bernard.IndyCar/, Apr. 5, 2010.

8. Ibid.

9. "Dallara, Others in Talks to Create Next IRL Chassis," *National Speed Sport News*, Feb. 10, 2010, 31.

10. Ibid.

11. Deltawing, http://www.deltawingracing.com/history/, accessed Dec. 30, 2013.

12. "Delta-wing Unveils 2012 IndyCar Concept," http://www.crash.net/indycar/news/156741/1/deltawing_unveils_revolutionary_indycar_concept.html, Feb. 11, 2010.

13. "Trio Throws Hat into Indy Car Design Ring," *National Speed Sport News*, Mar. 10, 2010, 10; "BAT Engineering Bids for IndyCar Business," http://www.crash.net/indycar/news/157460/1/bat_engineering_submits_fifth_indycar_proposal.html, Mar. 5, 2010.

14. Martin, "Bernard: Series Too Vanilla," *National Speed Sport News*, Apr. 21, 2010, 23.

15. Martin, "'Shootout' Time Trials Coming to Indy 500," *National Speed Sport News*, Apr. 21, 2010, 3.

16. Martin, "Fastest of the Fast," *National Speed Sport News*, May 26, 2010, 5.

17. Martin, "Bernard Forms Panel to Determine New IndyCar Chassis," *National Speed Sport News*, Mar. 24, 2010, 3.

18. Martin, "Dallara Tabbed for IndyCar's 2012 Chassis," *National Speed Sport News*, July 21, 2010, 3.

19. Martin, "Dallara's Concept Far from Spec," *National Speed Sport News*, July 21, 2010, 26.

20. Martin, "Dallara Tabbed for IndyCar's 2012 Chassis," *National Speed Sport News*, July 21, 2010, 3.

21. Martin, "Teams Torn on Implementing New 2012 Car," *National Speed Sport News*, Sept. 1, 2010, 3.

22. Martin, "Chevrolet Returns to IndyCar Scene," *National Speed Sport News*, Nov. 17, 2010, 6.

23. "Chevrolet Returns as Engine Supplier in 2012," http://www.crash.net/indycar/news/165008/1/chevrolet_engines_return_to_indycar_in_2012.html, Nov. 12, 2010.

24. Martin, "Bernard Answers Call for American Involvement," http://www.nationalspeedsportnews.com/latest-headlines/bernard-answers-call-for-american-involvement/, Nov. 16, 2010.

25. "Chevrolet Returns as Engine Supplier in 2012," http://www.crash.net/indycar/news/165008/1/chevrolet_engines_return_to_indycar_in_2012.html, Nov. 12, 2010.

26. Ibid.

27. "Lotus Join Honda and Chevrolet in Supplying Engines," http://www.crash.net/indycar/news/165186/1/lotus_to_supply_engines_for_indycar_in_2012.html, Nov. 19, 2010.

28. "Firestone to Quit US Open-Wheel Racing," http://www.crash.net/indycar/news/167161/1/firestone_to_quit_us_open-wheel_racing.html, Mar. 4, 2011.

29. "Firestone Reverses Decision to Quit IndyCar," http://www.crash.net/indycar/news/167349/1/firestone_reverses_decision_to_quit_series.html, Mar. 11, 2011.

30. "Firestone to Quit US Open-Wheel Racing," http://www.crash.net/indycar/news/167161/1/firestone_to_quit_us_open-wheel_racing.html, Mar. 4, 2011.

31. Ibid.

32. "Firestone Reverses Decision to Quit IndyCar," http://www.crash.net/indycar/news/167349/1/firestone_reverses_decision_to_quit_series.html, Mar. 11, 2011.

33. Schottle, "Deal with Flip-Flopping Firestone Big Risk for Miles," http://www.ibj.com/the-score-2013-01-02-deal-with-flip-flopping-firestone-big-gamble-for-mark-miles/PARAMS/post/38782, Jan. 2, 2013.

34. "Firestone Reverses Decision to Quit IndyCar," http://www.crash.net/indycar/news/167349/1/firestone_reverses_decision_to_quit_series.html, Mar. 11, 2011.

35. "Bespoke Aero Kits Postponed Until 2013," http://www.crash.net/indycar/news/172100/1/bespoke_aero_kits_postponed_until_2013.html, Aug. 14, 2011.

Chapter 15

1. Associated Press, "IndyCar Steals from NASCAR: Double File Restarts Planned," http://www.thatsracin.com/2011/01/11/53709/indycar-series-plans-double-file.html, Jan. 11, 2011.
2. "Injuries Add Edge to Double File Restart Row," http://www.crash.net/indycar/news/167922/1/injuries_add_edge_to_double-file_restart_row.html, Mar. 29, 2011.
3. "Recriminations Fly After Toronto," http://www.crash.net/indycar/news/171134/1/recriminations_rage_on_after_toronto.html, July 11, 2011.
4. "Power Blasts Race Director Barnhart," http://www.crash.net/indycar/news/172103/1/power_blasts_race_director_barnhart.html, Aug. 15, 2011.
5. "Power Fined $30,000 over New Hampshire," http://www.crash.net/indycar/news/172360/1/power_fined_30000_over_new_hampshire.html, Aug. 25, 2011.
6. "Barnhart Discusses Controversial Call," http://www.crash.net/indycar/news/172162/1/barnhart_discusses_controversial_restart_call.html, Aug. 16, 2011.
7. "New Hampshire Race Protest Denied," http://www.crash.net/indycar/news/172322/1/new_hampshire_results_protest_denied.html, Aug. 24, 2011.
8. "Helio Slams Barnhart over Officiating," http://www.crash.net/indycar/news/173399/1/helio_slams_circus_clown_barnhart.html, Sept. 26, 2011.
9. "Castroneves Fined $30K for Barnhart Comments," http://www.crash.net/indycar/news/173430/1/castroneves_fined_30k_for_comments.html, Sept. 27, 2011.
10. "IndyCar Numbers on the Rise," http://www.nationalspeedsportnews.com/indy/izod-indycar/indycar-numbers-on-the-rise/, Dec. 1, 2011.
11. Schoettle, "IndyCar CEO May Take Control of More Races," *Indianapolis Business Journal*, July 11, 2011, A-3.
12. Ibid.
13. Ibid.
14. Ibid.
15. Cavin, "$5 Million Challenge Is Not Quite," *Indianapolis Star*, Oct. 11, 2011, C-1.
16. "'Perfect Storm' Led to Vegas Tragedy," http://www.crash.net/indycar/news/175518/1/report_finds_perfect_storm_led_to_vegas_tragedy.html, Dec. 15, 2011.

17. Cavin, "Drivers Defend Bernard," *Indianapolis Star*, Oct. 25, 2011, C-2.
18. "'Perfect Storm' Led to Vegas Tragedy," http://www.crash.net/indycar/news/175518/1/report_finds_perfect_storm_led_to_vegas_tragedy.html, Dec. 15, 2011.
19. Schoettle, "IndyCar's Big New Wheels," *Indianapolis Business Journal*, Mar. 19, 2012, A-3.
20. "Barnhart out of Race Control for 2012," http://www.crash.net/indycar/news/175269/1/barnhart_out_of_race_control_in_2012.html/ Nov. 30, 2011.
21. "Beaux Barfield Hired by IndyCar," http://espn.go.com/racing/indycar/story/_/id/7420121/beaux-barfield-hired-indycar-race-director, Jan. 4, 2012.
22. "New Trophy to IndyCar Champion," http://www.nationalspeedsportnews.com/indy/izod-indycar/new-trophy-to-indycar-champion/, Oct. 13, 2011.
23. "Newman/Haas Quits IndyCar Series," http://www.crash.net/indycar/news/175289/1/newmanhaas_quits_indycar_series.html, Dec. 1, 2011.
24. "Series Set for New Chinese Flyaway," http://www.crash.net/indycar/news/174824/1/series_set_for_new_chinese_flyaway.html, Nov. 11, 2011.
25. "IndyCar Revamps Leaders Circle Program," http://www.nationalspeedsportnews.com/indy/izod-indycar/indycar-revamps-leaders-circle-program/, Feb. 10, 2012.
26. "Firestone Extends Pact with IndyCar," http://www.nationalspeedsportnews.com/indy/izod-indycar/firestone-extends-pact-with-indycar/, Feb. 12, 2012.
27. "Hulman & Company Expands Board," http://www.nationalspeedsportnews.com/indy/indycar-development-series/skip-barber-indycar-academy-created/, Mar. 8, 2012.
28. "Skip Barber IndyCar Academy Created," http://www.nationalspeedsportnews.com/indy/indycar-development-series/skip-barber-indycar-academy-created/, Mar. 28, 2012.
29. "Chevy Orders All Teams to Change Engines," http://www.crash.net/indycar/news/178508/1/chevy_orders_all_teams_to_change_engines.html, Apr. 12, 2012.
30. "Engine Penalties 'Will Stay' Says IndyCar," http://www.crash.net/indycar/news/178582/1/engine_penalties_will_stay_says_indycar.html, Apr. 14, 2012.
31. "No Engine Starting Grid Penalties During Indy," http://www.crash.net/indycar/news/178980/1/no_engine_grid_penalties_during_indy_500.html, Apr. 25, 2012.
32. Oreovicz, "Turbogate Fuels Indy Car Unrest," http://espn.go.com/racing/indycar/story/_/id/7900409/ May 8, 2012.

33. "IndyCar Expected to Rule on Friday on Chevrolet's Protest of Honda Turbocharger," http://www.autoweek.com/article/20120426/indycar/120429835, Apr. 26, 2012.

34. "Honda Wins Chance to Upgrade Turbochargers," http://www.crash.net/indycar/news/179024/1/honda_wins_right_to_upgrade_turbochargers.html, Apr. 27, 2012.

35. "Chevrolet Loses Final Turbocharger Appeal," http://www.crash.net/indycar/news/179587/1/chevy_loses_final_turbocharger_appeal.html, May 11, 2012.

36. "IndyCar Fines Panther Owner $25,000 for Disparaging Tweet," http://www.autoweek.com/article/20120428/INDYCAR/120429801, Apr. 27, 2012.

37. "Lotus Confirms Split with BHA and DRR," http://www.crash.net/indycar/news/178954/1/lotus_confirms_split_with_bha_and_drr.html, Apr. 24, 2012.

38. "New Rule to Stop Mid-Season Engine Swaps," http://www.crash.net/indycar/news/179228/1/new_rule_to_stop_mid-season_engine_swaps.html, May 2, 2012.

39. "Reports: Dragon 'Suing Lotus for Contractual Fraud,'" http://www.crash.net/indycar/news/179456/1/dragon_suing_lotus_for_contractual_fraud.html, May 7, 2012.

40. Martin, "Dragon Dumping Lotus for Chevrolet," http://www.nationalspeedsportnews.com/category/indy/page/78/, May 16, 2012.

41. Ibid.

42. Martin, "IndyCar Fines 11 Teams," http://www.nationalspeedsportnews.com/indy/izod-indycar/indycar-fines-11-teams/, May 20, 2012.

43. "Chevy Teams Grow Restless with Bernard," http://www.crash.net/indycar/news/180309/1/chevy_teams_grow_restless_with_bernard.html, May 30, 2012.

44. Ibid.

45. Ibid.

46. "Bernard 'Wanted to Get in Front of the Problem,'" http://www.crash.net/indycar/news/180447/1/bernards_strategy_pulls_owners_into_line.html, June 4, 2012.

47. Cavin, "Turmoil Surrounds Series Boss Bernard," *Indianapolis Star*, May 31, 2012, C-1.

48. "Bernard 'Wanted to Get in Front of the Problem,'" http://www.crash.net/indycar/news/180447/1/bernards_strategy_pulls_owners_into_line.html, June 4, 2012.

49. "Owners Want Further Delays to Aero Kits," http://www.crash.net/indycar/news/180508/1/owners_want_further_delay_to_aero_kits.html, June 5, 2012.

50. Fenech, "Faulty Asphalt Takes Lengthy Repair Job," *Detroit Free Press*, June 4, 2012, B-11; Lage, "Track Trouble Spoils Detroit Grand Prix," *Journal Gazette*, June 4, 2012, B-2.

51. Cavin, "Wilson Stays Close, Wins After Rahal's Late Mistake, Crash," *Indianapolis Star*, June 10, 2012, C-1.

52. Cavin, "Wilson's Team Fined, but He Keeps Win," *Indianapolis Star*, June 12, 2012, C-5.

53. Kravitz, "Give Bernard Some Credit—and Plenty of Blame Too," *Indianapolis Star*, June 24, 2012, C-1.

54. Cavin, "IndyCar Weekend Belongs to Andretti," *Indianapolis Star*, June 17, 2012, C-1.

55. "IndyCar Endures Another Embarrassing Mistake," *USA Today*, June 18, 2012, C-2.

56. "China Round Dropped—Replacement Being Sought," http://www.crash.net/indycar/news/180816/1/china_round_dropped_-_replacement_sought.html, June 13, 2012.

57. "No Extra Race to Replace China, Says IndyCar," http://www.crash.net/indycar/news/181211/1/no_replacement_for_china_says_indycar.html, June 25, 2012.

58. Oreovicz, "Tony George News Fuels Speculation," http://www.sportsbusinessdaily.com/Journal/Issues/2012/10/01/Leagues-and-Governing-Bodies/IndyCar.aspx, Sept. 27, 2012.

59. Mikell, "Tony George Leads Offer for IndyCar Series," http://www.sportsbusinessdaily.com/Journal/Issues/2012/10/01/Leagues-and-Governing-Bodies/IndyCar.aspx, Oct. 1, 2012.

60. "Official: Randy Bernard Exits as Series CEO," http://www.crash.net/indycar/news/185607/1/official_randy_bernard_exits_as_series_ceo.html, Oct. 29, 2012.

61. Cavin, "Bernard's Bumpy Ride," *Indianapolis Star*, Oct. 27, 2012, C-2.

62. "Official: Randy Bernard Exits as Series CEO," http://www.crash.net/indycar/news/185607/1/official_randy_bernard_exits_as_series_ceo.html, Oct. 29, 2012.

63. "Interim CEO Insists Bernard Was Not Sacked," http://www.crash.net/indycar/news/185722/1/interim_ceo_insists_bernard_was_not_sacked.html, Nov. 2, 2012.

64. Associated Press, "Randy Bernard Steps Down as IndyCar CEO; Will Stay with Series in an Advisory Role," http://www.foxnews.com/sports/2012/10/28/randy-bernard-steps-down-as-indycar-ceo-will-stay-with-series-in-advisory-role/, Oct. 28, 2012.

65. "Interim CEO Insists Bernard Was Not Sacked," http://www.crash.net/indycar/news/185722/1/interim_ceo_insists_bernard_was_not_sacked.html, Nov. 2, 2012.

66. Oreovicz, "Tony George News Fuels Speculation," http://www.sportsbusinessdaily.com/Journal/Issues/2012/10/01/Leagues-and-Governing-Bodies/IndyCar.aspx, Sept. 27, 2012.

67. Mikell, "Tony George Leads Offer for

IndyCar Series," http://www.sportsbusiness daily.com/Journal/Issues/2012/10/01/Leagues-and-Governing-Bodies/IndyCar.aspx, Oct. 1, 2012.

68. Cavin, "Tony George's Offer to Buy Indy-Car Wasn't Considered," http://www.usatoday. com/story/sports/motor/2012/10/30/tony-geor ge-bid-on-indycar-series/1669401/, Jan. 8, 2013.

69. Schoettle, "IndyCar Confronts 'Defining Moment.'" *Indianapolis Business Journal*, Nov. 5, 2012, A-3.

70. Ibid.

71. "Takeover Rumours Persist Despite Denials," http://www.crash.net/indycar/news/185 300/1/tony_george_quits_board_of_series_ owners.html, Oct. 3, 2012.

Chapter 16

1. "Takeover Rumours Persist Despite Denials," http://www.crash.net/indycar/news/ 185300/1/tony_george_quits_board_of_series_ owners.html, Oct. 3, 2012.

2. Schoettle, "IndyCar Execs: Distractions Mask Progress," *Indianapolis Business Journal*, Oct. 8, 2012, 3.

3. Schoettle, "Signs Point to Internal Hire to Replace Bernard as IndyCar CEO," http:// www.ibj.com/the-score-2012–11–02-all-signs-point-to-internal-hire-to-replace-bernard-as-indycar-ceo/PARAMS/post/37693, Nov. 2, 2012.

4. Kirby, "The Way It Is: Can Mark Miles Turn IndyCar Around?" http://www.gordon kirby.com/categories/columns/theway/2013/ the_way_it_is_no387.html, 2013; Schoettle, "Signs Point to Internal Hire to Replace Bernard as IndyCar CEO," http://www.ibj.com/the-score-2012-11-02-all-signs-point-to-internal-hire-to-replace-bernard-as-indycar-ceo/PARA MS/post/37693, Nov. 2, 2012; WTHR.com, "Mark Miles Tapped to Be CEO of Hulman & Company," http://www.wthr.com/story/201465 54/indycar-owners-set-for-announcement, Nov. 20, 2012.

5. Cavin and Murray, "IndyCar Chief Says He'll Try to Build Trust," *Indianapolis Star*, Nov. 21, 2012, A-1.

6. "Study Says IMS Generates $510 Million Impact," http://www.nationalspeedsportnews. com/indy/izod-indycar/study-says-ims-generates-510-million-impact/, Mar. 10, 2013.

7. Oreovicz, "Hulman CEO Miles Good for IndyCar?" http://espn.go.com/racing/blog/_/ name/oreovicz_john/id/8657254/indycar-hulman-ceo-mark-miles-good-indycar, Nov. 20, 2012.

8. Cavin and Murray, "IndyCar Chief Says He'll Try to Build Trust," *Indianapolis Star*, Nov. 21, 2012, A-1.

9. Oreovicz, "Hulman CEO Miles Good for IndyCar?" http://espn.go.com/racing/blog/_/ name/oreovicz_john/id/8657254/indycar-hul man-ceo-mark-miles-good-indycar, Nov. 20, 2012.

10. Ibid.

11. "IndyCar to Face Challenge from F1 Support Series?" http://www.crash.net/indycar/ news/186061/1/new_fl_challenge_looms_for_ indycar.html, Nov. 12, 2012.

12. Oreovicz, "Hulman CEO Miles Good for IndyCar?" http://espn.go.com/racing/blog/_/ name/oreovicz_john/id/8657254/indycar-hul man-ceo-mark-miles-good-indycar, Nov. 20, 2012.

13. Schottle, "Hulman & Co. Seeks to Overhaul IndyCar Management," http://www.ibj. com/the-score-2012-11-29-hulman-co-ceo-seeks-new-indycar-management-structure-team/PARAMS/post/38192, Nov. 29, 2012.

14. "Lotus out of IndyCar Racing," http:// www.nationalspeedsportnews.com/indy/izod-indycar/lotus-out-of-indycar-racing/, Dec. 17, 2012.

15. Schottle, "Deal with Flip-Flopping Firestone Big Risk for Miles," http://www.ibj.com/ the-score-2013-01-02-deal-with-flip-flopping-firestone-big-gamble-for-mark-miles/PARA MS/post/38782, Jan. 2, 2013.

16. "Cost-Cutting Deal Agreed with Dallara," http://www.crash.net/indycar/news/1873 48/1/cost-cutting-deal-agreed-with-dallara. html, Jan. 18, 2013.

17. Schoettle, "New Speedway President Asked to 'Save Our Track,'" http://www.ibj. com/the-score-2013-07-10-new-speedway-president-asked-to-save-our-track/PARAMS/ post/42365, July 10, 2013.

18. Schoettle, "Needs Exceed Subsidy," *Indianapolis Business Journal*, Feb. 13, 2013, 1.

19. "Study Says IMS Generates $510 Million Impact," http://www.nationalspeedsportnews. com/indy/izod-indycar/study-says-ims-generates-510-million-impact/, Mar. 10, 2013.

20. "IMS Racing Initiative Gets Approval," http://www.nationalspeedsportnews.com/ indy/izod-indycar/imsc-gets-legislative-approval-of-racing-initiative/, Apr. 13, 2013.

21. Fryer, "Consulting Group Suggests IndyCar Changes," *Press* (Sheboygan, Wisconsin), Mar. 2, 2013, 2.

22. Wikipedia, "Arie Luyendyk," http://en. wikipedia.org/wiki/Arie_Luyendyk.

23. Fryer, "Consulting Group Suggests IndyCar Changes," *Press* (Sheboygan, Wisconsin), Mar. 2, 2013, 2.

24. Associated Press, "IndyCar Courting Just Marketing Founder Zak Brown for CEO," http:// sportsillustrated.cnn.com/racing/news/201303 23/indycar-zak-brown-ceo.ap/, Mar. 23, 2013.

25. "Walker Ready for New IndyCar Challenge," http://www.nationalspeedsportnews.com/indy/izod-indycar/walker-ready-for-new-indycar-challenge/, May 13, 2013.

26. Associated Press, "IndyCar Courting Just Marketing Founder Zak Brown for CEO," http://sportsillustrated.cnn.com/racing/news/20130323/indycar-zak-brown-ceo.ap/, Mar. 23, 2013.

27. "Walker Ready for New IndyCar Challenge," http://www.nationalspeedsportnews.com/indy/izod-indycar/walker-ready-for-new-indycar-challenge/, May 13, 2013.

28. Ibid.

29. Martin, "IndyCar open to More Technical Innovation," http://www.nationalspeedsportnews.com/indy/izod-indycar/indycar-open-to-more-technical-innovation/, May 23, 2013.

30. Glendenning, "IndyCar and Indianapolis Nears Restructure—Mark Miles," http://www.autosport.com/news/report.php/id/108700, July 9, 2013; "Motorsports Media Green Becomes CEO of IMS Production," http://www.theautochannel.com/news/2011/07/14/540665-motorsports-media-green-becomes-ceo-ims-productions.html, July 14, 2013.

31. Weaver, "IndyCar Mandates Twin Turbos for All Engine Suppliers in 2014," http://www.sbnation.com/indycar/2013/7/25/4557438/indycar-mandates-twin-turbos-for-all-engine-suppliers-in-2014 July 25, 2013.

32. Schoettle, "Honda Wants IndyCar Officials to Find New Engine Suppliers," http://www.ibj.com/the-score-2013-10-14-honda-wants-indycar-officials-to-find-new-engine-suppliers/PARAMS/post/44044, Oct. 13, 2013.

33. Schoettle, "IndyCar Ponders Overseas Expansion to Counter Troubles at Home," http://www.ibj.com/the-score-2013-08-28-indycar-ponders-overseas-expansion-to-counter-troubles-at-home/PARAMS/post/43237, Aug. 28, 2013.

34. Schoettle, "New Boss Ready to Overhaul the Month of May in Indy," http://www.ibj.com/the-score-2013-09-03-new-boss-ready-to-overhaul-month-of-may-in-indy/PARAMS/post/43332, Sept. 3, 2013.

35. "IMS Reveals IndyCar Road Race Details," http://www.nationalspeedsportnews.com/indy/izod-indycar/ims-reveals-indycar-road-race-details/Oct. 1, 2013.

36. Carpenter, "IndyCar's Mark Miles on TV Ratings, New Markets and Improving Indianapolis Motor Speedway," http://www.sportsbusinessdaily.com/SB-Blogs/On-The-Ground/2013/12/MMF-Mark-Miles-IndyCar-Indianapolis-Motor-Speedway.aspx, Dec. 4, 2013.

Bibliography

Books

Clymer, Floyd. *Indianapolis 500 Mile Race History: A Complete Detailed History of Every Indianapolis Race Since 1909.* Los Angeles: Floyd Clymer, 1946.

Ludvigsen, Karl. *Dan Gurney: The Ultimate Racer.* Sparkford, Nr Yeovil, Somerset, UK: Haynes, 2000.

Shaffer, Rick. *CART: The First 20 Years, 1978–1998.* Richmond, UK: Hazelton, 1999.

Wallen, Dick, Dan Fleisher, and Dan Harker. *United States Auto Club: 50 Years of Speed and Glory.* Glendale, AZ: Dick Wallen's Racing Classic, 2006.

Newspapers

"ABC-TV Wins Rights to Show Indy 500 Live." *National Sport Speed News,* Aug. 21, 1985, 3.

"Absolutely, Positively, FedEx Signs to be CART's Sponsor." *National Speed Sport News,* Dec. 10, 1997, 2.

"ACCUS Accepts CART." *National Sport Speed News,* Sept. 14, 1988, 3.

"ACCUS Refusal to Hear Andretti Gives Unser 500." *National Speed Sport News,* Feb. 3, 1982, 2.

"Administration's Energy Saving Plan Could Halt US Auto Racing." *National Speed Sport News,* Mar. 7, 1979, 3.

Allyn, Ronnie. "CART Eliminates Skirts in Move to Slow Cars." *National Speed Sport News,* Sept. 1, 1982, 3.

_____. "Foyt Easy Ontario Victor as USAC Fields 21 Cars." *National Speed Sport News,* Mar. 28, 1979, 3.

"Andretti Green Promotions Secures 2009 IndyCar Series Date for GP of Toronto." *National Speed Sport News,* May 21, 2008, 42.

"Andretti Indy Appeal to ACCUS." *National Speed Sport News,* Nov. 11, 1981, 3.

"Another $15.5 Million Year for CART Series." *National Speed Sport News,* Feb. 25, 1987, 3.

"Another Missed Opportunity for Open-Wheel Merger." *National Speed Sport News,* Feb. 6, 2008, 3.

"Are Car Owners Bidding for Control of USAC?" *National Speed Sport News,* Oct. 25, 1978, 3.

"Arie, Roberto Head 77-Car Indy Entry List." *National Speed Sport News,* Apr. 17, 1996, 3.

"Attendance at Major U.S. Race Events Jumps 11%." *National Sport Speed News,* Jan. 6, 1988, 3.

"Attendance Upswing Noted at U.S. Events." *National Speed Sport News,* Dec. 15, 1982, 2.

"Auto Racing Attendance Continues to Climb." *National Sport Speed News,* Jan. 10, 1990, 2.

Ballard, Steve. "CART Board Votes to Accept Buyout." *Indianapolis Star,* Dec. 16, 2003, D-1.

_____. "CART Needs Deal to Continue." *Indianapolis Star,* Aug. 15, 2003, D-6.

_____. "Coming to Grips." *Indianapolis Star,* July 5, 2001, C-1.

_____. "Fans Will Get HD Views from Cars." *Indianapolis Star,* Mar. 28, 2008, D-8.

_____. "5 Things Needed to Boost Success of IRL's IndyCar." *Indianapolis Star,* May 4, 2008, C-1.

_____. "IRL Won't Get Chance to Pull Plug on CART." *Indianapolis Star,* Jan. 29, 2004, A-1.

_____. "Open-Wheel Series Entering New Eras, CART Moves Forward with Eyes on 2005." *Indianapolis Star,* Jan. 17, 2003, D-1.

_____. "Open-Wheel Unity: Desirable, Difficult." *Indianapolis Star,* May 24, 2005, D-1.

_____. "Philosophies to Clash as Judge Hears CART case." *Indianapolis Star,* Jan. 28, 2004, D-1.

_____. "With Judge's Ruling, Race Begins for Circuit." *Indianapolis Star,* Jan. 30, 2004, D-1.

Bignotti, Mary. "Open-Wheel Support Systems

Are Growing." *National Speed Sport News,* June 13, 2007, 2.

"Board Hears Sneva Case." *Indianapolis Star,* May 22, 1981, 37.

Cadou, Jep, Jr. "Ban a Shock to CART." *National Speed Sport News,* Apr. 25, 1979, p 3, 16.

_____. "CART Petitions Federal Court to Upset USAC's Indy Turndown." *National Speed Sport News,* May 2, 1979, 3.

_____. "CART Puts Pocono 500 Off Limits." *National Speed Sport News,* June 10, 1981, 3.

_____. "Cooper Decides: USAC to Stay On at Indy." *National Sport Speed News,* Sept. 3, 1980, 2.

_____. "Exotic Engines OK for Indy '82—USAC." *National Speed Sport News,* Aug. 5, 1981, 2.

_____. "Goodyear Indicates USAC Pullout May Be Near." *National Speed Sport News,* Sept. 20, 1978, 3.

_____. "Much Bitterness in First 2 Days of Indy Hearing." *National Speed Sport News,* June 10, 1981, 3.

_____. "Now It Comes Out—the Money (and Secrets)." *National Speed Sport News,* May 23, 1984, 3.

_____. "Oversupply of Race Cars Is Talk of Indy Town." *National Speed Sport News,* Apr. 25, 1984, 3.

_____. "A Slowdown at Indy Goal of USAC and CART." *National Sport Speed News,* June 5, 1985, 3.

_____. "USAC Loses Eight Officials in Air Crash." *National Speed Sport News,* Apr. 26, 1978, 3.

_____. "USAC Rules Out Participants on Board." *National Sport Speed News,* Aug. 20, 1980, 3.

_____. "USAC's Declaration of Independence May Mean War." *National Speed Sport News,* July 2, 1980, 3.

_____. "USAC's New Rules, What Do They Mean?" *National Speed Sport News,* Jan. 3, 1979, 3.

"CART and PPG Set $1 Million Point Fund." *National Sport Speed News,* Nov. 12, 1980, 3.

"CART Backs Extra Qualifying." *Indianapolis Star,* May 24, 1979, 1.

"CART Ban Set Aside." *National Speed Sport News,* July 1, 1981, 3.

"CART Chairman: Entertainment Thrust Needed." *National Sport Speed News,* Jan. 11, 1991, 2.

"CART Drops Detroit, Adds Australian Run." *National Sport Speed News,* Aug. 22, 1990, 3.

"CART Enters 44 Cars in Record Indy 500 Field." *National Speed Sport News,* Apr. 18, 1979, 3.

"CART Expands Board, Retains Pres. Capon-igro." *National Sport Speed News,* Nov. 1, 1989, 3.

"CART Fires Back." *National Speed Sport News,* Apr. 3, 1996, 3.

"CART Gets PPG as Sponsor, 4 NBC TV Races." *National Speed Sport News,* Oct. 31, 1979, 3.

"CART Is Back in Business." *Indianapolis Star,* July 2, 1980, 15.

"CART Issues Pink Slip to Caponigro, Picks Capels to Lead Club through '90." *National Sport Speed News,* Dec. 20, 1989, 3.

"CART Loses $9 Million." *National Speed Sport News,* May 14, 2003, 2.

"CART Names Bill Stokkan Chairman." *National Sport Speed News,* Apr. 11, 1990, 3.

"CART Network to Broadcast Sixteen Races." *National Sport Speed News,* Dec. 18, 1985, 3.

"CART Plans Acquisition Meeting." *National Speed Sport News,* Nov. 26, 2003, 2.

"CART, Pocono Make Peace; Set Aug. 15 500." *National Speed Sport News,* May 5, 1982, 2.

"CART Prize $ Jumps 15% to Record $11.5 Million." *National Speed Sport News,* Jan. 16, 1985, 3.

"CART Reveals Engine Specs." *Indianapolis Star,* Sept. 8, 1983, 35.

"CART Sponsor PPG Backs 500." *Indianapolis Star,* May 30, 1982, 2-D.

"CART Studying FISA Ban on Out-of-Country Races." *National Sport Speed News,* Nov. 2, 1988, 2.

"CART Wins over USAC in Apr. 22 TV Battle." *National Speed Sport News,* Mar. 28, 1979, 3.

"CART Won't Return to England for Now." *National Sport Speed News,* Nov. 27, 2002, 6.

"CART-IRL Talks Continue, May Resolution Unlikely." *National Speed Sport News,* Feb. 28, 1996, 3.

"CART's Japanese Race Scrubbed." *National Sport Speed News,* Dec. 14, 1988, 3.

"CART's Reply: Definite 'Maybe.'" *Indianapolis Star,* Feb. 23, 1980, 29.

"CART's Rules Rhubarbs Resurface at Detroit GP." *National Sport Speed News,* June 20, 1990, 3.

Cavin, Curt. "Bernard's Bumpy Ride." *Indianapolis Star,* Oct. 27, 2012, C-2.

_____. "Champ Car's Walker Considers Switch to IRL." *Indianapolis Star,* Feb. 13, 2008, D-3.

_____. "The Changing Face of Open-Wheel Racing." *Indianapolis Star,* Dec. 14, 2001, D-3.

_____. "Drivers Defend Bernard." *Indianapolis Star,* Oct. 25, 2011, C-2.

_____. "Era of Unity: Start the Excitement." *Indianapolis Star,* May 4, 2008, A-1.

_____. "500, IRL Drop USAC as Sanctioning Body." *Indianapolis Star,* June 17, 1997, A-1.

_____. "$5 Million Challenge Is Not Quite." *Indianapolis Star,* Oct. 11, 2011, C-1.

_____. "George Eager for New Era to Begin." *Indianapolis Star,* Mar. 28, 2008, D-1.

_____. "IndyCar Weekend Belongs to Andretti." *Indianapolis Star,* June 17, 2012, C-1.

_____. "IRL Closer to Deal with Champ Car." *Indianapolis Star,* Feb. 20, 2008, D-1.

_____. "IRL Meeting Draws Full Lineup of Champ Car Teams." *Indianapolis Star,* Feb. 26, 2008, D-1.

_____. "IRL Won't Push CART Merger." *Indianapolis Star,* Feb. 9, 2001, D-1.

_____. "'95 Marked the End of an Era at Speedway." *Indianapolis Star,* May 25, 2003, R-9.

_____. "No Deal Yet, but It's Closer." *Indianapolis Star,* Feb. 22, 2008, D-1.

_____. "No Merger News but Many Questions." *Indianapolis Star,* Feb. 15, 2008, D-6.

_____. "Only 16 '95 Indy Drivers Vying at MIS." *Indianapolis Star,* May 10, 1996, E-2.

_____. "Strong Words at 'Other 500.'" *Indianapolis Star,* May 11, 1996, D-1.

_____. "Turmoil Surrounds Series Boss Bernard." *Indianapolis Star,* May 31, 2012, C-1.

_____. "Unification." *Indianapolis Star,* Feb. 23, 2008, D-1.

_____. "Unifying Series Isn't Cheap." *Indianapolis Star,* Feb. 28, 2008, D-1.

_____. "U.S. Auto Club Still Part of Speedway Despite Debacle." *Indianapolis Star,* May 22, 1998, J-9.

_____. "Wilson Stays Close, Wins After Rahal's Late Mistake, Crash." *Indianapolis Star,* June 10, 2012, C-1.

_____. "Wilson's Team Fined, but He Keeps Win." *Indianapolis Star,* June 12, 2012, C-5.

Cavin, Curt, and Steve Ballard. "Champ Car's Tracy Looks for a Ride." *Indianapolis Star,* Feb. 29, 2008, D-5.

_____. "IRL, CCWS Execs Plan to Meet." *Indianapolis Star,* Feb. 21, 2008, D-3.

Cavin, Curt, and Jon Murray. "IndyCar Chief Says He'll Try to Build Trust." *Indianapolis Star,* Nov. 21, 2012, A-1.

"Champ Car, IRL Nearing Merger." *Indianapolis Star,* June 25, 2006, A-1.

"Champ Car to Pay Molson for TV Production." *National Speed Sport News,* Jan. 26, 2005, 10.

"Chassis Regs Complete IRL's 1997 Car Plans." *National Speed Sport News,* Apr. 3, 1996, 3.

Clayton, John. "GM Cutting Spending." *National Speed Sport News,* July 23, 2008, 2.

Collins, Bob. "Rising Costs Making Owners Restless." *Indianapolis Star,* May 28, 1978, sect. 2, 2.

"Controversy Surfaces in CART as Sponsor Unhappy with Head." *National Sport Speed News,* Nov. 29, 1989, 3.

"Cooper New Indianapolis Head, Reaction Favorable." *National Speed Sport News,* Oct. 24, 1979, 3.

"Cooper Quits as Speedway President." *Indianapolis Star,* May 8, 1982, 1.

"Dallara, Others in Talks to Create Next IRL Chassis." *National Speed Sport News,* Feb. 10, 2010, 31.

"Details Made Known of Indy's CART Suit." *National Speed Sport News,* May 15, 1996, 3.

"Details of Failed IRL-IndyCar Discussions Now Made Public." *National Speed Sport News,* July 19, 1995, 2.

"Dissent over CART Regs, Some Look to Detroit." *National Sport Speed News,* July 13, 1988, 3.

"Does USAC Vote Signal the End?" *National Speed Sport News,* July 9, 1980, 3.

"Drivers Seek CART Sanction for Indy 500." *National Speed Sport News,* Nov. 10, 1982, 3.

Economaki, Chris. "Battle Lines Forming in CART-FISA Feud." *National Sport Speed News,* Nov. 16, 1988, 3.

_____. "Business Pages, Not Sports Pages." *National Speed Sport News,* May 13, 2009, 4.

_____. "Racing Suffers Body Blow." *National Speed Sport News,* Jan. 7, 2009, 4.

_____. "Survey Says NFL Is Leading American Sport." *National Speed Sport News,* Jan. 16, 2008, 27.

_____. "Wherefore the Americans." *National Speed Sport News,* Jan. 9, 2008, 4.

Economaki, Chris, and Bill Oursler. "CART Big Guns Shell USAC, Key Defensive Move Seen." *National Speed Sport News,* Jan. 10, 1979, 3.

_____. "CART Chief, Indy 500 Boss in Hush-Hush Rules Parley." *National Speed Sport News,* July 18, 1984, 3.

_____. "CART-SCCA Deal Triggers Indy Stock-Block Thinking." *National Speed Sport News,* Dec. 13, 1978, 3.

_____. "CART Schedule Announced; Rift with USAC Widens." *National Speed Sport News,* Nov. 29, 1978, 3.

_____. "Champ Racing in Turmoil, CART Quits USAC." *National Speed Sport News,* Nov. 22, 1978, 3.

_____. "Major Obstacle to CART-USAC Peace Removed." *National Speed Sport News,* Feb. 28, 3.

_____. "New CART-USAC Reconciliation Plan Being Presented in Indy by Smartis." *National Speed Sport News,* June 13, 1979, 3.

_____. "Penske Offers 'Performance Bond.'" *National Speed Sport News,* Apr. 25, 1979, 3.

_____. "Six Tracks Remain USAC; Indy Goes Stock Block!" *National Speed Sport News,* Jan. 3, 1979, 3.

_____. "USAC Sets Stock-Block Formula at

600 Horses." *National Speed Sport News,* Jan. 24, 1979, 3.

"'84 CART Year at $10 Million!" *National Speed Sport News,* Feb. 29, 1984, 3.

"11 'Bumped' Cars Can Requalify Today." *Indianapolis Star,* May 26, 1979, 1.

"Fans to Join Paul Newman in His Return to Indy 500?" *Indianapolis Star,* Mar. 25, 2008, D-2.

"Fastest Indy 500 Field Set, Average Speed up 4 MPH." *National Sport Speed News,* May 15, 1985, 3.

Fenech, Anthony. "Faulty Asphalt Takes Lengthy Repair Job." *Detroit Free Press,* June 4, 2012, B-11.

_____. "Road to Indy Bridges Open-Wheel Gap." *National Speed Sport News,* Dec. 16, 2009, 2.

Franck, Lewis. "CART-FISA Negotiations On but TV Rights Pose Problem." *National Sport Speed News,* July 5, 1989, 3.

_____. "Detroit Indy Car Race May Not Be Dead." *National Sport Speed News,* Sept. 5, 1990, 3.

_____. "Penske Takes Issue with USAC." *National Sport Speed News,* Sept. 6, 1989, 3.

Freudenthal, Kurt. "Vollstedt Appeal Denied; Drivers Meet at 11 a.m." *Indianapolis Star,* May 23, 1981, 31.

Fryer, Jenna. "Consulting Group Suggests IndyCar Changes." *Press* (Sheboygan, Wisconsin), Mar. 2, 2013, 2.

"George Scoffs at Merger Rumors." *National Speed Sport News,* Mar. 1, 2006, 2.

"George Tackles Role of Team Owner." *National Speed Sport News,* Feb. 16, 2005, 2.

Guehler, Gary. "CART Spells Out Its $1 Million 500-Mile Michigan Race July 19." *National Speed Sport News,* Mar. 4, 1981, 3.

"Honda Indy Car Project Gets Green Light for '94." *National Speed Sport News,* Sept. 15, 1993, 3.

"Honda's Indy Decision Imminent." *National Speed Sport News,* Sept. 8, 1993, 2.

"Impasse in Indy-Car Talks; Goodyear Sharply Critical." *National Speed Sport News,* Jan. 23, 1980, 3.

"IMS Picks Tony George." *National Sport Speed News,* Jan. 10, 1990, 5.

"IMS' Tony George Joins USAC's Board." *National Speed Sport News,* Jan. 28, 1987, 3.

"Indy Car Owners Meet, Seek Restructuring of CART." *National Sport Speed News,* Oct. 11, 1989, 3.

"Indy Car 'Peace Conference' Falls Apart After Walkout." *National Speed Sport News,* Jan. 16, 1980, 2.

"Indy Head Cloutier Heart Victim at 81." *National Sport Speed News,* Dec. 13, 1989, 3.

"Indy Inks 'Lend-Lease' Deal with Pocono."

National Speed Sport News, Nov. 7, 1979, 3.

"Indy Is Open to All: TV Pact Is Key Issue." *National Speed Sport News,* Jan. 17, 1979, 3.

"Indy Qualifying Format Reduced to One Weekend." *National Speed Sport News,* Jan. 6, 2010, 9.

"IndyCar Endures Another Embarrassing Mistake." *USA Today,* June 18, 2012, C-2.

"IndyCar Girds for IMS Fight." *National Speed Sport News,* June 15, 1994, 3.

"IndyCar–IRL War of Words Hits New High." *National Speed Sport News,* June 21, 1995, 2.

"IndyCar Plans Huge '93 Fines for Rules Sins." *National Speed Sport News,* Nov. 18, 1992, 2.

"Indy's 500 Winner of TV Battle." *National Speed Sport News,* June 12, 1996, 2.

"IRL, Champ Car Make Up." *Indianapolis Star,* Feb. 23, 2008, 1.

"IRL, Dan Andersen Reviving U.S. F2000 Series." *National Speed Sport News,* Oct. 28, 2009, 9.

"IRL Engine Delay." *National Speed Sport News,* Mar. 15, 1995, 3.

"IRL's Long: Indy Control Key Issue." *National Speed Sport News,* July 26, 1995, 2.

"IRL's 'Look to Europe.'" *National Speed Sport News,* Apr. 10, 1996, 2.

"Key Meeting Friday on USAC's Troubles." *National Speed Sport News,* Aug. 16, 1978, 3.

Koenig, Bill. "Auto Circuit Ready to Race on Wall Street." *Indianapolis Star,* Mar. 8, 1998, L-6.

_____. "Both Races Suffer from Racing Civil War." *Indianapolis Star,* May 27, 1996, S-9.

_____. "CART/IRL Split Has Stalled Sport's Economic Growth." *Indianapolis Star,* Sept. 22, 1996, E-1.

_____. "CART, IRL TV Ratings Continue to Slide." *Indianapolis Star,* May 9, 1997, C-4.

_____. "CART Ordered to Drop IndyCar Name." *Indianapolis Star,* Mar. 20, 1996, F-1.

_____. "CART Stock Has a Fast Start." *Indianapolis Star,* Mar. 11, 1998, C-1.

_____. "Course of Change." *Indianapolis Star,* July 31, 1994, A-1.

_____. "Fans Shouldn't Hold Breath Waiting for CART's Return to Indianapolis." *Indianapolis Star,* May 18, 1997, C-7.

_____. "For Racing Sponsors, It's Time to Choose." *Indianapolis Star,* July 13, 1996, D-1.

_____. "Indy-Car Racing Split Also Brings Division of Sponsor's Spending." *Indianapolis Star,* May 19, 1996, E-1.

_____. "Indy-Car Racing Split Makes Engine Firms Shift Allegiances." *Indianapolis Star,* Feb. 25, 1996, E-1.

_____. "IRL May Earn $101 Million in Sponsorships." *Indianapolis Star,* Feb. 13, 1998, D-10.

_____. "NASCAR Takes Lead in Race for Sponsors." *Indianapolis Star,* Mar. 8, 1996, F-1.

_____. "The Race Is On for Indy-Car Sponsors." *Indianapolis Star,* Mar. 1, 1996, C-1.

Koenig, Bill, and Mary Francis. "Indy-Car Feud's Fallout Still Being Felt." *Indianapolis Star,* June 1, 1996, D-1.

Knutson, Ben. "Will CART Become an F-1 Feeder Series?" *National Speed Sport News,* Oct. 16, 2002, 2.

Kravitz, Bob. "Give Bernard Some Credit—and Plenty of Blame Too." *Indianapolis Star,* June 24, 2012, C-1.

_____. "Open-Wheeling Racing Begins Rebuilding After Unification." *Indianapolis Star,* May 4, 2008, C-1.

_____. "Racing Merger Must Not Stall." *Indianapolis Star,* July 7, 2006, D-1.

Lage, Larry. "Track Trouble Spoils Detroit Grand Prix." *Journal Gazette,* June 4, 2012, B-2.

Lemasters, Ron, Jr. "All Sweetness and Life at CART; Bonus in Change to For-Profit." *National Speed Sport News,* Jan. 29, 1992, 3.

_____. "The Big Day Is Finally Here for New Tony George Series." *National Speed Sport News,* Jan. 24, 1996, 3.

_____. "CART Gains Indy's George as Ally in FISA Tiff." *National Sport Speed News,* Dec. 12, 1990, 3.

_____. "CART Race a Reality." *National Speed Sport News,* Apr. 15, 1998, 3.

_____. "CART Returns to 'Big Board' Status; Still Hunting New CEO." *National Speed Sport News,* Nov. 17, 1993, 2.

_____. "CART Rule Forces Honda to Reevaluate Indy Car Program." *National Speed Sport News,* Feb. 10, 1993, 3.

_____. "Firestone Picks '95 for Indy Car Return." *National Speed Sport News,* May 19, 1993, 3.

_____. "IMS Cuts Week of Practice, 2nd Time Trial Weekend Next Year." *National Speed Sport News,* Sept. 17, 1997, 3.

_____. "IMS' George Pleased with NASCAR Test." *National Sport Speed News,* July 1, 1992, 3.

_____. "IMS-USAC Plans Rock Indy Car Set." *National Speed Sport News,* Mar. 16, 1994, 3.

_____. "Indy Speaks Out on Rule Changes." *National Sport Speed News,* Aug. 1, 1990, 3.

_____. "Indy Walls to Come Tumbling Down." *National Sport Speed News,* June 3, 1992, 2.

_____. "IndyCar's Craig Speaks of Conciliation, IRL, TV." *National Speed Sport News,* Feb. 8, 1995, 3.

_____. "Indy-CART Marriage Off." *National Sport Speed News,* Dec. 4, 1991, 3.

_____. "Indy's George Moves Ahead with Plan to Solve Indy Car Woes." *National Sport Speed News,* Feb. 19, 1992, 2.

_____. "Is CART-IRL Resolution Near?" *National Speed Sport News,* Apr. 7, 1999, 2.

_____. "New Indy Proposal Leaves CART Cold." *National Sport Speed News,* June 10, 1992, 2.

_____. "$1 Million IRL Bow for DisneyWorld." *National Speed Sport News,* Jan. 25, 1995, 3.

_____. "Round-Trip Detroit GP Ride for Stokkan." *National Sport Speed News,* Sept. 19, 1990, 3.

_____. "Rules Issue at Indy Won't Die." *National Sport Speed News,* May 16, 1990, 3.

_____. "Turbos May Go Says Indy Boss." *National Sport Speed News,* May 29, 1991, 3.

_____. "TV, Sponsor and Date Problems Face IndyCar." *National Sport Speed News,* Mar. 11, 1992, 3.

_____. "U.S. 500 Race Shocks Fans and Sponsors." *National Speed Sport News,* Jan. 10, 1996, 3.

_____. "Valvoline Out at IMS; Pennzoil Takes Over." *National Speed Sport News,* Mar. 13, 1996, 3.

"Letterman, Newman Side with CART in Indy War," *Indianapolis Star,* May 10, 1996, Q-6.

"'Make Cloutier Talk,' Court Asked." *Indianapolis Star,* May 2, 1979, 31.

Martin, Bruce. "After Volatile Month of May, Time to Move on for CART?" *National Speed Sport News,* June 12, 1996, 2.

_____. "Andretti Takes Three Cars to IRL." *National Speed Sport News,* Sept. 25, 2002, 2.

_____. "Bernard Forms Panel to Determine New IndyCar Chassis." *National Speed Sport News,* Mar. 24, 2010, 3.

_____. "Bernard: Series Too Vanilla." *National Speed Sport News,* Apr. 21, 2010, 23.

_____. "Briscoe at Ganassi; Is Texas in Trouble?" *National Speed Sport News,* Jan. 19, 2005, 5.

_____. "CART and IRL Champs to Share 500 Front Row." *National Speed Sport News,* May 24, 2000, 2.

_____. "Castroneves Keeps Point Lead." *National Speed Sport News,* July 3, 2002, 23.

_____. "Champ Car, IRL Merging Closer." *National Speed Sport News,* Feb. 13, 2008, 2.

_____. "Chevrolet Returns to IndyCar Scene." *National Speed Sport News,* Nov. 17, 2010, 6.

_____. "Chevy Will Leave the IRL." *National Speed Sport News,* Aug. 24, 2005, 25.

_____. "Dallara Tabbed for IndyCar's 2012 Chassis." *National Speed Sport News,* July 21, 2010, 3.

_____. "Dallara's Concept Far from Spec." *National Speed Sport News,* July 21, 2010, 26.

_____. "DirecTV to Come on Board as Indy-Car Series Title Sponsor." *National Speed Sport News,* Apr. 2, 2008, 3.

_____. "Dispute Not Straining Family." *National Speed Sport News,* Aug. 5, 2009, 29.

_____. "Engines Going Turbo in 2011." *National Speed Sport News,* Aug. 27, 2008, 2.

_____. "Fans Cheer Unser upon Indy Return." *National Speed Sport News,* May 17, 2000, 2.

_____. "Fastest of the Fast." *National Speed Sport News,* May 26, 2010, 5.

_____. "Forsythe to Enter Indy Lights." *National Speed Sport News,* July 23, 2008, 27.

_____. "George: Engine Availability Not an Issue." *National Speed Sport News,* Feb. 27, 2008, 25.

_____. "George, Kalkhoven Merger Comes to a Standstill." *National Speed Sport News,* July 5, 2006, 25.

_____. "George on CART: 'We Won't Change.'" *National Speed Sport News,* Sept. 29, 1999, 3.

_____. "George Ousted from Speedway, Indy-Car Roles." *National Speed Sport News,* July 8, 2009, 3.

_____. "George Outlines Future IRL Plans." *National Speed Sport News,* Apr. 9 2008, 30.

_____. "George Resigns from Speedway Board; Belskus: IMS Not for Sale." *National Speed Sport News,* Jan. 17, 2010, 3.

_____. "George: Role a Life-Long Position." *National Speed Sport News,* July 15, 2009, 22.

_____. "George's 'Vision' Now Over." *National Speed Sport News,* Feb. 3, 2010, 8.

_____. "Gossage, IRL at Odds over Future Texas Events." *National Speed Sport News,* June 11, 2008, 29.

_____. "Gossage: No Texas CART Race." *National Speed Sport News,* Sept. 18, 1996, 3.

_____. "Handshake Seals Open-Wheel Deal." *National Speed Sport News,* Mar. 5, 2008, 2.

_____. "Honda Says It's Ready to Power All of IRL in '07." *National Speed Sport News,* Oct. 19, 2005, 4.

_____. "IMS Fires Back with New Suit." *National Speed Sport News,* May 8, 1996, 3.

_____. "IMS Returns to Traditional Schedule." *National Speed Sport News,* July 12, 2000, 2.

_____. "IMS Tells CART 'Nix the Name.'" *National Speed Sport News,* Mar. 27, 1996, 2.

_____. "Indy 500 Fanfare Boosting IRL's Image." *National Speed Sport News,* June 8, 2005, 6.

_____. "IndyCar Board Rebuffs Roger on Peace Plan." *National Speed Sport News,* Feb. 28, 1995, 3.

_____. "IndyCar Series Signs 6-Year Pact with IZOD." *National Speed Sport News,* Nov. 11, 2009, 3.

_____. "IndyCar Teams Unified in Show of Support for George." *National Speed Sport News,* June 3, 2009, pp. 5, 33.

_____. "IRL and ABC/ESPN Extend Through '07." *National Speed Sport News,* Sept. 5, 2001.

_____. "IRL Car Specs Preclude Running in IndyCar Events." *National Speed Sport News,* Apr. 10, 1996, 2.

_____. "IRL Pleased, CART Owners Miffed." *National Speed Sport News,* Nov. 25, 1998, 2.

_____. "IRL Ready to Use IndyCar Again!" *National Speed Sport News,* Jan. 8, 2003, 3.

_____. "IRL Signs Northern Light to $50 Million Sponsorship." *National Speed Sport News,* Feb. 2, 2000, 3.

_____. "IRL's George Warms Up to Unification." *National Speed Sport News,* Mar. 29, 2006, 5.

_____. "Is Open-Wheel Peace at Hand?" *National Speed Sport News,* Aug. 19, 1998, 39.

_____. "'Little Al' Opens Up on CART-IRL Move." *National Speed Sport News,* Mar. 22, 2000, 3.

_____. "Luyendyk Puts Hammer Down for 2nd Indy Score." *National Speed Sport News,* June 4, 1997, 2.

_____. "Merger Not Coming Any Time Soon." *National Speed Sport News,* May 17, 2006, 20.

_____. "Merger Talks Crawling Along." *National Speed Sport News,* May 31, 2006, 3.

_____. "More Road Courses for IndyCar." *National Speed Sport News,* Aug. 6, 2008, 6.

_____. "New IndyCar CEO Faces Steep Learning Curve." *National Speed Sport News,* Feb. 10, 2010, 11.

_____. "New IRL Engine Rules Rile Penske." *National Speed Sport News,* Aug. 17, 1994, 3.

_____. "Open Indy Quals to All or We Strike!" *National Speed Sport News,* Sept. 27, 1995, 3.

_____. "Paul Tracy Wants to Race." *National Speed Sport News,* Apr. 9, 2008, 25.

_____. "Penske Indy Posture Divides CART Teams." *National Speed Sport News,* Mar. 5, 1997, 3.

_____. "Penske Not Buying Unification." *National Speed Sport News,* Mar. 29, 2006, 23.

_____. "Penske Ponders IRL Indy Run." *National Speed Sport News,* Feb. 19, 1997, 3.

_____. "Penske Researching Indianapolis Return." *National Speed Sport News,* June 7, 2000, 2.

_____. "Penske Says 'No' to Rival 500 at Michigan." *National Speed Sport News,* Oct. 11, 1995, 3.

_____. "Pep Boys Adds to IRL Season Opener." *National Speed Sport News,* Jan. 28, 1998, 3.

_____. "Race Date Leaves IRL, PIR at Crossroads." *National Speed Sport News*, Apr. 27, 2005, 2.

_____. "Ray Garners Championship; Brack Wins 500! As IRL Endure Season of Triumph and Tragedy," *National Speed Sport News*, Dec. 15, 1999, 8.

_____. "Reebok Will Not Sponsor IRL Tour." *National Speed Sport News*, Jan. 7, 1998, 3.

_____. "Reunited." *National Speed Sport News*, May 21, 2008, MD-2.

_____. "'Shootout' Time Trials Coming to Indy 500." *National Speed Sport News*, Apr. 21, 2010, 3.

_____. "Strong Words as CART-IRL Tiff Heats Up." *National Speed Sport News*, Jan. 10, 1996, 14.

_____. "Taking a Hard Look at the IndyCar Rumor Mill." *National Speed Sport News*, July 29, 2009, 23.

_____. "Team-Owner Penske Says CART's Days Are Numbered." *National Speed Sport News*, July 2, 2003, 24.

_____. "Teams Torn on Implementing New 2012 Car." *National Speed Sport News*, Sept. 1, 2010, 3.

_____. "Three Killed by Debris; IRL Cancels Race." *National Speed Sport News*, May 5, 1999, 3.

_____. "Tony G. at PIR?" *National Speed Sport News*, June 29, 1994, 3.

_____. "Transition of Equipment a 'Challenge.'" *National Speed Sport News*, Feb. 27, 2008, 3.

_____. "Walker Has Seen It from Both Sides Now." *National Speed Sport News*, Feb. 27, 2008, 27.

_____. "War Over, 'Now the Work Starts.'" *National Speed Sport News*, Feb. 27, 2008, 3.

_____. "Will It Be Turbos in 2011 for Indy Cars?" *National Speed Sport News*, July 2, 2008, 3.

Mayer, Steve. "Analyst Questions CART's Survival." *National Speed Sport News*, Mar. 19, 2003, 21.

_____. "Buys by CEO Heitzler, Others Raise Questions" *National Speed Sport News*, June 20, 2001, 3.

_____. "CART Attendance Questioned." *National Speed Sport News*, Jan. 29, 2003, 3.

_____. "CART Discloses $1.4 Million in Extra Expenses." *National Speed Sport News*, Oct. 31, 2001.

_____. "CART Loses $8.3 Million in Third Quarter." *National Speed Sport News*, Nov. 20, 2002, 2.

_____. "CART Losing Numbers Game." *National Speed Sport News*, Mar. 19, 2003, 2.

_____. "CART-NASCAR Tie?—Not Likely: France." *National Speed Sport News*, Dec. 15, 1999, 3.

_____. "CART Seeks up to $84 Million in IPO." *National Speed Sport News*, Jan. 7, 1998, 3.

_____. "CART Stock Hits New Low." *National Speed Sport News*, Mar. 12, 2003, 2.

_____. "CART Sues Road America." *National Speed Sport News*, Feb. 19, 2003, 2.

_____. "CART TV? Not Yet, but Possible." *National Speed Sport News*, Aug. 1, 2001, 3.

_____. "CART's Future Addressed." *National Speed Sport News*, June 11, 2003, 3.

_____. "CART's 10-K Poses Questions." *National Speed Sport News*, Apr. 2, 2003, 2.

_____. "CEO Heitzler Is No. 1 Target as CART Directors Sit Down." *National Speed Sport News*, Dec. 5, 2001, 2.

_____. "Controversy Swirls Around CART; Leadership Quality Is Questioned." *National Speed Sport News*, July 18, 2001, 2.

_____. "Despite Losing Forecast, Wall Street Backs CART CEO," *National Speed Sport News*, Mar. 13, 2002, 3.

_____. "Ecclestone on CART: 'No Interest.'" *National Speed Sport News*, June 12, 2002, 22.

_____. "Expensive New CART TV Pact Offers More Hours," *National Speed Sport News*, Aug. 22, 2001, 3.

_____. "Financial Trouble for CART?" *National Speed Sport News*, Aug. 21, 2002, 3.

_____. "The Heitzler File, Part 1." *National Speed Sport News*, July 25, 2001, 3.

_____. "If You Sue Me, I'll Sue You." *National Speed Sport News*, Apr. 3, 2002, 2.

_____. "Is CART Shareholder Planning Lawsuits?" *National Speed Sport News*, Nov. 20, 2002, 29.

_____. "It All Boils Down to Numbers and Shareholders." *National Speed Sport News*, May 19, 1999, 3.

_____. "Major Changes Possible for 'New CART.'" *National Speed Sport News*, Dec. 12, 2001, 3.

_____. "Major Investor Seeks Break Up, or Sale of CART." *National Speed Sport News*, Sept. 11, 2002, 3.

_____. "New Era Begins for CART Shareholders." *National Speed Sport News*, Dec. 11, 2002, 2.

_____. "No 'Poison Pill' for CART's Forsythe." *National Speed Sport News*, Sept. 18, 2002, 3.

_____. "Penske Sells Nearly All!" *National Speed Sport News*, Apr. 21, 1999, 3.

_____. "Racing in Europe Is Costly for CART." *National Speed Sport News*, Jan. 15, 2003, 14.

_____. "Words May Come Back to Haunt CART." *National Speed Sport News*, Oct. 23, 2002, 2.

"Membership of New Indy-Car Board Under Debate." *Indianapolis Star*, Oct. 13, 1991, D-2.

Miller, Robin. "Angry Foyt Turns In USAC Card." *Indianapolis Star*, Feb. 5, 1980, 21.

_____. "Bank Denies Lease to Save Pocono." *Indianapolis Star*, Mar. 1, 1981, sect. 4, 6.

_____. "The Battle Lines Have Been Drawn. With CART Teams Racing at Michigan in Protest, the Indianapolis 500 Is … A RACE DIVIDED." *Indianapolis Star*, May 24, 1996, S-1.

_____. "CART Calls Truce to Talk Peace." *Indianapolis Star*, June 12, 1979, 23.

_____. "CART Chairman Favors Democratic Indy-Car Board." *Indianapolis Star*, Oct. 28, 1991, D-1.

_____. "CART Finally Has a Price Tag: How Does $275 Million Sound?" *Indianapolis Star*, Mar. 15, 1998, C-8.

_____. "CART Has Much to Gain in Deal with Indy." *Indianapolis Star*, Sept. 6, 1991, B-3.

_____. "CART-IRL Boiler Is Cooling." *Indianapolis Star*, Aug. 11, 1996, B-9.

_____. "CART May Ask George to Re-vamp Racing." *Indianapolis Star*, Sept. 6, 1991, A-1.

_____. "CART Mired in Legal Lumbering." *Indianapolis Star*, May 5, 1979, 19.

_____. "CART Not Ready to Relinquish Sovereignty to George." *Indianapolis Star*, Nov. 10, 1991, D-3.

_____. "CART Officials Say They May Not Be Making May Pit Stop in Indy." *Indianapolis Star*, Oct. 11, 1995, B-1.

_____. "CART Owners Offer Plan for Return to the '500.'" *Indianapolis Star*, Nov. 8, 1998, A-1.

_____. "CART Says 'Let's Go,' USAC Shows E-Z Board." *Indianapolis Star*, Mar. 2, 1980, sect. 2, 1.

_____. "CART Still Waiting on IMS Reply." *Indianapolis Star*, Apr. 24, 1979, 23.

_____. "CART Teams to Get Indy Invites." *Indianapolis Star*, Jan. 25, 1980, 37.

_____. "CART to Steer Around Showdown." *Indianapolis Star*, Oct. 4, 1996, F-1.

_____. "CART Vows to Continue War with Indy." *Indianapolis Star*, June 2, 1996, B-1.

_____. "Cooper Declares Independence." *Indianapolis Star*, June 24, 1980, 24.

_____. "Don Is a Dandy at 205.198." *Indianapolis Star*, May 12, 1983, 37.

_____. "82 USAC Rules Eliminate Cosworth." *Indianapolis Star*, Jan. 7, 1981, 35.

_____. "First Court Victory Goes to CART." *Indianapolis Star*, May 4, 1979, 33.

_____. "500 Miles of an Unfunny Folly." *Indianapolis Star*, Sept. 7, 1978, 40.

_____. "Foyt Quits CART: Rejoins USAC." *Indianapolis Star*, Feb. 1, 1979, 33.

_____. "George Has a Take-It-or-Leave-It Deal for CART." *Indianapolis Star*, Oct. 31, 1991, D1.

_____. "George Plan Sent Back Once Again." *Indianapolis Star*, June 7, 1992, E-1.

_____. "George Takes Huge Risk to Unify Racing." *Indianapolis Star*, July 26, 1992, E-1.

_____. "George Unveils Name, Leaders for New Circuit." *Star*, July 9, 1994, E-1.

_____. "George's Change of Heart Bleeds Hypocrisy." *Indianapolis Star*, Sept. 12, 1997, C-1.

_____. "George's IRL Plans Will Damage Indy's Respectability." *Indianapolis Star*, July 5, 1995, B-1.

_____. "Goodyear Enters Indy-Car Battle." *Indianapolis Star*, Jan. 24, 1980, 37.

_____. "IndyCar, CART Spell Out, Settle Differences for Racing Acronym." *Indianapolis Star*, Dec. 22, 1996, C-10.

_____. "IRL, CART Sit, but No Fire in Peace Pipe." *Indianapolis Star*, Feb. 25, 1996, C-2.

_____. "IRL Is Competitive, but It's Certainly Not Major-League Racing." *Indianapolis Star*, Jan. 29, 1996, D-2.

_____. "IRL Retools the Rules, Opens Doors for CART." *Indianapolis Star*, May 17, 1997, A-1.

_____. "Judge Gives CART Go Sign." *Indianapolis Star*, May 6, 1979, 1.

_____. "Lack of Drivers Familiar to Racing Fans Casts a Major Cloud over IRL, CART." *Indianapolis Star*, May 15, 1998, D-1.

_____. "Major '500' Rules Changes Coming." *Indianapolis Star*, May 26, 1991, B-1.

_____. "May Daze Prompts Numerous Questions." *Indianapolis Star*, Sept. 14, 1997, C-7.

_____. "More Animosity Than Honesty at Speedway." *Indianapolis Star*, May 21, 1981, 47.

_____. "NASCAR's TV Success Puts CART, IRL to Shame." *Indianapolis Star*, July 1, 1998, B-1.

_____. "New CART Season Strong on Competition." *Indianapolis Star*, Feb. 25, 1996, C-2.

_____. "New IRL Rules Likely to Dash Reunion Hope." *Indianapolis Star*, Nov. 18, 1998, A-1.

_____. "Ontario Hitches Ride on CART." *Indianapolis Star*, July 3, 1979, 24.

_____. "Owners, Drivers Favor Changes." *Indianapolis Star*, Sept. 12, 1997, C-4.

_____. "Race Talks Fail; Hearing Today." *Indianapolis Star*, May 3, 1979, 35.

_____. "The Rejected 6 Ask Cloutier 'What For?'" *Indianapolis Star*, Apr. 22, 1979, sect. 2, 1.

_____. "6 Top '500' Entries Rejected." *Indianapolis Star*, Apr. 21, 1979, 1.

_____. "Speedway Message to CART Regulars Is 'Suite Dreams.'" *Indianapolis Star*, July 14, 1996, B-9.

_____. "Speedway President Offers CART, USAC Peace Plan." *Indianapolis Star*, Feb. 16, 1980, 31.

_____. "This Indy War Much Different Than '79 Split to Form CART." *Indianapolis Star,* July 13, 1994, B-1.

_____. "USAC-CART Talks Flag." *Indianapolis Star,* Feb. 1, 1980, 32.

_____. "USAC Focus on Sprint, Dirt Cars." *Indianapolis Star,* Sept. 25, 1980, 35.

_____. "USAC Nixes CRL; Reopens War?" *Indianapolis Star,* July 1, 1980, 26.

_____. "USAC's Life Threatened by CART." *Indianapolis Star,* Nov. 19, 1978, sect. 2, 1.

Miller, Robin, Curt Cavin, and Bill Koenig. "New IRL Rules Likely to Dash Reunion Hope." *Indianapolis Star,* Nov. 18, 1998, A-1.

"Milwaukee Vote Goes to CART." *Indianapolis Star,* July 9, 1980, 19.

Mittman, Dick. "Circuit Leaving Some Confused." *Indianapolis Star,* July 9, 1994, D-1.

_____. "George Ignites Car Wars." *Indianapolis Star,* Mar. 12, 1994, D-1.

_____. "Indy-Car War on For Real." *Indianapolis Star,* Dec. 20, 1995, G-1.

_____. "Indy-Only Format for 500 May Open Door for CART." *Indianapolis Star,* May 9, 1997, C-4.

_____. "No Real Winners in IRL, CART Feud; Tony George Says IRL Not at War with Anyone, Hopes in Time People Will View Series Differently." *Indianapolis Star,* May 24, 1997, D-1.

_____. "Road Course at Speedway Is 'Feasible.'" *Indianapolis Star,* Sept. 18, 1997, D-1.

Moore, George. "CART Files Suit vs. USAC, IMS." *Indianapolis Star,* Apr. 27, 1979, 31.

_____. "Cooper's Plan for Speedway: Evolution, Not Revolution." *Indianapolis Star,* Oct. 19, 1979, 39.

_____. "It's USAC's Responsibility: Cloutier." *Indianapolis Star,* Apr. 25, 1979, 53.

_____. "Racing Factions Seek Settlement." *Indianapolis Star,* May 24, 1979, 39.

_____. "USAC, CART Bomb Out." *Indianapolis Star,* June 16, 1979, 27.

_____. "USAC Makes Rulings for Equivalency." *Indianapolis Star,* Jan. 21, 1979, sect. 2, 1.

"New IRL Pact Has FOX with ABC for '99." *National Speed Sport News,* Jan. 6, 1999, 3.

"New USAC Regs Allow Single-Example Indy Engines." *National Speed Sport News,* Mar. 10, 1993, 2.

"Newly Formed CART Is Sanctioned by SCCA." *Indianapolis Star,* Dec. 11, 1978, 30.

"1979 Poor Year at Gate: Goodyear." *National Speed Sport News,* Jan. 9, 1980, 2.

"'90 CART/PPG Series Worth $20 Million; Car Specs Continue as Major Problem." *National Sport Speed News,* Jan. 17, 1990, 2.

"No CART Appeal on Pocono 7 Suspensions." *National Speed Sport News,* July 8, 1981, 3.

"No IRL Sked as Yet, But '96 TV Is All Set." *National Speed Sport News,* Jan. 18, 1995, 2.

"No Nissan Indy Effort, Massive Cuts in NPTI Staff." *National Speed Sport News,* Mar. 3, 1993, 3.

Oreovicz, John. "Appeals Panel Rebuffs CART on Disputed Popoff Valve." *National Speed Sport News,* July 11, 2001, 2.

_____. "Around the Bend." *National Speed Sport News,* May 7, 2008, 2.

_____. "Big Business: Ford Pulls Out of Champ Car." *National Speed Sport News,* Jan. 31, 2007, 2.

_____. "Bridgestone Sticking with CART." *National Speed Sport News,* Nov. 6, 2002, 22.

_____. "CART Alters Engine Regs, Ford and Honda Cry 'Foul.'" *National Speed Sport News,* June 20, 2001, 3.

_____. "CART Announces Assistance Program for Struggling Teams." *National Speed Sport News,* June 19, 2002, 27.

_____. "CART Announces Sked, SEC Filings." *National Speed Sport News,* Nov. 19, 2003, 29.

_____. "CART Axes Road America." *National Speed Sport News,* Mar. 12, 2003, 2.

_____. "CART Back to Turbos." *National Speed Sport News,* June 19, 2002, 3.

_____. "CART Begins Rebuilding Process." *National Speed Sport News,* Jan. 22, 2003, 27.

_____. "CART Board Ousts Craig." *National Speed Sport News,* June 21, 2000, 3.

_____. "CART Engine Suppliers Resist Plans to Cut Power." *National Speed Sport News,* July 26, 2000, 3.

_____. "CART Gets Offer for Shares." *National Speed Sport News,* Aug. 20, 2003, 3.

_____. "CART Looks for Private Investors." *National Speed Sport News,* June 18, 2003, 3.

_____. "CART Merge Vote Called Off." *National Speed Sport News,* Dec. 10, 2003, 2.

_____. "CART Stays Silent About Critical Board Meeting." *National Speed Sport News,* July 23, 2003, 4.

_____. "CART Stock Falls Below NYSE Criteria." *National Speed Sport News,* Oct. 8, 2003, 33.

_____. "CART Takes On Promoter's Role." *National Speed Sport News,* Mar. 6, 2002, 31.

_____. "CART Takes Strides to Help Competitors." *National Speed Sport News,* Aug. 21, 2002, 21.

_____. "CART Turns On the Lights." *National Speed Sport News,* Jan. 22, 2003, 23.

_____. "CART's Future Still Remains Uncertain." *National Speed Sport News,* July 16, 2003, 3.

_____. "CART's Popoff Problem Solved." *National Speed Sport News,* July 18, 2001, 2.

_____. "CEO Pook Defends CART's Position." *National Speed Sport News,* May 21, 2003, 3.

_____. "Champ Car Can't Clear Obstacles, Axes Ansan." *National Speed Sport News,* Oct. 5, 2005 3.

_____. "Champ Car Finalizes TV with Networks." *National Speed Sport News,* Jan. 19, 2005, 18.

_____. "Champ Car Firm Files for Bankruptcy." *National Speed Sport News,* Mar. 12, 2008, 2.

_____. "Champ Car Lands Television Deal with ABC/ESPN." *National Speed Sport News,* Nov. 22, 2006, 10.

_____. "Champ Car Locks Up Long Beach Grand Prix." *National Speed Sport News,* June 1, 2005, 3.

_____. "Champ Car to Talk with Honda." *National Speed Sport News,* May 25, 2005, 44.

_____. "Champ Car's First 'Turbo Tour' Takes Drivers to Media Masses." *National Speed Sport News,* Mar. 15, 2006, 37.

_____. "Chris Pook Clears Air on CART and Bernie." *National Speed Sport News,* Oct. 30, 2002, 2.

_____. "Conspiracy? Attendance Dips to New Low." *National Speed Sport News,* Aug. 31, 2005, 2.

_____. "Despite 22 Events CART Targets 500." *National Speed Sport News,* Nov. 10, 1999, 2.

_____. "Finally, CART Has Its Man!" *National Speed Sport News,* Dec. 6, 2000, 2.

_____. "Ford Announces Support for CART." *National Speed Sport News,* Nov. 27, 2002, 6.

_____. "Future of CART Being Decided Behind Closed Doors." *National Speed Sport News,* Aug. 6, 2003, 7.

_____. "Groups Take Wait-And-See Approach." *National Speed Sport News,* Feb. 20, 2008, 2.

_____. "Heitzler Goes, Pook Is Eyed as New CEO." *National Speed Sport News,* Dec. 12, 2001, 3.

_____. "Honda Appears Ready to Join IRL." *National Speed Sport News,* May 1, 2002, 3.

_____. "Is CART Saved by New Deal, or Not?" *National Speed Sport News,* Sept. 17, 2003, 6.

_____. "Kalkhoven: 'Leave It Alone.'" *National Speed Sport News,* Feb. 13, 2008, 2.

_____. "Mercedes Orders End to CART Engine Supply." *National Speed Sport News,* Sept. 13, 2000, 3.

_____. "New Champ Car Chassis Lightens Financial Strain." *National Speed Sport News,* Oct. 12, 2005, 3.

_____. "OWRS Deal Under Review." *National Speed Sport News,* Oct. 1, 2003, 2.

_____. "Pook Claims CART Is Moving Forward." *National Speed Sport News,* June 5, 2002, 25.

_____. "Pook Swings into Action as CART Strengthens Plan." *National Speed Sport News,* Jan. 30, 2002, 3.

_____. "Russell's CART Tenure Ends." *National Speed Sport News,* Oct. 3, 2001, 3.

_____. "Series VP Resigns; Matos Chooses IPS." *National Speed Sport News,* Jan. 23, 2008, 3.

_____. "Several New Teams Commit." *National Speed Sport News,* Jan. 8, 2003, 11.

_____. "Strategic Series." *National Speed Sport News,* Nov. 9, 2005, 20.

_____. "Top Jag F-1 Job Steals CART Boss." *National Speed Sport News,* Sept. 20, 2000, 3.

Oreovicz, John, and Bruce Martin. "No More Turbos for Toyota." *National Speed Sport News,* Oct. 3, 2001, 3.

Oursler, Bill. "As CART's Rules Expire, What to Do Is Question." *National Speed Sport News,* July 20, 1983, 3.

_____. "CART Replaces F-1 in Detroit, Sets Japan Bow." *National Sport Speed News,* Nov. 9, 1988, 3.

_____. "Formula One Owners Pan CART-Like Move." *National Speed Sport News,* Feb. 21, 1979, 6.

_____. "$6.3 Million Conspiracy Suit Is Filed by Pocono." *National Speed Sport News,* Sept. 5, 1979, 3.

_____. "Tensions Are Rising in CART-FISA Feud." *National Sport Speed News,* Oct. 10, 1990, 3.

Overpeck, Dave. "Extra Qualifications Voted Out." *Indianapolis Star,* May 25, 1979, 1.

_____. "1980 '500' by Invitation Only." *Indianapolis Star,* June 2, 1979, 1.

_____. "35 Cars Await Starting Flag." *Indianapolis Star,* May 27, 1979, 1.

_____. "USAC, CART Form New Racing League." *Indianapolis Star,* Apr. 4, 1980, 28.

"Peace Proposal Pleases Most, Not CART Head." *National Speed Sport News,* Feb. 20, 1980, 3.

"Penske: 'Indy Return Not a Closed Book.'" *National Speed Sport News,* June 26, 1996, 2.

"Penske Says Solution Close in CART-USAC Wrangling." *Indianapolis Star,* Mar. 28, 1980, 23.

"Pit Pass." *Indianapolis Star,* May 25, 1979, 33.

"Pit Pass." *Indianapolis Star,* May 27, 1979, sect. 2, 3.

"Pocono-CART Lawsuit Now at $9.9 Million." *National Speed Sport News,* July 15, 1981, 3.

"Pocono Entries Out, CART Cars Absent." *National Speed Sport News,* May 20, 1981, 3.

"Pocono Rejoins '81 USAC Sked." *Indianapolis Star,* Mar. 4, 1981, 19.

"Pocono Talks Are On." *National Speed Sport News,* May 30, 1979, 3.

"Principals Speak as IRL-IndyCar Battle Heats

Up." *National Speed Sport News,* Oct. 25, 1995, 3.

"Racing Attendance Jumps Despite Sluggish Economy." *National Sport Speed News,* Jan. 8, 1992, 5.

"Record Set for Indy 500 Entries." *National Speed Sport News,* Apr. 15, 1981, 2.

"Renew Detroit GP, Denver Site Issue." *National Sport Speed News,* Oct. 3, 1990, 3.

"Safer and Slower Cars for Indy's 1990 500: See USAC-CART Peace." *National Sport Speed News,* Jan. 31, 1990, 2.

"SCCA Seeking ACCUS' Intervention." *Indianapolis Star,* Apr. 23, 1979, 22.

Schoettle, Anthony. "IndyCar CEO May Take Control of More Races." *Indianapolis Business Journal,* July 11, 2011, A-3.

_____. "IndyCar Confronts 'Defining Moment.'" *Indianapolis Business Journal,* Nov. 5, 2012, A-3.

_____. "IndyCar Execs: Distractions Mask Progress." *Indianapolis Business Journal,* Oct. 8, 2012, 3.

_____. "IndyCar's Big New Wheels." *Indianapolis Business Journal,* Mar. 19, 2012, A-3.

_____. "Needs Exceed Subsidy." *Indianapolis Business Journal.* Feb. 13, 2013, 1.

"7 '500' Trials Protests Denied." *Indianapolis Star,* May 22, 1979, 1.

"Several Technical Changes Coming to Indy-Car in 2010." *National Speed Sport News,* Jan. 20, 2010, 2.

"Speedway's Cooper Lauds Move to Stock Engine." *Indianapolis Star,* Jan. 8, 1981, 34.

Stevens, John D. "Speedway Saga Began in Paris Hotel Room." *Indianapolis Star,* May 29, 1959, 4.

Stilley, Al. "Crash Tests Coming for Future Indy Cars." *National Speed Sport News,* Aug. 26, 1987, 3.

_____. "Indy Entries Jump to 77 as April 5 Deadline Passes." *National Sport Speed News,* Apr. 10, 1985, 2.

_____. "Only 15 'Old' Cars Among Indy Entries." *National Sport Speed News,* Apr. 17, 1985, 3.

_____. "Return Indy Car Racing to the Ovals—CART's Patrick." *National Speed Sport News,* Aug. 1, 1984, 3.

"Stock Blocks Are Cornerstone of New All-U.S. Indy Car Series." National Speed Sport News, Nov. 18, 1987, 3.

"13 CART Shows for '81 Season." *National Sport Speed News,* Oct. 8, 1980, 3.

"Three CART Races for TV; Indy Stick w/ USAC Regs." *National Sport Speed News,* Jan. 31, 1979, 3.

"Tobacco Money Makes Its Move into Auto Racing." *National Sport Speed News,* Jan. 20, 2010, 17.

"Tracy to Test for Germain Racing." *National Speed Sport News,* May 28, 2008, 12.

"Trials Sham of Speed." *Indianapolis Star,* May 21, 1979, 22.

"Trio Throws Hat into Indy Car Design Ring." *National Speed Sport News,* Mar. 10, 2010.

Turner, B. J. "CART's New Rules 'a Kick in the Face' Says Buick." *National Sport Speed News,* July 3, 1985, 3.

_____. "GM Believes It Has a Better Idea for Indy." *National Sport Speed News,* May 15, 1985, 3.

_____. "New CART Indy Car Rules Cut Downforce, Not Power." *National Sport Speed News,* July 3, 1985, 3.

"An Unanimous 'Nay' Vote on IRL Edict." *National Speed Sport News,* July 12, 1995, 3.

"U.S. Race Fans Jammed Speedways During 1984." *National Speed Sport News,* Jan. 9, 1985, 5.

"USAC and CART Meet to Discuss Ways of Slowing Indy Cars." *National Speed Sport News,* Sept. 3, 1986, 3.

"USAC Board Sets Emergency Meeting." *National Speed Sport News,* Nov. 8, 1978, 3.

"USAC, CART Like Looks of Cooper Proposal." *National Speed Sport News,* Feb. 27, 1980, 3.

"USAC Claims CART Violated Antitrust Act." *Indianapolis Star,* June 12, 1979, 23.

"USAC Directors Make 3 Changes." *Indianapolis Star,* Sept. 8, 1978, 33.

"USAC OK's Modified Cooper Peace Plan." *Indianapolis Star,* Feb. 21, 1980, 32.

"USAC OKs New Try for bumped Racers." *Indianapolis Star,* May 23, 1979, 1.

"USAC Panel OKs Fuel, Power Plan." *Indianapolis Star,* Aug. 19, 1978, 26.

"USAC Retains Indy 500 Sanction." *National Speed Sport News,* Jan. 12, 1983, 3.

"USAC Says No to Andretti." *National Speed Sport News,* Nov. 18, 1981, 3.

"USAC Schedule Claims Two '500s.'" *Indianapolis Star,* Dec. 13, 1980, 38.

"USAC's New Rules Parallel to CART's." *National Speed Sport News,* Oct. 6, 1982 2.

Waltz, Keith, "CART Rules Dispute Hot Topic at Pocono." *National Sport Speed News,* Aug. 21, 1989, 3.

Waters, Doug, "CART Plans for 1990 Include Canada, Europe, Japan." *National Sport Speed News,* Feb. 15, 1989, 2.

Web

"ABC, Versus to Screen IndyCar." http://www.crash.net/indycar/news/26187/1/series_celebrates_new_tv_deals.html. Aug. 8, 2008.

"AGR Backs Merger." http://www.crash.net/

indycar/news/25767/1/andretti_its_a_huge_ day.html. Feb. 23, 2008.

"Apex-Brazil Signs On as New IRL Fuel Partner." http://www.crash.net/indycar/news/ 26358/1/series_hits_apex_with_new_fuel_ partner.html. Nov. 19, 2008.

Associated Press. "Indy 500 Field Expanded to 35; Johnny Unser, St. James Back In." http:// articles.latimes.com/1997-05-19/sports/sp-60301_1_johnny-unser. May 19, 1997.

_____. "IndyCar Courting Just Marketing Founder Zak Brown for CEO." http://sports illustrated.cnn.com/racing/news/201303 23/indycar-zak-brown-ceo.ap/. Mar. 23, 2013.

_____. "IndyCar Steals from NASCAR: Double File Restarts Planned." http://www.thatsra cin.com/2011/01/11/53709/indycar-series-plans-double-file.html. Jan. 11, 2011.

_____. "Randy Bernard Steps Down as Indy-Car CEO; Will Stay with Series in an Advisory Role." http://www.foxnews.com/sports/ 2012/10/28/randy-bernard-steps-down-as-indycar-ceo-will-stay-with-series-in-adviso ry-role/. Oct. 28, 2012.

"Barnhart Discusses Controversial Call." http:// www.crash.net/indycar/news/172162/1/barn hart_discusses_controversial_restart_call. html. Aug. 16, 2011.

"Barnhart Out of Race Control for 2012." http://www.crash.net/indycar/news/175269/ 1/barnhart_out_of_race_control_in_2012. html/ Nov. 30, 2011.

"BAT Engineering Bids for IndyCar Business." http://www.crash.net/indycar/news/157460/ 1/bat_engineering_submits_fifth_indycar_ proposal.html. Mar. 5, 2010.

"Beaux Barfield Hired by IndyCar." http://espn. go.com/racing/indycar/story/_/id/7420121/ beaux-barfield-hired-indycar-race-director, Jan. 4, 2012.

"Bernard 'Wanted to Get in Front of the Problem.'" http://www.crash.net/indycar/news/ 180447/1/bernards_strategy_pulls_owners_ into_line.html. June 4, 2012.

"Bespoke Aero Kits Postponed Until 2013." http://www.crash.net/indycar/news/172100/ 1/bespoke_aero_kits_postponed_until_ 2013.html. Aug. 14, 2011.

Carpenter, Josh. "IndyCar's Mark Miles on TV Ratings, New Markets and Improving Indianapolis Motor Speedway." http://www.spo rtsbusinessdaily.com/SB-Blogs/On-The-Ground/2013/12/MMF-Mark-Miles-Indy Car-Indianapolis-Motor-Speedway.aspx. Dec. 4, 2013.

Carraccio, Brian. "A Look at IndyCar's Revolving Door of CEOs." http://www.autoracing1. com/article.asp?id=3873. Nov. 19, 2012.

Case, Dean. "Revolution at Indianapolis." http://

allamericanracers.com/revolution-at-india napolis/. Accessed Dec. 20, 2013.

"Castroneves Fined $30K for Barnhart Comments." http://www.crash.net/indycar/news/ 173430/1/castroneves_fined_30k_for_comm ents.html. Sept. 27, 2011.

Cavin, Curt. "Tony George's Offer to Buy IndyCar Wasn't Considered." http://www. usatoday.com/story/sports/motor/2012/10/ 30/tony-george-bid-on-indycar-series/ 1669401/. Jan. 8, 2013.

"Chevrolet Loses Final Turbocharger Appeal." http://www.crash.net/indycar/news/179587/ 1/chevy_loses_final_turbocharger_appeal. html. May 11, 2012.

"Chevy Orders All Teams to Change Engines." http://www.crash.net/indycar/news/178508/ 1/chevy_orders_all_teams_to_change_engi nes.html. Apr. 12, 2012.

"Chevrolet Returns as Engine Supplier in 2012." http://www.crash.net/indycar/news/165008/ 1/chevrolet_engines_return_to_indycar_in_ 2012.html. Nov. 12, 2010.

"Chevy Teams Grow Restless with Bernard." http://www.crash.net/indycar/news/180309/ 1/chevy_teams_grow_restless_with_ bernard.html. May 30, 2012.

"China Round Dropped—Replacement Being Sought." http://www.crash.net/indycar/ne ws/180816/1/china_round_dropped_-_re placement_sought.html. June 13, 2012.

"Cost-Cutting Deal Agreed with Dallara." http://www.crash.net/indycar/news/187348/ 1/cost-cutting-deal-agreed-with-dallara. html. Jan. 18, 2013.

"Cotman Confirmed at IRL." http://www.crash. net/indycar/news/25730/1/cotman_switch_ confirmed.html. Feb. 6, 2008.

"Dallara to Cut Prices in '09." http://www.crash. net/indycar/news/26379/1/dallara_to_cut_ costs_for_teams.html. Dec. 13, 2008.

Deltawing. http://www.deltawingracing.com/ history/. Accessed December 30, 2013.

"Delta-wing Unveils 2012 IndyCar Concept." http://www.crash.net/indycar/news/156741/ 1/deltawing_unveils_revolutionary_indy car_concept.html. Feb. 11, 2010.

"Engine Penalties 'Will Stay' Says IndyCar." http://www.crash.net/indycar/news/178582/ 1/engine_penalties_will_stay_says_indycar. html. Apr. 14, 2012.

"Firestone Extends Pact with IndyCar." http:// www.nationalspeedsportnews.com/indy/ izod-indycar/firestone-extends-pact-with-indycar/. Feb. 12, 2012.

"Firestone Reverses Decision to Quit IndyCar." http://www.crash.net/indycar/news/167349/ 1/firestone_reverses_decision_to_quit_ser ies.html. Mar. 11, 2011.

"Firestone to Quit US Open-Wheel Racing."

http://www.crash.net/indycar/news/167161/1/firestone_to_quit_us_open-wheel_racing.html. Mar. 4, 2011.

"Forsythe Scales Back to Atlantic Effort." http://www.crash.net/indycar/news/25792/1/forsythe_bows_out_but_stays_in_atlantics.html. Feb. 29, 2008.

"George Continues to Seek Reason for Exit." http://www.crash.net/indycar/news/150400/1/george_wants_reason_for_push.html. July 26, 2009.

"George Denies IMS 'Oust' Claims." http://www.crash.net/indycar/news/147501/1/george_still_at_ims_focused_on_irl.html. May 27, 2009.

Glendenning, Mark. "IndyCar and Indianapolis Nears Restructure—Mark Miles." http://www.autosport.com/news/report.php/id/108700. July 9, 2013.

Hawkins, Steve. "Extreme G-forces Prompt Race Cancellation." Apr. 30, 2001. www.abcnews.com/US/story?id93412&page.

"Helio Slams Barnhart over Officiating." http://www.crash.net/indycar/news/173399/1/helio_slams_circus_clown_barnhart.html. Sept. 26, 2011.

Hollingsworth, Joe. "IRL and CART." www.aut{}omedia.com/IRL_and_CART/pht20030901.

"Honda Gets Five More Years in the IRL." http://www.crash.net/indycar/news/26021/1/honda_extends_engine_deal.html. May 24, 2008.

"Honda Wins Chance to Upgrade Turbochargers." http://www.crash.net/indycar/news/179024/1/honda_wins_right_to_upgrade_turbochargers.html. Apr. 27, 2012.

"Honda's US Programme to Continue." http://www.crash.net/indycar/news/26376/1/honda_to_continue_us_programme.html. Dec. 7, 2008.

"Hulman and Company Expands Board." http://www.nationalspeedsportnews.com/indy/indycar-development-series/skip-barber-indycar-academy-created/. Mar. 8, 2012.

"IMS Racing Initiative Gets Approval." http://www.nationalspeedsportnews.com/indy/izod-indycar/imsc-gets-legislative-approval-of-racing-initiative/. Apr. 13, 2013.

"IMS Reveals IndyCar Road Race Details." http://www.nationalspeedsportnews.com/indy/izod-indycar/ims-reveals-indycar-road-race-details/. Oct. 1, 2013.

"Indianapolis, IRL Announces Job Cuts." http://www.crash.net/indycar/news/154689/1/ims_irl_announces_job_cuts.html. Nov. 16, 2009.

Indianapolis Motor Speedway. http://www.indianapolismotorspeedway.com/indy500/history/stats/results/?year=2000.

"IndyCar Expected to Rule on Friday on Chevrolet's Protest of Honda Turbocharger." http://www.autoweek.com/article/20120426/indycar/120429835. Apr. 26, 2012.

"IndyCar Fines Panther Owner $25,000 for Disparaging Tweet." http://www.autoweek.com/article/20120428/INDYCAR/120429801. Apr. 27, 2012.

"IndyCar Numbers on the Rise." http://www.nationalspeedsportnews.com/indy/izod-indycar/indycar-numbers-on-the-rise/. Dec. 1, 2011.

"IndyCar Rating Up 53%." http://www.nationalspeedsportnews.com/indy/izod-indycar/indycar-rating-up-53-percent/. Mar. 27, 2013.

"IndyCar Revamps Leaders Circle Program." http://www.nationalspeedsportnews.com/indy/izod-indycar/indycar-revamps-leaders-circle-program/. Feb. 10, 2012.

"IndyCar to Face Challenge from F1 Support Series?" http://www.crash.net/indycar/news/186061/1/new_f1_challenge_looms_for_indycar.html. Nov. 12, 2012.

"Indy Introduces 'Push to Pass.'" http://www.crash.net/indycar/news/150529/1/indycar_series_introduces_push_to_pass.html. July 29, 2009.

"Indy Racing League Appoints New CEO." http://www.crash.net/indycar/news/156523/1/league_reveals_new_ceo.html. Feb. 3, 2010.

"Injuries Add Edge to Double File Restart Row." http://www.crash.net/indycar/news/167922/1/injuries_add_edge_to_double-file_restart_row.html. Mar. 29, 2011.

"Interim CEO Insists Bernard Was Not Sacked." http://www.crash.net/indycar/news/185722/1/interim_ceo_insists_bernard_was_not_sacked.html. Nov. 2, 2012.

"IRL Becomes Indy Racing League IndyCar Series." http://www.crash.net/indycar/news/16966/1/irl_becomes_indy_racing_league_indycar_series.html. Jan. 8, 2003.

"IRL Happy with Momentum." http://www.crash.net/indycar/news/26108/1/irl_happy_with_unification_upswing.html. July 4, 2008.

"IZOD IndyCar Series Page." http://racing-reference.info/irl.htm.

Kallman, Dave. "Push to Pass Gets First Use at Indy." http://www.jsonline.com/sports/autoracing/95164034.html. May 28, 2010.

Kaplan, Daniel. "ISL Files Countersuit Against Ex-partner CART." http://www.sportsbusinessdaily.com/Journal/Issues/2001/04/20010416/No-Topic-Name/ISL-Files-Countersuit-Against-Ex-Partner-CART.aspx. Apr. 16, 2001.

Kirby, Gordon. "The Way It Is: Can Mark Miles Turn IndyCar Around?" http://www.gordonkirby.com/categories/columns/theway/2013/the_way_it_is_no387.html#top. 2013.

Kirby, Gordon. "The Way It Is: Debating the Great Spec Car Plague." http://www.gordon

kirby.com/categories/columns/theway/2006/the_way_it_is_no7.html. May 15, 2006.

_____. "The Way It Is: Looking at the Challenges Facing America's Open-Wheel Racing." http://www.gordonkirby.com/categories/columns/theway/2006/the_way_it_is_no1.html. Apr. 6, 2006.

_____. "The Way It Is: The Tragedy of History Repeating Itself." http://www.gordonkirby.com/categories/theway/2012/the_way_it_is_no350.html. August 27, 2012.

_____. "The Way It Is: Tony George's Dystopian Vision Is upon Us." http://www.gordonkirby.com/categories/columns/theway/2006/the_way_it_is_no9.html. May 29, 2006.

_____. "The Way It Is: Why Dan Gurney Is America's Greatest Racing Man." http://www.gordonkirby.com/categories/columns/theway/2006/the_way_it_is_no38.html. Dec. 18, 2006.

"Lotus Confirms Split with BHA and DRR." http://www.crash.net/indycar/news/178954/1/lotus_confirms_split_with_bha_and_drr.html. Apr. 24, 2012.

"Lotus Join Honda and Chevrolet in Supplying Engines." http://www.crash.net/indycar/news/165186/1/lotus_to_supply_engines_for_indycar_in_2012.html. Nov. 19, 2010.

"Lotus out of IndyCar Racing." http://www.nationalspeedsportnews.com/indy/izod-indycar/lotus-out-of-indycar-racing/. Dec. 17, 2012.

Martin. Bruce. "Bernard Answers Call for American Involvement." http://www.nationalspeedsportnews.com/latest-headlines/bernard-answers-call-for-american-involvement/. Nov. 16, 2010.

_____. "Dragon Dumping Lotus for Chevrolet." http://www.nationalspeedsportnews.com/category/indy/page/78/. May 16, 2012.

_____. "IndyCar Fines 11 Teams." http://www.nationalspeedsportnews.com/indy/izod-indycar/indycar-fines-11-teams/. May 20, 2012.

_____. "IndyCar Open to More Technical Innovation." http://www.nationalspeedsportnews.com/indy/izod-indycar/indycar-open-to-more-technical-innovation/. May 23, 2013.

_____. "New CEO Bernard Could Deliver Much Needed Boost to the IndyCar." http://sportsillustrated.cnn.com/2010/writers/bruce_martin/04/05/Randy.Bernard.IndyCar/. Apr. 5, 2010.

"Merger Plans Hit Standstill?" http://www.crash.net/indycar/news/25744/1/merger_talks_stall.html. Feb. 10, 2008.

Mikell, Tripp. "Tony George Leads Offer for IndyCar Series." http://www.sportsbusiness daily.com/Journal/Issues/2012/10/01/Leagues-and-Governing-Bodies/IndyCar.aspx. Oct. 1, 2012.

"Motorsports Media Green Becomes CEO of IMS Production." http://www.theautochannel.com/news/2011/07/14/540665-motorsports-media-green-becomes-ceo-ims-productions.html. July 14, 2013.

Mylenski, Skip. "Risk-Taking Rogue Pat Patrick Strikes It Big in Oil—and Racing." http://articles.chicagotribune.com/1998-08-14/sports/9808140060_1_championship-auto-racing-teams-american-racing-series-united-states-auto-club. Aug. 14, 1998.

"New Trophy to IndyCar Champion." http://www.nationalspeedsportnews.com/indy/izod-indycar/new-trophy-to-indycar-champion/. Oct. 13, 2011.

"Newman/Haas Quits IndyCar Series." http://www.crash.net/indycar/news/175289/1/newmanhaas_quits_indycar_series.html. Dec. 1, 2011.

"New Hampshire Race Protest Denied." http://www.crash.net/indycar/news/172322/1/new_hampshire_results_protest_denied.html. Aug. 24, 2011.

"New Rule to Stop Mid-season Engine Swaps." http://www.crash.net/indycar/news/179228/1/new_rule_to_stop_mid-season_engine_swaps.html. May 2, 2012.

"No Engine Starting Grid Penalties During Indy." http://www.crash.net/indycar/news/178980/1/no_engine_grid_penalties_during_indy_500.html. Apr. 25, 2012.

"No Extra Race to Replace China, says IndyCar." http://www.crash.net/indycar/news/181211/1/no_replacement_for_china_says_indycar.html. June 25, 2012.

"No Resolution to Merger Talks." http://www.crash.net/indycar/news/25765/1/still_ground_to_cover_before_unity.html. Feb. 22, 2008.

"Official: Randy Bernard Exits as Series CEO." http://www.crash.net/indycar/news/185607/1/official_randy_bernard_exits_as_series_ceo.html. Oct. 29, 2012.

Oreovicz, John. "Hulman CEO Miles Good for IndyCar?" http://espn.go.com/racing/blog/_/name/oreovicz_john/id/8657254/indycar-hulman-ceo-mark-miles-good-indycar. Nov. 20, 2012.

_____. "Tony George News Fuels Speculation." http://www.sportsbusinessdaily.com/Journal/Issues/2012/10/01/Leagues-and-Governing-Bodies/IndyCar.aspx. Sept. 27, 2012.

_____. "Turbogate Fuels Indy Car Unrest." http://espn.go.com/racing/indycar/story/_/id/7900409/. May 8, 2012.

"Owners Want Further Delays to Aero Kits." http://www.crash.net/indycar/news/180508/

1/owners_want_further_delay_to_aero_kits. html. June 5, 2012.

"Paul Tracy Confirms IndyCar Comeback with Walker." http://www.crash.net/indycar/news/26132/1/tracy_confirms_indycar_return. html. July 14, 2008.

"'Perfect Storm' Led to Vegas Tragedy." http://www.crash.net/indycar/news/175518/1/report_finds_perfect_storm_led_to_vegas_tragedy.html. Dec. 15, 2011.

"Power Blasts Race Director Barnhart." http://www.crash.net/indycar/news/172103/1/power_blasts_race_director_barnhart.html. Aug. 15, 2011.

"Power Fined $30,000 over New Hampshire." http://www.crash.net/indycar/news/172360/1/power_fined_30000_over_new_hampshire.html. Aug. 25, 2011.

Professional Bull Riders. http://www.pbr.com/en/news/press-releases/2009/2/pbrs-live-attendance-up-in-2009-season.aspx.

"Recriminations Fly After Toronto." http://www.crash.net/indycar/news/171134/1/recriminations_rage_on_after_toronto.html. July 11, 2011.

"Reports: Dragon Suing Lotus for Contractual Fraud." http://www.crash.net/indycar/news/179456/1/dragon_suing_lotus_for_contractual_fraud.html. May 7, 2012.

Rudeen, Kenneth. "British Bullet at Indy." http://sportsillustrated.cnn.com/vault/article/magazine/MAG1072607/index.htm. May 29, 1961.

Schoettle, Anthony. "Deal with Flip-Flopping Firestone Big Risk for Miles." http://www.ibj.com/the-score-2013-01-02-deal-with-flip-flopping-firestone-big-gamble-for-mark-miles/PARAMS/post/38782. Jan. 2, 2013.

_____. "Honda Wants Indycar Officials to Find New Engine Suppliers." http://www.ibj.com/the-score-2013-10-14-honda-wants-indycar-officials-to-find-new-engine-suppliers/PARAMS/post/44044. Oct. 13, 2013.

_____. "Hulman and Co. Seeks to Overhaul IndyCar Management." http://www.ibj.com/the-score-2012-11-29-hulman-co-ceo-seeks-new-indycar-management-structure-team/PARAMS/post/38192. Nov. 29, 2012.

_____. "IndyCar CEO May Take Control of More Races." *Indianapolis Business Journal*, July 11, 2011, A-3.

_____. "IndyCar Ponders Overseas Expansion to Counter Troubles at Home." http://www.ibj.com/the-score-2013-08-28-indycar-ponders-overseas-expansion-to-counter-troubles-at-home/PARAMS/post/43237. Aug. 28, 2013.

_____. "IndyCar's Big New Wheels." *Indianapolis Business Journal*, Mar. 19, 2012, A-3.

_____. "New Boss Ready to Overhaul the Month of May in Indy." http://www.ibj.com/the-score-2013-09-03-new-boss-ready-to-overhaul-month-of-may-in-indy/PARAMS/post/43332. Sept. 3, 2013.

_____. "New Speedway President Asked to 'Save Our Track.'" http://www.ibj.com/the-score-2013-07-10-new-speedway-president-asked-to-save-our-track/PARAMS/post/42365. July 10, 2013.

_____. "Signs Point to Internal Hire to Replace Bernard as IndyCar CEO." http://www.ibj.com/the-score-2012-11-02-all-signs-point-to-internal-hire-to-replace-bernard-as-indycar-ceo/PARAMS/post/37693. Nov. 2, 2012.

Securities and Exchange Commission. CART 10-Q for 6/30/2002. http://www.sec.gov/Archives/edgar/data/1051825/000095015202006428/l95551ae10vq.txt.

_____. CART 10-Q for 6/30/2003. http://www.sec.gov/Archives/edgar/data/1051825/000095015203007658/l02333ae10vq.txt.

_____. CART 10-K for 12/31/2003. http://www.sec.gov/Archives/edgar/data/1051825/000095015204006473/l09292ae10vk.txt.

"Series Set for New Chinese Flyaway." http://www.crash.net/indycar/news/174824/1/series_set_for_new_chinese_flyaway.html. Nov. 11, 2011.

"Series to File for Bankruptcy?" http://www.crash.net/indycar/news/25749/1/confusion_amid_bankruptcy_rumours.html. Feb. 13, 2008.

"Skip Barber IndyCar Academy Created." http://www.nationalspeedsportnews.com/indy/indycar-development-series/skip-barber-indycar-academy-created/. Mar. 28, 2012.

"Study Says IMS Generates $510 Million Impact." http://www.nationalspeedsportnews.com/indy/izod-indycar/study-says-ims-generates-510-million-impact/. Mar. 10, 2013.

"Takeover Rumours Persist Despite Denials." http://www.crash.net/indycar/news/185300/1/tony_george_quits_board_of_series_owners.html. Oct. 3, 2012.

"Tracy Takes Forsythe to Court." http://www.crash.net/indycar/news/26303/1/tracy_sues_for_breach_of_contract.html. Oct. 7, 2008.

"US Open-Wheel Merger Agreed?" http://www.crash.net/indycar/news/25756/1/us_poised_for_unity_at_last.html. Feb. 19, 2008.

"US Open Wheel Merger Close for 2008?" http://www.crash.net/indycar/news/25744/1/merger_talks_stall.html. Feb. 8, 2008.

"Walker: It's What People Wanted." http://www.crash.net/indycar/news/25768/1/walker_its_back_to_the_future.html. Feb. 28, 2008.

"Walker Ready for New IndyCar Challenge." http://www.nationalspeedsportnews.com/

indy/izod-indycar/walker-ready-for-new-indycar-challenge/. May 13, 2013.

"Walker to Move Regardless?" http://www.crash.net/indycar/news/25746/1/walker_to_go_regardless.html. Feb. 11, 2008.

Waltz, Keith. "Andy Granatelli Unveils Turbine Powered Indy Car." http://www.nationalspeedsportnews.com/racing-history/torn-from-the-headlines/andy-granatelli-unveils-turbine-powered-indy-car/. Accessed Dec. 21, 2013.

Weaver, Matt. "IndyCar Mandates Twin Turbos for All Engine Suppliers in 2014." http://www.sbnation.com/indycar/2013/7/25/4557438/indycar-mandates-twin-turbos-for-all-engine-suppliers-in-2014. July 25, 2013.

Wikipedia. "Arie Luyendyk." http://en.wikipedia.org/wiki/Arie_Luyendyk. Accessed Jan. 1, 2014.

_____. "Dario Franchitti." http://en.wikipedia.org/wiki/Dario_Franchitti. Accessed Jan. 1, 2014.

_____. "Kelley Racing." http://en.Wikipedia.org/wiki/Kelley_racing.

_____. "1965 Indianapolis 500." http://en.wikipedia.org/wiki/1965_Indianapolis_500. Accessed Dec. 20, 2013.

_____. "Professional Bull Riders." http://en.wikipedia.org/wiki/Professional_Bull_Riders.

WTHR.com. "Mark Miles Tapped to Be CEO of Hulman and Company." http://www.wthr.com/story/20146554/indycar-owners-set-for-announcement. Nov. 20, 2012.

"Xtrac to Offer Cheaper Support." http://www.crash.net/indycar/news/142832/1/xtrac_cuts_cost_for_teams.html. Feb. 10, 2009.

Index

Page numbers in **bold italics** indicate pages with illustrations.